Wellness Management in Hospitality and Tourism

Bendegul Okumus and Heather Linton Kelly

Goodfellow Publishers Ltd

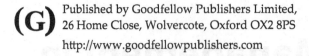 Published by Goodfellow Publishers Limited,
26 Home Close, Wolvercote, Oxford OX2 8PS
http://www.goodfellowpublishers.com

British Library Cataloguing in Publication Data: a catalogue record for this title is available from the British Library.

Library of Congress Catalog Card Number: on file.

ISBN: 978-1-915097-22-4

DOI: 10.23912/978-1-915097-24-8-5275

 Design and typesetting by P.K. McBride, www.macbride.org.uk

Cover design by Cylinder

Printed by Printforce, Biggleswade

Distributed by UK Marston Book Services, www.marston.co.uk

Contents

Preface

The first edition of *Wellness Management in Hospitality and Tourism* is written to be a textbook for students in tourism and hospitality programs as well as in culinary and restaurant programs. After the devastating onset of Covid-19, the importance of health, wellness and well-being topics has increased and many educational institutions, industries, organizations and academics are paying more attention to these subjects. As new academic courses and certificate programs commence, the problem of resources arises. For that reason, this book was written in textbook format to support students and instructors in schools and institutions that offer health, wellness and well-being-related courses.

This book is one of the first books in the health and wellness area in terms of accessible content and practical use. Considering the limited literature available at the time of this book's creation, the authors pulled from many written and online resources, student feedback was obtained and new literature and online sources were added regularly to update the content since its inception in 2019. In addition, the authors have used clear language and expression while writing this book. *Wellness Management in Hospitality and Tourism* is organized into 14 chapters. Each chapter is enriched with learning outcomes, case studies, definitions of key terms, discussion questions and a question bank.

In the first chapter, wellness management is introduced and the overall concept of wellness management in hospitality and tourism as a foundation for the rest of this book is explained. In the second chapter, we discuss how wellness in hospitality and tourism affects individual travelers and the destinations they visit. Chapter 3 looks at the spectrum of health and wellness in hospitality and tourism that exists across the globe. In the fourth chapter, we cover some of the historically known wellness destinations and discuss the emerging regions and what they have to offer tourists. While the fifth chapter introduces the concept of segmentation in wellness in foodservice, hospitality, and tourism, Chapter 6 discusses the concept of health and wellness food and beverages as well as health and wellness food trends in foodservice, hospitality, and tourism. The seventh chapter explains spa and hot spring development and management and the eighth chapter covers health and wellness events, festivals, and activities in foodservice, hospitality, and tourism. Chapter 9 provides information about how to design, operate, and manage a wellness event; Chapter 10 discusses the management and development of health and wellness destinations, facilities, and amenities in foodservice, hospitality, and tourism businesses; and Chapters 11 and 12 analyze the management of health and wellness programs and offerings in foodservice, hospitality, and tourism businesses. Then Chapter 13 discusses wellness management during times of crisis, and Chapter 14 draws conclusions from the previous chapters and offers suggestions for current and future wellness management in foodservice, hospitality, and tourism businesses.

We are grateful for the help of all the tourism and hospitality undergraduate students who provided constructive comments and Sally North of Goodfellow Publishers who supported the completion of this book project.

Bendegul Okumus

Heather Linton Kelly

Acknowledgment

We would like to express our deepest gratitude to Ms. Frances Sherlock, who assisted us in the editing and preparation of this book and teaching materials.

About the authors

Dr. Bendegul Okumus is an Associate Professor at the University of Central Florida's Rosen College of Hospitality Management. She has a degree in Nutrition and Home Economics, along with a master's and Ph.D. degrees in Food Science and Technology, and a master's in Hospitality and Tourism Management. She has work experience at theme parks and hotels in Orlando, particularly in food preparation, foodservices, restaurant management, and event management. She also worked at Florida's Orange County Health Department in the Women, Infants, and  Children Division as a nutritionist. Her main research areas include food/culinary tourism, healthy eating, eating behavior in different age groups, food safety in restaurants and food trucks, health and wellness in hospitality and tourism, mental health and wellness and food waste. She has over 20 years of academic and teaching experience at four universities in two countries. Her multidisciplinary and multicultural experiences have emboldened her to develop and teach numerous courses such as Nutrition Concepts and Issues in Food Services, Wellness Management in Hospitality and Tourism, International Cuisine and Culture, Sanitation in the Food Service Industry, Food Sanitation, Event Industry, Marketing in Hospitality and Tourism, and Principles of Management and Leadership in Hospitality and Tourism.

Heather Linton Kelly is the Director of Research and Sustainability for the Adventure Travel Trade Association (ATTA). Heather holds a master's in Business Administration from Suffolk University, and a master's in Hotel Administration from the Cornell Hotel School. She has taught business, marketing, and communications courses at four universities in New York state and Heidelberg, Germany. After working for a hospitality research firm and in a hotel sales office, Heather went  on to spend 3.5 years as Marketing Manager for the Aruba Convention Bureau for North America, and one year as a consultant with Discover the Palm Beaches, Florida. Heather also spent 7 years with Hotel Link Solutions, part of the WHL Group, working with small hotels in developing tourism economies to build their online presence. She has worked on consulting projects with the World Bank, TripAdvisor, the European Travel Commission, the Discover England Fund, and others. Heather brings her industry and research experience, along with her love for authentic and meaningful travel, to her current role at ATTA. Her research supports the adventure travel industry in its belief and commitment to sustainable tourism and a responsible and profitable future, especially concerning women, indigenous peoples, and developing tourism destinations.

To my mother Ehlizar Aras, my father Ilyas Aras, my children Ezgi and Eda Okumus and my husband Fevzi Okumus

Bendegul Okumus

To my daughter Ayla, my light and inspiration every day

Heather Linton Kelly

1 Introduction to Wellness Management in Hospitality and Tourism

This chapter introduces the overall concept of wellness management in hospitality and tourism as a foundation for the rest of this book. First, it discusses the concept of health and wellness. Next, it looks at what wellness tourism is and how it differs from medical tourism. Primary and secondary wellness tourism are defined, and the impact of wellness travel on the global economy is introduced.

Learning outcomes

By the end of reading this chapter, students should be able to do the following:

1. Define health and wellness.
2. Define wellness tourism and medical tourism.
3. Discuss the differences between wellness tourism and medical tourism.
4. Discuss the impact of wellness travel on the global economy.
5. Define primary and secondary wellness travelers.
6. Identify core motivations for wellness tourism.
7. Identify the main beneficiaries/stakeholders of wellness activities in the hospitality and tourism industry.

Case study: Bucuti & Tara Beach Resort, Aruba

"Wellness" has become a buzzword in the hospitality and tourism industry and for many good reasons. However, some organizations and destinations have been focusing on wellness principles for decades before the movement became mainstream. One example is Bucuti & Tara Beach Resort on the Caribbean island of Aruba.

While the numerous large branded hotel chains on the island have been moving beyond the fitness center and spa, Bucuti & Tara Beach Resort has been taking steps to maximize its wellness efforts from its opening in 1987. Their concept of wellness starts with environmental sustainability. The resort hotel is the first carbon-neutral property in the Caribbean. Much of their produce is locally grown, they have eliminated almost all single-use plastic on the property, and they generate electricity through solar panels and their fitness facility equipment. Starting with a strong foundation of environmental wellness, the hotel is better able to offer personal wellness services and guarantees to its guests.

Bucuti & Tara Beach Resort offers wellness amenities like a tranquil adults-only environment, a Daily Healthy Hour with reduced price smoothies and mocktails, free daily wellness activities on the property, exercise classes and nutritional counseling, non-smoking rooms with additional air purification, an on-site restaurant with healthy ingredients and portions, and of course, spa treatments focused on balancing mind, body, and spirit.

Another important concept in wellness travel is connecting with new people, other travelers, and locals alike, to expand one's mental well-being and interact with the local community. Bucuti & Tara Beach Resort not only employs local Aruban people, they also open their classes and restaurants to the community and are happy to connect guests to events run by other local organizations, such as stand up paddleboard yoga. Many tourism entities are incorporating a range of wellness programs and activities into their business, from sustainability to physical health; Bucuti & Tara Beach Resort in Aruba is one example of a hotel that has focused on this from its inception.

Discussion questions

1. What types of wellness programs and activities can hotels offer to their guests?
2. How can tourism entities go beyond spa treatments to offer a more holistic wellness experience?
3. How can hotels and other service providers incorporate local people and traditions into the guest experience in a way that enhances wellness?
4. Do you know any hospitality and tourism organization offering unique wellness experiences? If yes, please provide a short description of these experiences.

Wellness management in hospitality and tourism.

According to Stara and Peterson (2017), there are five main themes surrounding research on wellness: (1) wellness as a state of being, (2) wellness as a process of personal growth, (3) wellness as an approach to professional care, (4) wellness as a matter of community, and (5) wellness as a global topic. This textbook broaches all five of these topics in one way or another as it explores wellness in regards to hospitality and tourism.

Health, wellness, and well-being

The concepts of health, wellness, and well-being are certainly not new. The World Health Organization (WHO) defines **health** as "a state of complete physical, mental and social well-being," taking care to further note that it is not only the absence of disease or illness (WHO, 2019). The Global Wellness Institute (GWI) more specifically defines **wellness** as "the active pursuit of activities, choices and lifestyles that lead to a state of holistic health" (GWI, 2019a and Yeung and Johnston 2018, p. iii). **Well-being,** on the other hand, tends to be more subjective in nature, focusing on happiness rather than health or wellness. Dillette et al. (2020, p. 795) sum up all three concepts by stating that "wellness can be thought of in congruence with prevention and health, while well-being with happiness." Throughout history, people of the world have participated in a shared search for health, wellness, and well-being (Tables 1.1 and 1.2.).

Table 1.1: History of wellness (summarized from GWI, 2019a; Pierre-Louis, 2019)

Ancient wellness	
3,000 – 1,500 BC	The practice of **Ayurveda** is developed as a holistic system that promotes harmony between body, mind, and spirit. This balance is unique for each person's own nutritional, exercise, social, and hygiene needs, and yoga and meditation are incorporated. Originally an oral tradition, Ayurveda was later recorded in the four sacred Hindu texts of the Vedas.
3,000 – 2,000 BC	**Traditional Chinese Medicine (TCM)** emerges as a holistic perspective to achieving health and well-being by fostering harmony. Influenced by Taoism and Buddhism, TCM incorporates healing methods like acupuncture, herbal medicine, qigong (which focuses on regulated breathing exercises, [Merriam Webster, 2020a]), and tai chi.
500 BC	In ancient Greece, Hippocrates argued that disease is due to poor diet, lifestyle, and environmental factors, and focused on preventing sickness instead of only treating disease.
50 BC	The ancient Romans adapted Greek beliefs that disease prevention is essential, and created a public health infrastructure with aqueducts, sewers, and public baths to prevent the spread of germs.
Wellness defined and homeopathy developed	
1650s	The Oxford English Dictionary traces the word "wellness" back to 1654, from the diary of Sir Archibald Johnston: "I … blessed God … for my daughter's wealnesse." A 1655 letter from Dorothy Osborne to her husband, Sir William Temple, is the first citation with the modern spelling of 'wellness.'
1790s	In Germany, physician Christian Hahneman develops a system that uses natural substances to encourage the body to heal itself, known as **homeopathy**.

19th Century intellectual and medical movements	
1860s	Sebastian Kneipp's "Kneipp Cure" is promoted, which combines hydrotherapy, herbalism, exercise, and nutrition. Phineas Quimby's theories of mentally aided healing spawn the New Thought movement.
1870s	The spiritual-healing-based Christian Science is founded by Mary Baker Eddy. Andrew Taylor Still develops a holistic healing approach to manipulating muscles and joints, known as **osteopathy**.
1880s	In Switzerland, physician Maximilian Bircher-Benner studies and promotes nutritional research, encouraging a balanced diet with lots of fruits and vegetables. The YMCA launches around a core principle of developing mind, body, and spirit.
1890s	**Chiropractic** practice, focusing on the body's structure and functioning, is developed by Daniel David Palmer.
20th Century: Wellness spreads and get serious	
1900s	John Harvey Kellogg, of Kellogg's cereal fame, directs a **sanatorium** in Battle Creek, Michigan. His facility and message promoted learning how to stay well through a healthy diet, fresh air, hydrotherapy, and exercise. **Naturopathy** spreads to the U.S. from Europe; this philosophy is focused on the body's ability to heal itself through dietary and lifestyle change, herbs, massage and joint manipulation.
1910	The Carnegie Foundation's *Flexner Report* is published, critiquing North America's medical education system. The report questions the validity of all medicine other than biomedicine, and most natural wellness systems are dropped from mainstream medical education.
1950s - 1970s	*Prevention* magazine, designed to promote alternative/preventative health, is launched by J.I. Rodale. Physician Halbert L. Dunn develops the idea of "high level wellness" through lectures and a book by the same title. This concept influences Dr. John Travis to open the world's first wellness center in California, along with a 12-dimension wellness assessment tool, *The Wellness Inventory* (1975), and *The Wellness Workbook* (1977). Other wellness centers, institutes, and conferences are launched around the country.
1980s - 2000s	Wellness comes to the mainstream through the fitness and spa industries, workplace wellness programs, and self-help programs.
21st Century & beyond	
2000-2010	Wellness begins to permeate and transform every industry in the world, including travel and hospitality. In 2002, Paul Zan Pilzer's book *The Wellness Revolution* helped define the industry's characteristics. In 2008, Bhutan implemented the world's first Gross National Happiness scale, endorsing happiness as a fundamental human right. The Consortium of Academic Health Centers for Integrative Medicine is created and accepted worldwide, with many prominent institutions joining.
2011-2020	Between 2011 and 2018, various cities and nations around the globe create laws taxing soda and sugary drinks. These countries include but are not limited to Finland, Hungary, France, UAE, Portugal, and South Africa. In 2012, the United Nations Sustainable Development Solutions Network released the inaugural World Happiness Report, and June 9, 2013 became the first annual Global Wellness Day. The focus on wellness continues to grow worldwide.

Oral and written records of the Ayurvedic connection between body, mind, and spirit originate as early as 3,000 B.C. Egyptian and Babylonian architecture show evidence in spas and baths as early as 3,000 B.C. (Kazakov & Oyner, 2019). In 500 B.C., the ancient Greek physician Hippocrates argued that disease develops out of diet, lifestyle, and environmental factors, and proposed the idea of preventing sickness rather than just curing disease. Native American, Alaskan, and Pacific Islander cultures view wellness in terms of balance and harmony of one's many facets. Whereas in Middle Eastern and Eastern Asian cultures, wellness is rooted in many of their natural cures and therapies like the Turkish hammam, a Thai massage, hot springs or onsen in Japan, tai chi in China, and many more (Stara & Peterson, 2017).

The Oxford English Dictionary traces the history of the word "wellness" to the 1650s, and homeopathy, herbalism, hydrotherapy, sanatoria, fresh air cures, and other "natural" cures for all types of physical, mental, and spiritual ailments have been sought for centuries.

Table 1.2: The short chronological order of wellness practices

Ayurveda	3000-1500 B.C.
Traditional Chinese Medicine	3000-2000 B.C.
Ancient Greek Medicine	500 B.C.
Homeopathy	1790s
Hydrotherapy	1860s
Chiropractic	1890s
The Flexner Report	1910
Organic Farming	1950s
High Level Wellness	1960s
First Wellness Center Opens	1970s
Wellness Goes Mainstream	1890s-2000
Bhutan Gross National Happiness	2008
Wellness Goes Global	2010
Legislation to Curb Obesity Diabetes	2011-2018
UN World Happiness Report	2012
Global Wellness Tourism Economy Report	2013
Global Wellness Institute and Global Wellness Economy Monitor	2014
The wellness Moonshot: A World Free of Preventable Disease	2017
GWI Build Well to Live Well Report	2018

Adapted from Global Wellness Institute (2019).

Importance of wellness

Wellness is important not only to individuals but also to businesses, societies, and governments. In the last 45 years, worldwide obesity has tripled, and the number of people with diabetes has quadrupled (WHO, 2018a; WHO, 2018b). These ailments cost billions of dollars a year to treat, a bill often paid by the government, and eventually, the taxpayer. Beyond physical manifestations of being unwell, workplace stress is high and rising rapidly, causing strain on productivity, job tenure, and happiness at work. In 2019, average health spending as a share of GDP reached around 9.9% worldwide, with the United States spending the highest share on health at 16.8% (OECD, 2021).

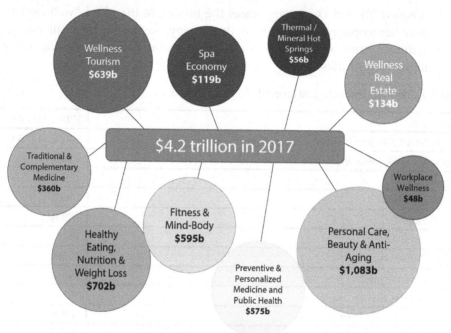

Figure 1.1: Value of the global wellness economy. Adapted from Yeung and Johnston (2018), Global Wellness Tourism Economy Monitor October 2018.

The wellness industry is growing fast (Figure 1.1). The global wellness economy is estimated to be over $4 trillion, representing more than 5% of global economic output. The Global Wellness Institute (2020) defines the **wellness economy** as 10 "industries that enable consumers to incorporate wellness activities and lifestyles into their daily lives." The largest of these sectors in terms of value is Personal Care, Beauty, and Anti-Aging, with Wellness Hospitality and Tourism coming in second at an annual value of well over $600 billion (GWI, 2019). Each of these factors assist people "in the active pursuit of activities, choices and lifestyles that lead to a state of holistic health" (Dillette et al., 2020, p. 796). Figure 1.1 highlights the value of the global wellness economy. With the development of technology, the use of social media has increased and people spend much of their time connecting digitally with each other and with organizations. This presents a good opportunity to convert users into potential customers, and digital transformation is redefining the business model by providing users and companies with a range of smart and connected products (Boccardelli & Peruffo, 2018). Recent research shows that Facebook and Instagram are prominent social media platforms for the beauty and wellness industry, followed by Snapchat, YouTube and LinkedIn (Kaur & Kumar, 2020).

What is wellness in hospitality and tourism?

In their literature review of wellness in the hospitality and tourism industry, Dillette, Douglas, and Andrzejewski (2020) use Voigt et al's (2011, p 17) definition of wellness tourism that it is "the sum of all the relationships resulting from a journey by people whose motive, in whole or in part, is to maintain or promote their health and well-being, and who stay at least one night at a facility that is specifically designed to enable and enhance people's physical, psychological, spiritual and/or social well-being." Keep this broad wellness tourism definition in mind as you make your way through this textbook.

One of the fastest-growing travel segments is **wellness in hospitality and tourism** or any travel associated with the pursuit of maintaining or enhancing one's personal well-being (GWI, 2019). Estimated at a value of $639.4 billion in 2017, this group is a large and lucrative one for hospitality providers. An annual growth rate of 6.5% from 2015-2017 was more than double the growth rate for the tourism industry as a whole, making it an important segment for study (Yeung & Johnston, 2018). Regions with the most indicative wellness tourism markets are Southeast Asia, North America, and the Germanic and Mediterranean countries in Europe (Stara & Peterson, 2017).

Traveling can have some negative connotations and ramifications. It often brings stress, from worrying about being on time to the airport, to leaving the office and other responsibilities behind. This stress, combined with a change in routine and location, can lead to poor sleeping and disruption to a fitness program. Many people eat too much while traveling, compounded with making less healthy food choices than they would at home, and travel can lead to excessive alcohol consumption. Consciously striving to avoid these pitfalls, wellness travel encourages rest and rejuvenation, extending and discovering healthier lifestyles, identifying authentic and transformative experiences, preventing and managing disease or illness, and overall finding meaning, connection, and joy (Yeung & Johnston, 2018). Many hospitality and tourism businesses also offer wellness experiences and facilities for the local population.

Primary and secondary wellness tourism

Wellness tourism attracts healthy tourists with a proactive interest in managing or strengthening their health (Stara & Peterson, 2017). Wellness travelers do some of the same activities as the more traditional tourist, but the main purpose of their trip may differ (Table 1.3).

A **primary wellness tourist's** destination choice is primarily motivated by wellness, whereas many traditional tourists may more accurately be classified as

secondary wellness tourists, who focus on wellness and participate in wellness experiences while traveling for leisure or business (Yeung & Johnston, 2018). A secondary wellness tourist takes steps to find healthy lodging, food and beverage and fitness facilities while traveling. This may include a day at a hot spring as part of a larger trip, a visit to a spa at a beach resort or receiving a traditional body treatment to explore the local culture, using the fitness center of a hotel or cruise ship, or other elements of wellness brought into a broader trip. On the other hand, the primary wellness tourist's main goal of a trip is to improve their mind, body, and/or spiritual wellness (Yeung & Johnston, 2018).

Table 1.3: Primary and secondary wellness tourists

Primary wellness tourists	Secondary wellness tourists
Vacationing at a destination spa or taking a weekend spa trip	A business or leisure traveler selects healthy lodging, food and beverage and fitness facilities while traveling
Staying at a hot springs resort for multiple days	A family taking a vacation stays at a hot springs resort
Going to a health and wellness facility for a health check-up	An adventure tourist spends a night at a spa after hiking
Staying at a spa resort	A vacationer staying at a beach resort who visits the spa during their trip
Spending time at an ashram or meditation or yoga	A member of a tour group who visits a hammam (a Turkish bath usually offered in a communal bath house, [Merriam Webster, 2020b]) or receives a Thai massage or reflexology treatment as part of their itinerary
Attending a yoga retreat with healthy food and beverage offerings	
Joining a wellness cruise	

Adapted from Yeung & Johnston (2018).

The global Covid-19 pandemic that started in 2020 had a massive impact on tourism, with over $1.3 trillion in lost revenues. Due to the inability to travel for a period of time, wellness tourism decreased along with the larger industry. This is likely a major contributor to the global wellness economy's reduction from an estimated high of $4.9 trillion in 2019 to $4.4 trillion in 2020 (GWI, 2020). However, the Covid-19 health crisis also led to a greater focus on health concerns, especially mental and spiritual health (WHO, 2022), which will likely translate to increased wellness tourism. More about Covid-19's impact will be discussed throughout this book.

As primary and secondary wellness travelers are important markets, hotels are being developed that target both types. Large brand-name hotel companies such as Marriott International, Hilton Worldwide, and Wyndham Hotel Group have all launched brands and programs focused on wellness. Amenities include guest rooms specially furnished with yoga props or other fitness equipment, healthy menus, cooking classes, seminars, fitness concierge services, and others. Other brands like InterContinental Hotels Group (IHG) and Hyatt Hotels & Resorts have begun building wellness-centric brands, such as IHG's EVEN Hotels and Hyatt's acquisitions of wellness resort and spa company Miraval Group and lifestyle center chain Exhale in 2017.

Case study: Secondary wellness tourists, the Bucket List Family

The Bucket List Family, consisting of Garrett, Jessica, Dorothy, Manilla, and Calihan Gee, is a family of five 'travel journalists' (Bucket List Family, 2019). They travel the world documenting 'bucket list' experiences on their YouTube channel and Instagram page and have amassed quite a following over the years (during the writing of this book, they had over one million subscribers on YouTube (Bucket List Family, n.d.a) and over 2.4 million followers on Instagram (Bucket List Family, n.d.b).

In their over three years of travel, they are perfect examples of secondary wellness travelers. At each destination they travel to, they make finding a local gym (whether it is at their hotel or down the street from their Airbnb), a local park, or a local farmers' market a priority. They also prioritize healthy foods over junk foods while traveling. As stated in their family blog, "health is a top priority for our family but travel can make it very difficult" (Gee, 2017). That blog post also discusses everything from why health is important to their family, to how to snack while traveling, to workout plans while traveling (both when a gym is available and when a gym is not available). But their main priority while traveling in not wellness, it is for bucket list-type experiences like swimming with whales in Tonga or seeing silverback gorillas in Rwanda.

Discussion questions

1. Do you think that secondary wellness tourism is a fad or trend, or do you think it is here for the long haul? Explain your reasoning.

2. In what ways can hotels and the hospitality industry accommodate secondary wellness tourists?

Wellness companies, like luxury fitness studio chain Equinox, are also venturing into the hotel industry and opening their own branded accommodations (Horwath, 2018). Another way to look at this is by viewing wellness as the road or what an individual can do every day to take care of themselves, like eat well, keep relationships, be mindful, manage stress, and strengthen the body. Wellbeing is the destination where all of these things align (Kyricos, 2019). This spectrum of wellness developments ranges from wellness-themed to authentic wellness offerings (Table 1.4).

Wellness travelers as markets for the hospitality industry

A wellness resort (also known as a wellness clinic) is an example of an authentic wellness development. This type of organization has four primary elements: (1) accommodation, (2) wellness activities, (3) healthy food and beverage options, and (4) wellness facilities. The wellness resort recreational ecosystem is specifically defined as "a spatial system of interconnected ecological, economic and social components, which allows for more accurate elaboration of the methodology basis of the wellness resort stable development concept" (Pavlenko et al, 2019, p. 1). Environmental factors are very important to maintain a healthy mind and body. Researchers have conducted many studies on the importance of the environment as a place to improve human health, and emphasize the special places where sick people can renew and clean their souls and bodies. The healing effect of the environment has been continuously examined and is shown to affect the importance of ecological health facilities especially after the Covid-19 pandemic (Abdo & Shokry, 2020). These resorts often offer guided wellness retreats, multi-day programs hosted by one or more facilitators, which are intention-driven and typically include learning and lifestyle workshops and fitness activities (Horwath, 2018). One important feature of wellness resorts is that they often bundle most elements of the stay as an all-inclusive package, so guests are guided through a specific controlled program and therefore achieve maximum results (Pierre-Louis, 2019).

Table 1.4: Spectrum of wellness developments

Wellness-themed developments	Authentic wellness developments	
In-room workout stations In-room fitness equipment Apps for guided training/meditation Supplements & shakes in minibars Adult coloring books/postcards	In-Room Features	In-room yoga & meditation stations Extension of the healing process (e.g. Vitamin C shower, Ozone-enriched air) No in-room snacks
Healthy food and beverage selection Private and group fitness & yoga classes Meditation programs Fitness concierge services & clubs Workout gear lending Bike rentals	Services/ Programming	Pre- & post-stay consultation Expert medical evaluations Custom food and beverage plans & workout sessions Twice-a-day meditation/yoga sessions Personal wellness concierge Educational workshops/seminars Sense of community Spiritual education
Collaboration with wellness/fitness brands Sustainability initiatives	Other Initiatives	Collaboration with medical clinics Wellness community standards Nature-oriented design standards Use of sustainable & 'healthy' materials

Adapted from Schweder and Modena (2018).

Motivations and offerings for wellness tourism

The Global Wellness Institute identifies six core motivations for seeking wellness tourism: social, physical, mental, spiritual, emotional, and environmental, and specifically calls out the fact that every destination has something to offer in at least one of these areas. Physical travelers might find health, fitness, and beauty through healthy eating resources, wellness centers, health resorts and sanatoria, spas, etc. Mental and spiritual seekers look for mind-body and spiritual connections through activities such as yoga and meditation, prayer, volunteering, time alone, and with family and friends. Emotional explorers might better connect with themselves through retreats, life coaching, music and arts, and stress reduction, and everyone can connect to the environment around them by spending time in nature (Yeung & Johnston, 2018).

Any hospitality and tourism organization, as well as a destination, can identify at least one item on this list as one of their offerings that can be promoted to wellness travelers (Yeung & Johnston, 2018) and each destination offers something different to each wellness traveler (GWI, 2020). In fact, most locations will have multiple resources that not only offer wellness benefits to individual travelers but also to the local community and the environment, all of which are tied closely to one another. This variety of options also helps demonstrate that participants and stakeholders in the wellness tourism industry go beyond hotels and spas, into many other segments of the economy, benefiting an extensive group of people, companies, and governments.

Table 1.5: Wellness travel values and activities

Value sought	Activities	Locations
Physical		
Fitness	Gym visits Fitness classes Stretching Pilates	Gyms Fitness centers
Healthy Eating	Nutrition Weight management Detoxing Culinary experiences	Organic and natural restaurants Health food stores
Health	Complementary and alternative medicine (CAM) Integrative medicine Diagnostics Health check-ups Chronic condition management	Integrative health centers CAM centers Wellness centers
Spa & Beauty	Massage Bathing Body treatments Facials Hair and nails	Spas Salons Baths and springs Thalasso (sea-related spa and beauty treatments)
Mental		
Mind-Body	Yoga Meditation Tai chi Qigong Biofeedback (a process whereby electronic monitoring of normal bodily functions is used to train someone to acquire voluntary control of that function) (OED, 2020)	Yoga studios Martial arts studios
Spiritual		
Spiritual & Connection	Prayer Volunteering Time with family and friends Time alone	Yoga retreats Spiritual retreats Ashrams

Emotional		
Personal Growth	Retreats Life coaching Stress reduction Reading Music and arts	Lifestyle retreats Wellness retreats
Environmental		
Eco & Adventure	Hiking Biking Taking walks Nature visits	Parks Wildlife sanctuaries Nature preserves
Social facets are incorporated in all of these aspects as needed. Some facilities, such as healthy hotels, wellness cruises, and health resorts and sanatoria offer multiple values and activities.		

Adapted from Yeung & Johnston (2018).

The most direct beneficiaries of wellness are in the hospitality and tourism infrastructure. Hotels and other types of lodging, transportation companies, restaurants, attractions, and destination management organizations (DMOs) all clearly benefit from increased tourism, as do gift shops, retail stores, and local artisans. Organizations and associations in the wellness lifestyle category also often receive a share of the wellness tourist's wallet, as they purchase healthy food, attend fitness and mind body studio programs, explore local nature and recreation amenities, visit community and spiritual institutions, and possibly purchase local real estate like a timeshare or vacation home. Spas and thermal/mineral springs have long been popular tourist attractions, and interest has developed further into health resorts and wellness retreats, and even centers for alternative medicine and alternative health (Table 1.5).

There is a bigger effect on the community infrastructure than just going beyond the immediate impact of the tourism dollar on businesses. Local governments benefit from tourist taxes levied, and the economy is boosted as businesses employ local people and purchase supplies. This promotes investment by third parties and the development of social programs and benefits. As the local economy is strengthened, and investment priorities become clear as destinations seek to attract more wellness travelers, environmental and sustainability programs are often encouraged and developed. It is clear that wellness tourism can provide many benefits to a destination, but as with all tourism, it must be measured and managed carefully.

Not only do tourists benefit from wellness offerings, local residents do as well. The industry brings in tourism dollars to the local economy and provides additional jobs for residents. Wellness travelers are often high-value, meaning they spend more than the average tourist and tend to care about sustainability and other positive aspects of tourism. In addition to increased tourism dollars and jobs, residents also benefit from the presence of wellness organizations. They are usually welcome to take advantage of the services, often at a local resident discounted price. This can mean overall improved health and well-being of their community as a whole (Figure 1.2).

Hospitality & Tourism Infrastructure
- Accommodation
- Dining establishments
- Destinations
- Attractions
- Arts & culture
- Retail, gift shops, artisans
- Transportation

Wellness Lifestyle
- Healthy food & markets
- Fitness & mind-body studios
- Real estate (e.g. timeshare, vacation homes)
- Nature & recreation amenities
- Community & spiritual institutions

Wellness & Prevention
- Spas
- Health resorts & wellness retreats
- Thermal/mineral hot springs
- Centers for alternative medicine & integrative health centers

Government
- Tourism
- Health
- Economic development
- Investment promotion
- Environment/sustainability
- Social development

Figure 1.2: Stakeholders that can collaborate and benefit from wellness tourism. Adapted from Yeung & Johnston (2018).

Measuring wellness tourism

In this era of overtourism, it is becoming increasingly important to attract not the highest number of visitors possible, but instead the right kind of tourists that allow the destination to flourish while still embracing its identity. Wellness travelers tend to be high-spend visitors, especially primary wellness travelers. Globally in 2017, 830 million trips (domestic and international combined) were taken, with a total spend of $639.4bn. The number-one wellness tourism destination in 2017 was the United States, capturing $226bn, followed by Germany ($65.7bn), China ($31.7bn), France ($30.7bn), and Japan ($22.5bn) (Table 1.6). These estimates include lodging, food and beverage, activities and excursions, shopping, in-country transportation, and other services (Yeung & Johnston, 2018). **International wellness tourism expenditures** include all receipts earned by a country from inbound wellness tourists visiting from abroad, with an overnight stay; domestic wellness tourism expenditures track all expenditures in a country made by wellness tourists who are traveling within their own country, with an overnight stay (Yeung & Johnston, 2019, p. 26).

Secondary wellness travelers are much more common than primary wellness travelers, accounting for 89% of trips and 86% of expenditures (compared to 11% and 14% respectively for primary wellness travelers). Domestic wellness travel also leads to international wellness travel, at 82% of trips, and 65% of expenditures (compared to 18% and 35% respectively for international wellness travel) (Yeung & Johnston, 2018).

Table 1.6: Top 15 Wellness tourism destination markets in 2017

Rank in 2017	Country	Number of Trips (millions)	Direct Employment (millions)	Expenditures (US$ billions)
1	United States	176.5	1.88	$226.0
2	Germany	66.1	1.13	$65.7
3	China	70.2	1.78	$31.7
4	France	32.4	0.31	$30.7
5	Japan	40.5	0.18	$22.5
6	Austria	16.8	0.16	$16.5
7	India	56.0	3.74	$16.3
8	Canada	27.5	0.29	$15.7
9	United Kingdom	23.2	0.20	$13.5
10	Italy	13.1	0.15	$13.4
11	Mexico	18.7	0.49	$12.8
12	Switzerland	9.7	0.10	$12.6
13	Thailand	12.5	0.53	$12.0
14	Australia	10.0	0.11	$10.5
15	Spain	18.8	0.10	$9.9

Note: These figures combine both international/inbound and domestic wellness tourism spending, and also include both primary and secondary wellness trips.

Adapted from Yeung & Johnston (2018, p. 24).

Wellness tourists tend to spend more than the average traveler. They are typically more wealthy, educated, and well-traveled, and keen on trying new wellness experiences. In 2017, the international wellness traveler spent 53% more than the average international traveler, and the domestic wellness tourist spent 178% more than the average domestic tourist. Primary wellness travelers outspent secondary wellness travelers in both categories (Yeung & Johnston, 2018). By 2022, the total wellness tourism industry is projected to be worth over $910bn, which will represent 18% of the global tourism market (Yeung & Johnston, 2018).

Wellness tourism vs. medical tourism

It is important to distinguish between wellness tourism and medical tourism. Although both are often combined under the umbrella of "health tourism," they serve very different purposes and target audiences. The confusion comes from not only consumers but also destination marketing. This misconception and miscommunication stems from poor understanding of these markets and inconsistent use of terminologies by destinations, government agencies and promotional agencies (GWI, 2022). **Medical tourism** is related to the "poor health" end of the spectrum, with patients traveling to another place for specific medical treatments or enhancements. These reactive events may include elective and necessary surgery and dental procedures. On the other side of the spectrum are the wellness tourists, seeking a proactive way to maintain and protect their health through healthy living, disease prevention, stress reduction, and more through voluntary non-medical activities. Not only are the motivations for these two types of travel quite different, but the resulting customer mindsets, resources needed, and beneficiaries differ drastically as well (Tables 1.7 and 1.8).

Table 1.7: Medical and wellness continuum

Reactive	Proactive
Medical tourism	**Wellness tourism**
Purpose is to receive treatment for a diagnosed disease, ailment, condition or to seek enhancement.	Purpose is to maintain, manage, or improve health and well-being.
Driven by a desire for lower cost of care, higher quality care, better access to care, and/or care not available at home.	Driven by a desire for healthy living, disease prevention, stress reduction, management of poor lifestyle habits, and/or authentic experiences.
Reactive to illnesses, medically necessary, invasive activities, and/or those overseen by a doctor.	Proactive, voluntary and non-invasive activities.

Adapted and developed from Yeung & Johnston (2018).

Table 1.8: Health continuum

Poor health	Optimal state of well-being
Medical paradigm	**Wellness paradigm**
Feel better	Thrive
Treat and cure illness	Maintain and improve health
Corrective	Preventive
Episodic	Holistic
Clinical-responsibility	Individual responsibility
Compartmentalized	Integrated into life

Adapted and developed from Yeung & Johnston (2018).

Wellness tourism and Covid-19

Crises such as Covid-19 create devastation and opportunities for tourism activities. Even before the severe global crisis caused by the Covid-19 pandemic in 2020, people were interested in finding health and wellness activities and places while traveling (Silva & Mayer, 2021). For example, travelers have long sought therapeutic environments and landscapes that encompass healing in natural areas. Researchers have begun to understand tourist behaviors toward these landscapes and their contributions to healing processes. Consequently, recent academic studies have focused on the potential of therapeutic environments and landscapes in order to reveal the importance of health and wellness tourism destinations after Covid-19 (Majeed & Ramkissoon, 2020).

Recent studies have also revealed the significant negative effects of Covid-19 on mental and physical health. However, the tourism industry is still in the early stages of investigating whether the current health and wellness concepts are effectively healing the psychological and physical devastations of Covid-19 (Ma et al., 2021). For instance, spa and thermal centers have unique healing effects on physical health issues but supply and demand has fluctuated in recent years. Therefore, the functionality of thermal centers, especially the use of mineral waters, should be reviewed by destinations due to a heightened need (Pinos Navarrete & Shaw, 2021). The pandemic has created big opportunities for thermal destinations and other wellness destinations to reposition their wellness activities, services and products by examining the functions and improvement potentials of these destinations.

Summary

Throughout history, people have searched for health and wellness. The Global Wellness Institute specifies that wellness differs from medicine, and defines wellness as "the active pursuit of activities, choices, and lifestyles that lead to a state of holistic health"(GWI, 2019a; Yeung & Johnston. 2018). The wellness industry is one of the fastest-growing and most lucrative segments of the global tourism market. The segment is comprised of primary wellness tourists and secondary wellness tourists, and the hospitality industry is responding with a variety of wellness-themed and authentic wellness developments. Many stakeholders benefit from wellness travel, including the local community.

Definition of key terms

Ayurveda – A holistic system that promotes harmony between body, mind, and spirit by balancing each person's nutritional, exercise, social, and hygiene needs (Global Wellness Institute, 2019b)

Chiropractic – A practice that focuses on the body's structure and functioning, developed by Daniel David Palmer (Global Wellness Institute, 2019b)

Domestic wellness tourism expenditures – All expenditures in a country made by wellness tourists who are traveling within their own country, with an overnight stay (Yeung and Johnston, 2018).

Health – A state of complete physical, mental, and social well-being.

Homeopathy – A system that uses natural substances to encourage the body to heal itself, developed by German physician Christian Hahneman (Global Wellness Institute, 2019a and 2019b).

International wellness tourism expenditures – All receipts earned by a country from inbound wellness tourists visiting from abroad, with an overnight stay (Yeung and Johnston, 2018).

Medical tourism – Related to the "poor health" end of the market, with people traveling to another place for medical treatments or enhancements.

Naturopathy – An approach focused on the body's ability to heal itself through dietary and lifestyle change, herbs, massage and joint manipulation (Global Wellness Institute, 2019a and 2019b).

Osteopathy – A holistic healing approach to manipulating muscles and joints, developed by Andrew Taylor Still (Global Wellness Institute, 2019a and 2019b).

Primary wellness tourist – A tourist whose trip or destination is primarily motivated by wellness (Yeung and Johnston, 2018).

Sanatorium – A medical facility for long-term illness or other healing practices.

Secondary wellness tourist – A tourist who seeks to maintain wellness while traveling or who participates in wellness experiences while taking any type of trip for leisure or business (Global Wellness Institute, 2019a and 2019b; Yeung and Johnston, 2018).

Traditional Chinese Medicine (TCM) – A holistic perspective to achieving health and well-being by fostering harmony and using techniques like acupuncture, herbal medicine, qigong, and tai chi (Global Wellness Institute, 2019a and 2019b).

Well-being – Closely associated with the intangible concept of happiness and is both subjective and psychological in nature (Dillette et al., 2020).

Wellness – The active pursuit of activities, choices and lifestyles that lead to a state of holistic health (Global Wellness Institute, 2019a).

Wellness economy – Industries that enable consumers to incorporate wellness activities and lifestyles into their daily lives (Global Wellness Institute, 2019a).

Wellness resort – Accommodation with four primary elements: (i) accommodation, (ii) a variety of wellness activities, (iii) healthy dining options, and (iv) wellness-related facilities (Schweder and Modena, 2018)

Wellness retreat – Multi-day programs hosted by one or more facilitators, which are intention-driven and typically include learning and lifestyle workshops and fitness activities.

Wellness tourism – Traveling for the purpose of maintaining and improving one's personal physical and mental wellbeing.

Discussion questions

1. Why is wellness becoming so important and popular in hospitality and tourism?
2. Who benefits from wellness in hospitality and tourism?
3. What is the monetary value of wellness travel?
4. What are the differences between wellness tourism and medical tourism?

5. What are the main stakeholders/beneficiaries the of wellness sector in the hospitality and tourism industry?

6. According to the CDC, traveling to another country to get medical care can be risky. Why is this, what can be the possible risks, and how can they be minimized?

Homework

Find an example of a hospitality and tourism organization or a destination that promotes wellness as one of their core offerings. In two pages, describe what they offer, discuss how the entities work together to support and improve the destination, and write about a few ways the local people benefit from the focus on wellness.

References

Abdo, A., & Shokry, M. (2020). Health and wellness resorts. *Journal of Critical Reviews*, 7(8).

Boccardelli, P., & Peruffo, E. (2018). How Technogym Created the Wellness Industry. In *Business Despite Borders* (pp. 65-76). Palgrave Macmillan, Cham.

Bucket List Family. (2019). About. Retrieved January 25, 2020, from https://www.thebucketlistfamily.com/about

Bucket List Family (n.d.a). YouTube Channel. Retrieved January 25, 2020, from https://www.youtube.com/channel/UCuAHfJyWROB4XRReS43EWUw

Bucket List Family (n.d.b). Instagram Page. Retrieved January 25, 2020, from https://www.instagram.com/thebucketlistfamily/

Centers for Disease Control and Prevention (2021). Medical Tourism: Travel to another Country for Medical Care. Retrieved March 11, 2022, from https://wwwnc.cdc.gov/travel/page/medical-tourism

Dillette, A.K, Douglas, A,.C., & Andrzejewski, C. (2020). Dimensions of holistic wellness as a result of international wellness tourism experiences. *Current Issues in Tourism*. 1-18. DOI: 10.1080/13683500.2020.1746247

Gee, G. (2017). The ultimate travel workout and diet plans by The Bucket List Family. Medium. Retrieved January 20, 2020 from https://medium.com/@garrettgee/the-bucket-list-family-travel-workout-and-diet-plan-61660c5533a1

Global Wellness Institute. (2019a). Wellness Definitions. Retrieved November 8, 2019, from https://globalwellnessinstitute.org/what-is-wellness/wellness-economy-definitions/

Global Wellness Institute. (2019b). History of Wellness. Retrieved January 1, 2020, from https://globalwellnessinstitute.org/industry-research/history-of-wellness/

Global Wellness Institute. (2020). What is wellness tourism? Retrieved January 25, 2020, from https://globalwellnessinstitute.org/what-is-wellness/what-is-wellness-tourism/

Global Wellness Institute (2021). The Global Wellness Economy: Looking Beyond Covid. Retrieved May 28, 2022 from https://globalwellnessinstitute.org/wp-content/uploads/2021/11/GWI-WE-Monitor-2021_final-digital.pdf

Global Wellness Institute. (2022). Wellness Tourism. Retrieved March 11, 2022, from https://globalwellnessinstitute.org/what-is-wellness/what-is-wellness-tourism/

Kaur, K., & Kumar, P. (2020). Social media usage in Indian beauty and wellness industry: a qualitative study. *TQM Journal*. 33(1), 17-32. https://doi.org/10.1108/TQM-09-2019-0216

Kazakov, S. & Oyner, O. (2019). Wellness tourism: A perspective article. *Tourism Review*. 1 – 6. DOI:10.1108/TR-05-2019-0154

Kyricos, M. (2019). The name game: Defining wellness and well-being. Retrieved January 2, 2020, from https://www.hotelmanagement.net/operate/name-game-defining-wellness-and-well-being-for-hospitality-industry

Organization for Economic Co-operation and Development (2021). OECD Health Statistics 2019. Retrieved May 28, 2022, from https://www.oecd.org/health/health-data.htm

Oxford Dictionary. (2020). Biofeedback. Retrieved May 19, 2020 from https://www.lexico.com/definition/biofeedback

Ma, S., Zhao, X., Gong, Y., & Wengel, Y. (2021). Proposing "healing tourism" as a post-Covid-19 tourism product. *Anatolia*, 32(1), 136-139.

Majeed, S., & Ramkissoon, H. (2020). Health, wellness, and place attachment during and post health pandemics. *Frontiers in Psychology*, 3026.

Merriam Webster. (2020a) Qigong. Retrieved January 20, 2020, from https://www.merriam-webster.com/dictionary/qigong

Merriam Webster. (2020b). Hamam. Retrieved January 20, 2020, from https://www.merriam-webster.com/dictionary/hammam

Pavlenko, I. G., Ostovskaya, A. A., & Kirenkina, E. S. (2019, June). Transition Model: to the Ecologically Balanced Development of the Ecosystem of Wellness Resort Territories. In *IOP Conference Series: Earth and Environmental Science* (272(2), 22072). IOP Publishing.

Pierre-Louis, A. (2019). How to integrate wellness into hospitality for guest satisfaction and owner return. Retrieved January 2, 2020, from https://insights.ehotelier.com/insights/2019/08/08/how-to-integrate-wellness-into-hospitality-for-guest-satisfaction-and-owner-return/

Pinos Navarrete, A., & Shaw, G. (2021). Spa tourism opportunities as strategic sector in aiding recovery from Covid-19: The Spanish model. *Tourism and Hospitality Research*, 21(2), 245-250.

Schweder, I & Modena, F. (2018). Industry Report: Wellness-Themed vs. Wellness Hospitality. Retrieved January 2, 2020, from https://horwathhtl.com/ publication/ industry-report-wellness-themed-vs-wellness-hospitality/

Silva, L. C. S., & Mayer, V. F. (2021). Wellness tourism: Conceptual analysis and trends. In *Rebuilding and Restructuring the Tourism Industry: Infusion of happiness and quality of life* (pp. 183-196). IGI Global.

Stara, J. & Peterson, C. (2017). Understanding the concept of wellness for the future of the tourism industry: A literature review. *Journal of Tourism and Services*, 14(1), 18-29.

World Health Organization (2018a). Obesity and Overweight: Key Facts. Retrieved November 9, 2019, from https://www.who.int/news-room/ fact-sheets/detail/obesity-and-overweight

World Health Organization (2018b). Diabetes: Key Facts. Retrieved November 9, 2019, from https://www.who.int/news-room/fact-sheets/detail/diabetes

World Health Organization (2019). Constitution. Retrieved November 8, 2019, from https://www.who.int/about/who-we-are/constitution

World Health Organization (2022). Covid-19 pandemic triggers 25% increase in prevalence of anxiety and depression worldwide. Retrieved May 28, 2022, from https://www.who.int/news/item/02-03-2022-covid-19-pandemic-triggers-25-increase-in-prevalence-of-anxiety-and-depression-worldwide

Yeung, O. & Johnston, K. (2018). Global Wellness Tourism Economy Monitor October 2018. Global Wellness Institute. Retrieved November 8, 2019, from https://globalwellnessinstitute.org/ industry-research/ global-wellness-tourism-economy/

2 | Quality of Life and Wellness in Hospitality and Tourism

This chapter discusses how wellness in hospitality and tourism affects individual travelers and the destinations they visit. First, it introduces the concept of quality of life and wellness and how it applies to hospitality and tourism. Then, it introduces mindfulness as an underlying concept of wellness travel and its benefits to the individual traveler and the destination. Finally, some trends in wellness hospitality and tourism are presented.

Learning outcomes

By the end of this chapter, students should be able to do the following:

1. Define and discuss the term 'quality of life'.
2. Define and discuss the domains of the Gross National Happiness Index (GNHI) and the World Happiness Report.
3. Discuss why some countries have higher World Happiness Report rankings than others.
4. Define and discuss the concept of quality of life and wellness in hospitality and tourism.
5. Define mindfulness within a hospitality and tourism context.
6. Discuss the benefits of mindfulness to travelers.
7. Discuss the benefits and drawbacks of mindfulness to the destination.
8. Discuss how the concept of quality of life and wellness can be improved through hospitality and tourism.
9. Define bleisure and discuss how hospitality and travel businesses can offer better bleisure packages.

Case study: Six Senses Bhutan

In 2018, the first of the Six Senses Bhutan lodges opened in the first carbon-negative country (one of only three as of May 2022, the others being Suriname and Panama). With a total of five lodges open in Bhutan as of May 2022, the brand offers an entirely new type of trip to travelers seeking a unique wellness experience. Described as a multi-lodge wellness circuit, guests can stay at one lodge or have the option to journey through all five properties (with 82 rooms total) in Thimphu (located next to pine forests and apple orchards), Punakha (a more austere lodge), Paro (the "Stone Ruins"), the Gangtey (in the Phobjikha Valley), and Bumthang (in the mountain district) (Six Senses, 2020).

These five lodges are spread around dramatically diverse topographies, climate zones, and cultural areas of the country and represent the five key pillars of Bhutan's unique "Gross National Happiness Index (GNHI)" declared in 1972 by then-King Jigme Singye Wangchuck to be more important than the Gross Domestic Product (GDP). The domains of the GNHI include psychological well-being, health, education, time use, cultural diversity and resilience, good governance, community vitality, ecological diversity and resilience, and living standards. Based on their responses to the index questions, people in a specific country are rated as unhappy, narrowly happy, extensively happy, or deeply happy.

• Psychological wellbeing • Cultural diversity and resilience • Good governance	• Ecological diversity and resilience • Education • Time use	• Health • Community vitality • Living standards

Figure 2.1: Gross National Health Index domains. Developed from Oxford Poverty & Human Development Initiative (2020).

The Six Senses Bhutan lodges were built on these GNHI domains (Figure 2.1), with each location being wholly focused on wellness, sustainability, culture, and spirituality, from the hotel design to their food and beverage offerings, to the spa experiences. The Six Senses guiding principles include their pioneering spa and wellness offerings, wholesome and sustainable cuisine, sleep health, and self-discovery (Six Senses, 2019a). The Six Senses Bhutan lodges offer their guests anywhere from four- to 10-night stays in the various lodges and even offer guests "tailored stays" where the lodge will accommodate guests' individual wants and needs (Six Senses, 2020).

Guests receive a bracelet at the beginning of their trip to mark their physical, mental, and spiritual journey. When they arrive at each of the five properties, they receive a card and guidance to set their intentions for the specific aspect of happiness promoted at that lodge (Yeung and Johnston, 2018). Six Senses also promotes wellness for its employees through programs to help everyone achieve optimal well-being (Six Senses, 2019b). Lastly, their sustainability principles incorporate green energy, employing and sourcing locally, keeping funds in the local community, and more (Six Senses, 2019c)·

Discussion questions

1. What are the domains of the Gross National Happiness Index (GNHI)?
2. How does the Six Senses Bhutan brand promote wellness to the local people and community?
3. How does the Six Senses Bhutan brand promote wellness to its guests?
4. Find similar lodging businesses in your city/region or country that operate in the same domain and discuss what they offer.

Quality of life and wellness

The WHO defines **quality of life** as, "an individual's perception of their position in life in the context of the culture and value systems in which they live and in relation to their goals, expectations, standards and concerns" (WHO, 2012). It can refer to the well-being of both societies and individuals and includes many factors like physical health, education, employment, wealth, safety and security, freedom, family, religious beliefs, and the environment. The **GNHI** offers a way to measure the general well-being of a population (on a scale from zero to one) across nine domains (Oxford Poverty & Human Development Initiative, 2020).

1. **Living Standards** – material comforts measured by income, financial security, housing, asset ownership.
2. **Health** – both physical and mental health.
3. **Education** – types of knowledge, values, and skills.
4. **Good governance** – how people perceive government functions.
5. **Ecological diversity and resilience** – people's perception of their environment.
6. **Time use** – how much time is spent on work, non-work, sleep; work-life balance.
7. **Psychological well-being** – quality of life, life satisfaction, and spirituality.
8. **Cultural diversity and resilience** – strength of cultural traditions and festivals.
9. **Community vitality** – relationships and interactions with community, social cohesion, and volunteerism.

Adapted from the 2015 GNH Survey Report (Centre for Bhutan Studies & GNH Research, 2020).

Currently, the GNHI method is only used in Bhutan. The country of Bhutan views the GNHI as more important to its country than the GNP, and its purpose is to ensure

Bhutan and its society is "just, equal and harmonious" (Centre for Bhutan Studies & GNH Research, 2020). The 2015 survey concluded that when compared to the 2010 survey, Bhutanese people are happier and healthier, which indicates that the lives of the Bhutanese people are getting better. The report also shows the government of Bhutan how the lives of its people can be improved to increase their overall wellness. The 2015 survey highlighted that the psychological well-being of the Bhutanese people needs to be improved to help increase the country's GNHI score.

The worldwide version of the GNHI is the World Happiness Report, published by the United Nations Sustainable Development Solutions Network since 2012. This report incorporates factors like GDP per capita, social support, healthy life expectancy, freedom to make life choices, generosity, and perceptions of corruption in its happiness score (World Happiness Report, 2019). This report is unique in that the scores are not based on an index for all six factors but instead on individuals in each country's assessment of those factors in their own lives in their country (World Happiness Report, 2022). The United Nations states that the GDP per capita and healthy life expectancy are the two factors that have the most significant impact on a country's happiness score. Table 2.1 lists the top 20 counties in the World Happiness Report and Table 2.2 lists the lowest ranking countries on the World Happiness Report.

Table 2.1: World Happiness Report Top 20 Countries, 2020.

Ranking	Country	Score (out of 10)
1	Finland	7.82
2	Denmark	7.64
3	Iceland	7.56
4	Switzerland	7.51
5	Netherlands	7.42
6	Luxembourg	7.40
7	Sweden	7.38
8	Norway	7.37
9	Israel	7.36
10	New Zealand	7.20
11	Austria	7.16
12	Australia	7.16
13	Ireland	7.04
14	Germany	7.03
15	Canada	7.03
16	United States	6.98
17	United Kingdom	6.94
18	Czechia	6.92
19	Belgium	6.81
20	France	6.69

Developed from the World Happiness Report (2022).

Table 2.2: World Happiness Report Lowest Ranking Countries (2020)

Ranking	Country	Score (out of 10)
130	Chad	4.25
131	Ethiopia	4.24
132	Yemen	4.20
133	Mauritania	4.15
134	Jordan	4.15
135	Togo	4.11
136	India	3.78
137	Zambia	3.76
138	Malawi	3.75
139	Tanzania	3.70
140	Sierra Leone	3.57
141	Lesotho	3.51
142	Botswana	3.47
143	Rwanda	3.27
144	Zimbabwe	3.00
145	Lebanon	3.00
146	Afghanistan	2.40

Developed from the World Happiness Report (2022).

Quality of life and wellness in hospitality and tourism

Although quality of life (QOL) research in tourism is new, it has been ongoing for many years in other disciplines. People have always developed new visions to live their lives in a better way, and scholars and practitioners are now learning more about QOL adaptation strategies for tourism. Individuals with economic advantages can travel easily, which may increase their satisfaction from travel, and therefore improve their overall QOL. However, individuals with socio-economic disadvantages cannot participate in leisure tourism frequently, so they prefer to do other travel activities such as visiting friends and relatives (VFR tourism) which may result in positive outcomes for their QOL (Backer & Weiler, 2018; Taheri et al., 2017).

Wellness in the hospitality and tourism movement is increasing quality of life not only for travelers but for the local people in their destinations as well (Figure 2.2). As mentioned in Chapter 1, wellness is about more than just spa treatments and hotel fitness centers. The global wellness economy reached an estimated $4.9 trillion in 2019 and is projected to snowball in the coming years as the world recovers from Covid-19 (Global Wellness Institute, 2021). The tourism segment of the global wellness economy was valued at $639 billion in 2017 (pre-Covid-19), offering a lucrative target market for many destinations across the globe (Global Wellness Institute, 2019).

As presented in Figure 2.2, lodging, although it is the largest segment, is not the only tourism category that benefits from wellness travel. In 2017, it was valued at $130.5 billion. This was followed by food and beverage at $111.5 billion, in-country transport at $109.9 billion, shopping at $98.3 billion, activities and excursions at $99.7 billion, and other services at $89.5 billion (Yeung and Johnston, 2018).

In-Country Transport **$109.9b** Airlines, Rental Cars, Public Transit, Trains, Taxis	Hotels/Motels Resorts Campgrounds	**Lodging** **$130.5b**	Destination Spas Health Resorts Ashrams | Retreats
	Restaurants Bars Snack Shops	**Food & Beverage** **$111.5b**	Spa Cuisine Healthy Cuisine Organic Cuisine
	Souvenirs | Gifts Clothing | Art	**Shopping** **$98.3b**	Fitness Wear | Spa Products Healthy Foods | Vitamins
Other Services **$89.5b** Telecom, Insurance, Travel Agencies, Concierges	Museums Tours | Theater	**Activities & Excursions** **$99.7b**	Spas | Bathing | Fitness Meditation | Life Coaching

Generic → Wellness-Specific

Figure 2.2: The Wellness Tourism Industry in 2017. Adapted from Global Wellness Summit (2020).

Benefits of wellness to guests in hospitality and tourism

While physical advantages to the body, through activities like hiking or swimming, are an essential component of wellness tourism, the mind can also benefit. **Mindfulness** is known as the practice of maintaining a nonjudgmental state of heightened or complete awareness of one's thoughts, emotions, or experiences on a moment-to-moment basis (Merriam-Webster, 2019). To travel more mindfully, people can take such actions as slowing down and noticing where they are and what is around them, feeling each step and engaging all of their senses, savoring the moment, and relaxing and resting. Simply walking out of the hotel with no plan, only the intention to wander, and notice everything going on, without the distraction of a screen, can be one way to engage mindfully and learn about a destination more completely (Mindful.org, 2017). Focusing on wellness while traveling can benefit both the traveler and the destination they are visiting.

When people visit hospitality and tourism businesses or while they travel, they often neglect the good habits they have in their everyday life. At home, they may have a consistent sleep schedule and monitor their nutritional intake. However, on vacation or a business trip, sleep routines may be disrupted, fitness schedules are neglected, and food and alcohol consumption can become excessive. These disruptions can lead to sickness, exhaustion, and feeling like the vacation was not refreshing. In addition, they may find it difficult to return to a normal schedule upon returning home.

On the other hand, concentrating on wellness while traveling, whether a primary or secondary focus, encourages tourists to maintain and enhance their quality of life even when out of their everyday routine. Even consciously making decisions such as limiting food and alcohol consumption, going for a nature walk daily, or setting aside time for creative activities will benefit a traveler. Overindulging in unhealthy options while traveling may give short-term gratification, but people often regret that decision soon after.

The external environment of the facility or location is important in aiding in the wellness of the tourist. The components of the facility consist of the overall tone created by staff, activities and dining, the tourist participation in said activities and the support instructors, and the variety and novelty of the activities like meditation or wellness seminars. This lays the foundation to support the guest's basic needs (i.e., relationships with other guests, facility staff, and instructors and their autonomy) as well as incorporates wellness-related values like mindfulness and intrinsic motivation. This leads to the facility creating psychological well-being in the guest through enhanced confidence and competence in wellness and their enhanced wellness-related abilities, which is the eventual goal of a wellness facility and wellness vacation or trip (Thal & Hudson, 2019).

A major goal of a wellness trip is to return home feeling better at check-out than at check-in. Traveling with wellness in mind not only encourages people to maintain their existing positive habits, but also offers opportunities to expand their awareness to learn about and incorporate new practices. Millennials, in particular, look for experiences that build on their existing daily wellness practices without replicating them. This generation already combines wellness into their everyday life with meditation, yoga classes, and cold-pressed juices, and is looking for more (Yeung and Johnston, 2018).

Possible activities to include on a wellness trip comprise those focused on the mind, such as different types of meditation, creative classes, relaxation techniques, Ayurvedic treatments, and spending time in nature. Complementary physical activities might include a unique type of yoga, walking or running, spa treatments, mineral or hot springs, healthy cooking, or dining at a local farm-to-table bistro. All of these behaviors could be added on to any trip by a secondary wellness traveler, or they could make up the bulk of a trip for a primary wellness traveler.

Even when traveling on business, it is possible to make time for wellness activities. In a break between meetings, a traveler can put on their walking shoes and explore the surrounding area on foot, instead of only seeing it from a vehicle window on the way to and from the airport. Many cities and hotels also offer bicycle rental for another convenient and healthy way to travel. Hotels also may have features like early-morning yoga classes and evening meditation sessions that can fit into a business traveler's day. The Walt Disney World Resort, in Orlando, Florida, advertises jogging paths around their resorts on their recreation page. Resorts on the property like the Boardwalk even offer "fun run" races for the guests staying at the resort. In addition to jogging, hotels at the Walt Disney World Resort, like the Boardwalk, offer their guests complimentary early morning yoga classes on select mornings during the week (Walt Disney World Resort, 2020a).

These activities are far more interesting than the hotel fitness room. In addition to making time for wellness activities throughout the day, business travelers want to be able to extend a business trip and enjoy a few personal days, a phenomenon known as **bleisure** travel. A Global Business Travel Association study found that almost 70% of those surveyed believe having the option to add a few personal days to a business trip is important (Global Business Travel Association, n.d.).

Wellness in hospitality and tourism does not need to be expensive. It is not about spending thousands of dollars at a luxury spa, but rather finding activities to heighten enjoyment and healthily relax the mind and body. This could be as easy and inexpensive as disconnecting from technology for a few hours and taking a nature walk in a nearby town. Anyone traveling can follow suggestions like staying hydrated, wearing sunscreen, eating well, and ensuring adequate sleep. Wellness in hospitality and tourism is simply a pause in everyday life, offering an opportunity to relax and return to daily activities in a more focused and refreshed frame of mind.

The benefits of wellness in hospitality and tourism continue even after returning home. A 2017 study found that after a weeklong wellness retreat, attendees saw sustained weight loss, lowered blood pressure, and psychological benefits for at least six weeks beyond their trip (Cohen et al., 2017).

Benefits of quality of life and wellness packages to destinations

Researchers are finding that high-end luxury travelers are more frequently seeking wellness vacations. The international wellness tourist spent 53% more than the average international tourist, and the domestic wellness tourist spent 178% more than the average domestic tourist in 2017 (Global Wellness Summit, 2019). Socially conscious high-net-worth consumers, especially those members of younger generations, look for sustainable, ethical living through inconspicuous and responsible consumption, rather than overt and traditional displays of wealth like designer labels (Quartz, 2017). There are also the "discerning affluents" who comprise twice the luxury market when compared to those who are considered "status seekers." This group is less likely to buy a Mercedes because it is a Mercedes and more likely to buy it because it is "the safest car in the world". Discerning affluents have a better understanding of their purchases when compared to status seekers. They are also more likely to do research on and justify luxury purchases like luxury wellness travel, which makes them a developing market for wellness tourism destinations (Michelli, 2008).

Younger generations (Millennials and Generation Z) are more willing to invest in sustainable and ethical brands than older generations (Generation X and Baby Boomers). This can be seen in the rise of ethical and sustainable brands like TOMs, Inkkas, KAVU, Serengetee, and many more who target these generations with their products. This, in turn, means than younger travelers (Millennials and Gen Z) are more willing to invest in sustainable luxury travel and ethical brands than older generations (Gen X and Baby Boomers), and future luxury travelers have more of a focus on philanthropy and giving back. However, while these travelers are willing to pay more for a sustainable hotel, they do not want to compromise on luxury or comfort (MATTER, 2019). This interest in wellness travel from high-end luxury travelers means that fewer visitors are needed to bring in the same amount of revenue, which can help destinations minimize their risk of overtourism. Wellness travel also encourages visitors to go beyond crowded cities and major tourist destinations and visit less "touristy" locations in areas that can benefit significantly from the economic boost and also helps to lessen the strain of overtourism on those popular tourist destinations. These more rural and underdeveloped areas have limited infrastructure and can only handle a limited number of visitors. Therefore, higher-spending travelers are a lucrative market.

Beyond suburbs and rural areas within easy traveling distance from a city, developing markets like Africa, Asia-Pacific, and Latin America are benefiting from travelers interested in their unspoiled and still truly authentic offerings (Powell, 2018a). For example, Singita luxury safari lodges in Africa feature not only a spa and a healthy menu, but a genuine opportunity to slow down, disconnect from digital devices, and reconnect with nature and one's self. According to Singita CEO Tom Fels, "what Singita offers is a holistic experience; in the space, the quiet, the integration with nature, our people, our purposeful conservation and community work, while accompanied by thoughtful and relevant food offerings and the opportunity to exercise or relax the body or mind. The total result of which is a transformative wellness experience" (Shankman, 2018).

Although there are few destinations almost wholly dedicated to wellness tourism, most locations already have some existing features to attract wellness travelers. These include promoting locally grown healthy food options, locally owned businesses with any health or sustainability focus, local nature areas, holistic health care providers, and more. This allows the region's people to share their local cultures and customs while protecting their environment and bringing income into their economy.

The marketing appeal of travelers going home in a healthier state than they arrived can be used by many destinations to bring visitors in the short term. At the same time, they work on further developing their wellness offerings. However, it is important to note that, like overtourism, promoting wellness travel to a destination does have potential drawbacks. Smaller communities with health-minded residents might be overwhelmed by visitors filling their yoga classes, hiking trails, and spas. Like with overtourism, local residents may feel like wellness tourists are pushing them out of their wellness activities while also increasing the price. Although wellness tourism does bring in tourist dollars to the economy, it may reduce residents' quality of life, decreasing the appeal of the destination as a wellness destination (Barrie, 2019).

Wellness trends in hospitality and tourism

Individual wellness travel is increasing

Women, in particular, are traveling alone to achieve their wellness goals. At the Fairmont Chateau Lake Louise in Canada's Banff National Park, solo female travelers were responsible for purchasing half of their one- or two-night wellness packages, and three-quarters of their three- and four-night stays. Half of the guests at Canyon Ranch, a brand of wellness resorts, retreats, and facilities, are solo travelers, often looking for an immersive and self-reflective experience. Guests want an experience that is private and personal, and solo wellness travel provides that for many (Craft, 2019; eHotelier, 2019).

Demand for flexibility in trip length

As each wellness journey is unique, travelers also look for an itinerary that fits their schedule. Some prefer an extended getaway, for example, eight to twelve weeks, to make significant life or health changes. Others like short trips throughout the year to recharge or maintain a commitment to long-term wellness (Craft, 2019; eHotelier, 2019). For secondary wellness tourists, this variation in trip length allows them to add supplementary wellness plans to their existing trips.

Higher awareness of value proposition

As mentioned, the wellness travel segment is growing more rapidly than the overall travel industry, and wellness travelers in particular are a high-value segment (Yeung and Johnston, 2018). Although these consumers are willing to spend more, in exchange they are requesting specific solutions that are the right fit for their needs. Their goals may be clearly defined as losing weight or establishing a healthy eating plan, or they may be less defined, such as a need to regroup internally after a significant life change (eHotelier, 2019). Wellness travelers are ready to pay to have their exact needs met, when they see a high life-enrichment potential.

Large hotels recognizing wellness

Hotels are also joining the wellness trends and developing their offerings. Some hotels are adding chromotherapy (a form of color therapy) to their spa lineup – for example, choose blue to reduce blood pressure or violet to stimulate your immune system. Others are incorporating salt float bath therapy, cryo skin slimming, infrared saunas, CBD treatments, trendy fitness equipment, and more. For example, Marriott International not only offers wellness-themed hotel rooms and many special features throughout its properties but has also developed an internally focused program for both guests and employees. TakeCare Level30 began in August 2019; the custom app-based well-being challenge allows players to partner and compete by incorporating rewarding behaviors into their daily routine. These behaviors include reading, meditating, drinking more water, and other habits that take 30 days to develop. The goal of this program is to improve users' overall happiness, personal wellness, interactions with others, and their impact on the community. The program was designed to appeal to users all around the world and to be a fun, opt-in way to interact with other employees and guests while improving overall well-being (Kohll, 2019).

Hyatt created a new position in August 2018, the Senior Vice President, Global Head of Well-Being, responsible for improving both guest and employee well-being. Hyatt has also invested heavily in well-being, with the acquisition of the Miraval and

Exhale resort, fitness, and spa brands. Miraval is about mindfulness getaways, and Exhale seeks to provide accessible wellness every day (Powell, 2018b).

Transformative travel

The benefits of experiences, including hospitality and tourism, have been heavily studied since the release of *Welcome to the Experience Economy* in 1998 (Pine & Gilmore, 1998). The experience economy is society moving away from purchasing just goods and services to purchasing customized experiences, and experiential travel is one way to customize a tourist's experience. Experiential travel has focused on authenticity by helping travelers live, dine, and explore like locals. Now, travelers are going beyond experiences and into **transformative travel**. Considered to be "hospitality and travel products that inspire and challenge travelers on a deeply personal level, creating emotions through the powerful medium of storytelling," this transformation happens through individual self-reflection, rather than just experiencing products and services. Customers are looking for more than disconnected treatments, programs, and classes; they want life-changing wellness journeys (Yeung and Johnston, 2018).

Wellness takes on overtourism

As the world becomes more affluent and the middle class continues to grow, more and more people are traveling, which takes a toll on popular tourist destinations like Barcelona, Venice, and Dubrovnik. Euromonitor International reports that 46% of tourists visit just 100 destinations; this leads to overcrowding and degradation of the destination (which are only a few of the side effects of overtourism). How does wellness address the issue of overtourism? Wellness tourism draws tourists to under-developed areas of each country, undeveloped regions, and even underdeveloped countries and can act as an "escape valve" for overtourism. The Global Wellness Summit gives the example of Tyrol in south Italy, which is a developing wellness destination that can help to alleviate some of the strains of overtourism felt by Venice. As wellness tourists continue to grow in their personal discovery for growth and wellness, their mindsets will change from consuming the resources a destination has to offer and tourism being commercial to a more meaningful two-way exchange between the destination and the tourist, thus helping combat the issue of overtourism (McGroarty et al., 2019).

China – uncovering the wealth in wellness

In the past few decades, China has emerged as a power player in the world economy, and its growing middle class and the sheer size of its market influence the global wellness industry. As China has opened its doors, pieces of its culture and its practices have become globalized. According to the 2019 Global Wellness Summit, "traditional Chinese medicine has reached 183 countries and regions around the world, expecting an estimated $50 billion global market." More wellness destinations worldwide will be incorporating Chinese traditional medicine into their wellness itineraries. China has increased its wellness tourism offerings to domestic and international tourists as well. According to the 2019 Global Wellness Summit, in recent years (pre-Covid-19), China has gone from 11th in wellness tourism to third, bringing in $31.7 billion in revenue and welcoming 70.2 million wellness stays. This increase in wellness tourism has seen resort brands like Alila, Aman, Banyan Tree, and Six Senses capitalize on the growing wellness hospitality industry in the country (McGroarty et al., 2019).

Food and healthy eating

Diet is considered an important contribution to health, so people associate healthy eating with wellness and well-being. Environmental conditions, psychological, social and cultural factors affect food choices (Falk et al., 2001). Authenticity, experiential values, and place attachment increase the intentions to re-purchase and recommend food among tourists (Chang et al., 2021). Ethnic food consumption also affects tourists' purchasing behavior and destination preferences. Therefore, food can be considered as a key marketing tool for destinations (Shi et al., 2022).

Exercise and a healthy diet can help improve negative moods, low energy levels and a lack of vitality in the human body. Food choices are often related to personal taste and unique body chemistry. Diet significantly affects a person's mood, sleep quality, social life and mental capacity. Excessive eating can lead to being overweight, and obesity that is associated with cancer, cardiovascular disease, and decreased physical function. Making healthy food choices is a key factor to optimize physical and mental health, but it is difficult to adhere to the right diet with diverse food and beverages to nourish body and mind.

Summary

This chapter started with an overview of the quality of life and wellness, including Bhutan's Gross National Happiness Index and the UN World Happiness Report score, and what quality of life means in hospitality and tourism. The concept of mindfulness was introduced, along with how practicing it in tourism can benefit travelers. A major goal of a wellness trip is to return home feeling better at check-out than at check-in, and each traveler goes about this transformation differently. Trends in wellness and tourism include solo wellness travel, the need for trip length flexibility, a higher awareness of the value proposition, the search for transformation in travel, and how large hotels are addressing this important segment.

Definition of key terms

Bleisure – The practice of combining business travel and leisure travel into one trip.

Gross National Happiness Index (GNHI) – Offers a way to measure the general well-being of a population across nine domains.

Mindfulness – "The practice of maintaining a nonjudgmental state of heightened or complete awareness of one's thoughts, emotions, or experiences on a moment-to-moment basis" (Merriam-Webster, 2019).

Quality of life – "An individual's perception of their position in life in the context of the culture and value systems in which they live and in relation to their goals, expectations, standards and concerns" (WHO, 2012).

Transformative travel – Travel products that challenge and inspire the sophisticated traveler on a deeply personal level, creating emotion through storytelling (McGroarty et al., 2018).

Discussion questions

1. What does the concept of quality of life mean, and why is it important?
2. How can we improve mindfulness for our guests and travelers?
3. Which countries have the highest World Happiness Report score, and why?
4. Which countries have the lowest World Happiness Report score, and why?
5. What wellness-related steps can be taken to help improve those scores?
6. What are the benefits of wellness travel for individual travelers?
7. What are the benefits of wellness travel for destinations?
8. What are the potential downfalls of wellness travel for destinations?
9. How can destinations mitigate these potential downfalls?
10. How can we improve the quality of life and wellness through hospitality and tourism?
11. What are the wellness trends in hospitality and tourism?
12. Find a local hospitality business and evaluate their bleisure options.

Homework

Think about how different types of travelers approach wellness activities. Consider business and leisure travelers, primary and secondary wellness travelers, and other categories. What might they be looking for? How can destinations appease them?

References

Backer, E., & Weiler, B. (2018). Travel and quality of life: Where do socio-economically disadvantaged individuals fit in? *Journal of Vacation Marketing*, 24(2), 159-171.

Barrie, L. (2019). Travel Megatrends 2019: Wellness is the new hook in travel marketing. Retrieved November 26, 2019, from https://skift.com/2019/02/26/travel-megatrends-2019-wellness-is-the-new-hook-in-travel-marketing/

Centre for Bhutan Studies & GNH Research. (2020). A compass towards a just and harmonious society: 2015 GNH Survey Report. Retrieved May 26, 2020 from http://www.grossnationalhappiness.com/wp-content/uploads/2017/01/Final-GNH-Report-jp-21.3.17-ilovepdf-compressed.pdf

Chang, J., Okumus, B., Li, Z. W., & Lin, H. H. (2021). What serves as the best bridge in food consumption: experiential value or place attachment? *Asia Pacific Journal of Tourism Research*, 26(12), 1302-1317.

Craft, D. (2019). Wellness travel trends – a niche category with broad appeal? Retrieved January 6, 2020, from www.wexinc.com/insights/blog/wex-travel/consumer/wellness-travel-trends-a-niche-category-with-broad-appeal/

Cohen, M. M., Elliott, F., Oates, L., Schembri, A. & Mantri, N. (2017). Do wellness tourists get well? An observational study of multiple dimensions of health and well-being after a week-long retreat. *Journal of Alternative and Complementary Medicine*, 23(2), 140-148.

eHotelier. (2019). Five wellness travel trends in 2019. Retrieved January 5, 2020, from https://insights.ehotelier.com/global-news/2019/01/17/five-wellness-travel-trends-in-2019/

Falk, L. W., Sobal, J., Bisogni, C. A., Connors, M., & Devine, C. M. (2001). Managing healthy eating: definitions, classifications, and strategies. *Health Education & Behavior*, 28(4), 425-439.

Global Business Travel Association. (n.d.) http://www.gbta.org/foundation/pressreleases/Pages/rls_02116.aspx

Global Wellness Institute. (2019) What is the Wellness Economy? Retrieved November 20, 2019, from https://globalwellnessinstitute.org/what-is-wellness/what-is-the-wellness-economy/

Global Wellness Institute (2021). The Global Wellness Economy: Looking Beyond Covid. Retrieved May 28, 2022 from https://globalwellnessinstitute.org/wp-content/uploads/2021/11/GWI-WE-Monitor-2021_final-digital.pdf

Global Wellness Summit. (2018). 2018 Global Wellness Trends Report. Retrieved November 20, 2019, from https://www.globalwellnesssummit.com/2018-global-wellness-trends/

Global Wellness Summit. (2019) 2018 Global Wellness Economy Monitor. Retrieved November 26, 2019, from https://globalwellnessinstitute.org/industry-research/2018-global-wellness-economy-monitor/

Kohll, A. (2019). How do you build a wellness program for 700,000+ employees? Retrieved November 26, 2019, from www.forbes.com/sites/alankohll/2019/08/04/how-do-you-build-a-wellness-program-for-700000-employees/#236dd61a45fe

MATTER. (2019). Sustainable luxury is the future: How travel brands must adapt to survive. Retrieved November 26, 2019, from https://matter.purelifeexperiences.com/

McGroarty, B., Isroelit, B., Cavanah, C. & Ellis, S. (2018). 2018 Wellness Trends, from Global Wellness Summit. Retrieved November 26, 2019 from https://www.globalwellnesssummit.com/wp-content/uploads/2018/03/2018GlobalWellnessTrends_GlobalWellnessSummit.pdf

McGroarty, B., Cavanah, C., Powell, L., Lo, J., Walsh, J., & Ellis, S. (2019). 2019 Wellness Trends, from Global Wellness Summit. Retrieved May 28, 2020 from https://www.globalwellnesssummit.com/2019-global-wellness-trends/

Merriam-Webster. (2019). Definition of mindfulness. Retrieved November 20, 2019, from https://www.merriam-webster.com/dictionary/mindfulness

Michelli, J.A. (2008). The new gold standard: 5 leadership principles for creating a legendary customer experience courtesy of The Ritz Carlton Hotel. New York: McGraw Hill.

Mindful.org. (2017). How to be a mindful traveler. Retrieved November 20, 2019, from https://www.mindful.org/how-to-be-a-mindful-traveler/

Oxford Poverty and Human Development Initiative (2019). Bhutan's Gross National Happiness Index. Retrieved November 26, 2019, from https://ophi.org.uk/policy/national-policy/gross-national-happiness-index/

Pine, B. J., & Gilmore, J. H. (1998). Welcome to the Experience Economy. *Harvard Business Review*, 76, 97-105.

Powell, L. (2018a). Can wellness provide an antidote to overtourism? Retrieved November 26, 2019, from https://skift.com/2018/10/10/can-wellness-provide-an-antidote-to-overtourism/

Powell, L. (2018b). Hyatt's new wellness exec talks strategy. Retrieved November 26, 2019, from skift.com/2018/12/18/hyatts-new-wellness-exec-talks-strategy/

Quartz. (2017). Millennials are making it luxe to be more ethical and environmentally aware. Retrieved January 5, 2020, from https://qz.com/999207/millennials-are-making-it-luxe-to-be-more-ethical-and-environmentally-aware/

Shankman, S. (2018). The rise of luxury wellness tourism in Africa. Retrieved November 26, 2019, from https://skift.com/2018/06/05/the-rise-of-luxury-wellness-tourism-in-africa/

Shi, F., Dedeoğlu, B. B., & Okumus, B. (2022). Will diners be enticed to be travelers? The role of ethnic food consumption and its antecedents. *Journal of Destination Marketing & Management*, 23, 100685.

Six Senses Bhutan. (2020). Six Senses Bhutan Lodges. Retrieved on January 25, 2020, from https://www.sixsenses.com/en/resorts/bhutan/lodges

Six Senses Bhutan. (2019a). Journeys. Retrieved November 26, 2019, from https://www.sixsenses.com/en/resorts/bhutan/journeys

Six Senses. (2019b). Introducing Mission Wellness. Retrieved November 26, 2019, from https://www.sixsenses.com/en/corporate/news/introducing-mission-wellness

Six Senses. (2019c). Six Senses Sustainability. Retrieved November 26, 2019, from https://www.sixsenses.com/en/sustainability

Taheri, B., Jafari, A., & Okumus, B. (2017). Ceremonious politeness in consuming food in VFR tourism: Scale development. *Service Industries Journal*, 37(15-16), 948-967.

Thal, K.I., & Hudson, S. (2019). A conceptual model of wellness destination characteristics that contribute to psychological well-being. *Journal of Hospitality and Tourism Research*, 43(1). 41-57. DOI: 10.1177/1096348017704498.

Walt Disney World Resort. (2020a). Jogging Trails. Retrieved January 25, 2020, from https://disneyworld.disney.go.com/recreation/jogging/

Walt Disney World Resort. (2020b). Disney's Boardwalk Inn. Retrieved January 25, 2020 from https://disneyworld.disney.go.com/resorts/boardwalk-inn/recreation/

World Happiness Report. (2019). World Happiness Report 2019. Retrieved January 5, 2020, from https://worldhappiness.report/ed/2019/

World Happiness Report. (2022). World Happiness Report 2022. Retrieved May 28, 2022, from https://worldhappiness.report/ed/2022/

World Health Organization. (2012). WHOQOL: Measuring Quality of Life. Retrieved May 28, 2022, from https://www.who.int/tools/whoqol

Yeung, O. & Johnston, K. (2018). Global Wellness Tourism Economy Monitor October 2018. Global Wellness Institute. Retrieved November 8, 2019, from https://globalwellnessinstitute.org/ industry-research/global-wellness-tourism-economy/

3 Typologies of Health and Wellness in Hospitality and Tourism

This chapter looks at the spectrum of health and wellness in hospitality and tourism that exists across the globe. Some types of wellness tourism are focused on physical well-being, while others seek to fulfill spiritual and psychological needs. In recent years, as tourists have begun looking for a multitude of offerings to improve their physical and mental wellness, defining and understanding the variety of health and wellness tourism offerings has increased. It will continue to do so in the future.

Learning outcomes

By the end of this chapter, students should be able to do the following:

1. Define and discuss the full spectrum of health tourism.
2. Define spas and thermal/mineral springs.
3. Define yoga and meditation practices.
4. Define spiritual tourism and holistic tourism.
5. Define and discuss occupational wellness.

Case study: Canyon Ranch

Canyon Ranch was founded in 1979 as a luxury high-end health and fitness destination, with its first location in Tucson, Arizona. The company uses an "integrative professional approach featuring board-certified physicians, registered dieticians, exercise physiologists, licensed therapists, and other highly-skilled, caring staff who work together to provide a 360° approach to wellness" (Canyon Ranch, 2019a). Staff at Canyon Ranch are professional, trained practitioners and certified physicians who incorporate both Western medicine and alternative therapies into their programs. The employees are knowledgeable about treatments used around the world and use this knowledge to identify the best plan for each guest. The company believes in combining fitness and movement, nutrition and food, health and healing, mind and spirit, and spa and beauty into one beautiful offering to give guests a single destination to reach their wellness goals (Canyon Ranch, 2019b).

A second location was opened in Lenox, Massachusetts, in 1989, and these two properties are billed as Wellness Resorts, which also includes Canyon Ranch Living® residential communities. The Canyon Ranch brand also includes a day spa and fitness center found at The Venetian® Resort in Las Vegas and can be found on board Cunard's Queen Mary 2® in addition to over 20 other ships, including Celebrity Cruises. Most recent to open (in 2019) is the Canyon Ranch Wellness Retreat location in Woodside, California. This center offers "three- and four-day customized, transformational and experiential paths for like-minded individuals or groups", (Canyon Ranch, 2019a) demonstrating Canyon Ranch's continued leadership in the wellness tourism arena. Canyon Ranch has gone beyond lodging and self-contained day spas and retreats. In 2018, the company announced a partnership with Singapore Airlines, intending to make the almost 19-hour non-stop flight (the longest flight in the world) between Singapore and New York (Newark, New Jersey) a healthier route. Canyon Ranch's contribution includes science-based balanced meals and activity recommendations to promote rest and relaxation and maintain healthy circulation and movement in-flight (Singapore Airlines, 2018; Canyon Ranch, 2019a). As the company continues to grow, they have stayed true to their mission of "creating environments and products that promote health and the highest enjoyment of life for all people."

Discussion Questions

1. How has Canyon Ranch become a leader in the wellness tourism industry?
2. What does Canyon Ranch offer its guests?
3. What does Singapore Airlines gain from partnering with Canyon Ranch?
4. What is a natural extension of the Canyon Ranch brand that still stays true to its mission statement?
5. What can we learn from this case study?

The spectrum of health and wellness tourism

Based on their current situation and motivations, customers can select from the variety of health and wellness offerings available to them from around the world. Primary wellness customers may have different desired outcomes from their wellness-focused trip than secondary wellness tourists, who are more likely to add components in a la carte manner. **Health tourism**, as defined by the World Health Organization (WHO), is "using services to improve physical or psychological health with the help of mineral water springs, climatic conditions, or medical intervention in an area outside one's place of residence for more than 24 hours and less than one year" (Amouzagar et al., 2016, p. 88).

Developing countries can benefit from implementing health tourism as a part of their tourism and economic strategies. According to a qualitative study on health tourism by Amouzagar et al., the benefits of health tourism to Iran include national development, economic growth, and changing the attitudes of other nations. They also found that the health tourism sector in Iran is challenged due to insufficient marketing, political instability, lack of insurance coverage, lack of qualified employees and managers, not having international standards and lack technology (Amouzagar et al., 2016). Developing countries across the world have similar benefits and challenges as Iran when it comes to health tourism.

Table 3.1: A spectrum of health tourism (Smith & Puczkó, 2008).

Physical Healing	Medical spas/ baths	Mofetta (1)	Surgery trips	Rehabilitation retreats
Beauty Treatments	Cosmetic surgery trips	Hotel/day spas		
Relaxation/ Rest	Pampering spas/ baths	Wellness hotels	Thalassotherapy centers	
Leisure/ Entertainment	Spa resorts with 'fun waters'	Sport/ fitness holidays		
Life/Work Balance	Holistic centers	Occupational wellness workshops		
Psychological	Holistic centers	Workshops, e.g., Hoffman (2), psycho-drama		
Spiritual	Meditation retreats	Yoga centers	Pilgrimage	

(1) Derived from Mofette, volcanic vent whose vapors can be used in spa treatments (Encyclopaedia Britannica, 2006).

(2) 7-day soul searching, healing treat of transformation and development for people who feel stuck in one or more important areas of their life (Hoffman Institute, 2020).

As presented in Table 3.1, Smith and Puczkó offer a spectrum and subcategories of health tourism. In health tourism, the body, mind, and spirit work together to satisfy a full range of wellness needs. Medical (therapeutic and surgical) tourism primarily focuses on the body, and spiritual tourism is mostly targeted toward mental health and growth. Other types that incorporate the mind and a complete approach to wellness tourism include Thalasso tourism, leisure spa tourism, yoga, and meditation tourism, occupational wellness tourism, and holistic tourism (Smith & Puczkó, 2008).

The same tourist may choose different options depending on their current situation. For example, when looking to undergo and recover from a cosmetic procedure like a facial peel, an individual may select a high-end day spa with a hotel attached, to spend a weekend being pampered while their skin recovers from the slight trauma. At a different time, the same individual may be undergoing a high amount of stress in their work and may need a holistic center that offers workshops on occupational wellness and work/life balance to help them cope with their current situation. In a third example for the same individual, perhaps they are on a work trip in a location known for its yoga retreats, and they decide to extend their trip for pleasure to spend a few days meditating and learning new yoga techniques. All of these are valid examples of health and wellness tourism encompassing the body, mind, and spirit, and could be undertaken in both primary and secondary situations.

Another distinction that may vary between travelers or within one individual in multiple situations is their level of participation in the wellness experience. Some physical wellness treatments, for example receiving a massage or relaxing in a hot spring, do not appear to require a lot of involvement. In contrast, others like meditation and workshops lend themselves better to more direct involvement. However, it is essential to consider that the level of desired commitment often varies from person to person, even when they are both undergoing a treatment (e.g., both lounging in a hot spring) at the same time. Also, the same person may be more engaged depending on the day, their current mindset, and personal situation at that moment in time. This varying level of involvement within and between people can offer challenges to wellness managers, as will be discussed in a future chapter.

Spas

Spas are "are places and facilities that offer a variety of professional services that provide the renewal of mind, body, and spirit." (International SPA Association, n.d.) The popularity of health and spa tourism is continuously increasing and becoming an important marketing area. Although tourism operators actively market the tourism resources in their region, spa tourism activities are still limited (Azman & Chan, 2010). Since the Covid-19 pandemic began, consumer profiles and needs have changed and health and wellness-related tourism has become preferred by travelers and consumers. The $119 billion spa economy, which represents about 41% of wellness tourism spending, includes not only the spa facilities and employees, but also spa consulting, associations, capital investors, education, and spa-related media and events (Global Wellness Institute, 2019a; 2019b; Han et al., 2019).

Spa visitors tend to be women, but there is a growing trend for men to visit spas. In 2004, men accounted for 30% of spa clients. Spas mostly cater to the Baby Boomer generation (those born between 1946 and 1964) and the average age of a spa visitor is 49 years old (Tawil, 2011). Guests who visit spas often share the following characteristics: "(i) a life full of intense anxiety, workload, and insecurity, (ii) a search for more intensive experiences of relaxation and rejuvenation, (iii) a wish to restore a balance between work and private life, thus improving quality of life, (iv) a high disposable income and willingness to reward themselves by visiting a wellness and spa centre, (v) requirements to enjoy personal service and care, cleanliness, hygiene and a pleasant atmosphere, reasonable waiting time for using equipment and facilities, and finally, continuous presence and support by skillful staff." On a similar note, the people who visit spas are typically motivated by "(i) an increased orientation to a healthy and aesthetic body, (ii) a general desire for a healthier lifestyle (healthy nutrition), (iii) the quest for spiritual experiences (meditation and yoga), (iv) the pursuit of happiness (as perceived by everyone), (v) the desire to look 'sexier' and healthier, and (vi) an increasing demand for non-surgical treatments" (Sotiriadis et al., 2016, p.6).

There are four broad categories of hotel spa tourists: Aristocrats, Explorers, Socializers, and Budgeters (Tawil, 2011). This may be a flexible starting point for the field; it is a useful way to begin thinking about spa tourists. This framework is based on three dimensions: health (reasons for going on a spa holiday), choice (factors in choosing a spa destination), and experience (facilities and treatments used and post-visit feedback).

- *Aristocrats* are high-class, tactful, and organized. They are often older people with a high income seeking to rest and relax, either by choice or by recommendation from their doctor to take a rehabilitation break. This group expects a clean space and polished design, with many facilities, high-end service, and attention to detail. Cost is generally not a big concern for them.

- *Explorers* are looking for a unique spa experience, possibly in an exotic location or with atypical treatment offerings. This group wants to try new activities and often prefers to travel alone.

- On the other hand, people in the *Socializer* category like to visit a spa with friends or family. They are often looking for a short break with opportunities to socialize with their group in a café, relaxation room, and shopping area.

- Lastly, the *Budgeters* are seeking to indulge themselves at a day spa, often through a core treatment like a massage, and then making full use of the included facilities like a swimming pool or sauna, to maximize their limited funds. They are more likely to visit a local day spa than to spend money on extras like an overnight stay. As mentioned earlier, all four of these groups may be present at one location at the same time, making it essential to cater to more than one type of visitor and to identify the likely needs of each guest. Figure 3.1 provides some of the major characteristics of Hotel Spa Tourists.

Figure 3.1: Hotel Spa Tourists. Adopted from Tawil, R. F. (2011).

Additionally, Table 3.2 highlights the seven different kinds of spa/wellness capacities as defined by the International Spa Association.

Table 3.2: Seven types of spa/wellness capacities (Adapted from Vukovic et al., 2015)

Type of Spa	Description
Club Spa	Primary use: fitness; also offers professional spa services
Cruise Ship Spa	Spa on a cruise ship that offers professional spa services, fitness, and wellness; also offers spa menu with carefully chosen meals
Day Spa	Offers professional spa services daily; best examples of these spas are in western Europe
Destination Spa	Offer guests the opportunity to improve lifestyle and health through professional spa services, fitness, education, and accommodation all within the spa
Medical Spa	Integrates spa services with conventional treatments and therapies to give guests a complete health and wellness experience
Mineral Springs Spa	Uses minerals, thermal or springs, or hydrotherapeutic in its spa services; most European spas are this type of spa
Resort/Hotel Spa	Similar to cruise ship spa in that it offers professional spa services, fitness, and wellness at a resort/hotel.

> **Discussion:** Through online research, list the top five spa businesses in your region as well as globally. Explain each of them briefly.

Active exploration in hospitality and tourism

Many people around the world, especially in developed Western economies, lack the level of activity in their everyday lives necessary to remain healthy. Others thrive on adventure and adrenaline and enjoy taking vacations for the sole purpose of exploring and pushing their physical limits. Activities like hiking, swimming, snorkeling, rock climbing, cycling, and others on land, in the air, and water, all encourage travelers to escape their daily routine. Even less intense activities are beneficial, such as stretching, walking, yoga; anything that keeps the body moving helps to maintain physical health.

> **Discussion:**
> 1. What are the leading destinations for active exploration in your state and/or country? What active activities can travelers undertake in these destinations?
> 2. What active activities can travelers and locals undertake in the city where you live?
> 3. Thalasso and thermal/mineral springs.

Thermal springs date back to the Roman era, where they were often places where people went for care and to socialize (Migliaccio, 2018). **Thalassotherapy** is the therapeutic use of seawater, marine algae, and marine mud in various body treatments (Travel to Wellness, 2019). Its name is derived from the Greek word for 'sea,' and the benefits of the sea were promoted in early writings by Euripides and Hippocrates. The water-based materials are said to tone and moisturize the skin and improve circulation when applied in treatments such as wraps and scrubs. It may treat ailments such as physical and emotional exhaustion, depression, obesity, cellulite, rheumatism, peripheral circulatory problems, and conditions dealing with the ear, nose, throat, and mouth.

It is believed that thalassotherapy is beneficial as a preventative health treatment and when recovering from surgery or illness. Seawater can be ionized with negative ions and sprayed onto the body or inhaled into the lungs. Extended exposure to open marine air may prove beneficial to the overall wellness of the body and mind. Thalassotherapy has strict requirements to maximize its health benefits; seawater must be drawn from a certain depth and distance offshore, it should be heated to around 96/98 degrees Fahrenheit (34-35 degrees Celsius) to keep the microorganisms alive, and it must be used within 48 hours of collection to ensure those same microorganisms retain their healing powers. For these reasons, the therapy needs to take place within a specific time frame, and places that offer thalassotherapy need to be near the sea like the Thalassotherapy Spa in the Mayan Riviera of Mexico (Travel to Wellness, 2019).

Similarly, **thermal/mineral springs,** or hot springs, are naturally occurring thermal springs of water hotter than 98°F (37°C); the water is usually heated by emanation from or passage near hot or molten rocks (Dictionary.com, 2019). They can be used for recreational, wellness, or therapeutic or curative purposes (Global Wellness Institute, 2019). Many of the popular hot springs in the United States are found in the western half of the country, in states like Oregon, California, Colorado, Idaho, Alaska, Arizona, Nevada, Washington, New Mexico, Wyoming, and Utah. Some eastern alternatives are found in Virginia, and the Hot Springs National Park is located in the city of Hot Springs, Arkansas (Local Adventurer, 2020). Globally, the most famous hot springs are Iceland's Blue Lagoon Geothermal Spa, the Banjar Hot Springs in Bali, the Pamukkale Thermal Pools in Turkey, British Columbia's Hot Springs Cove, the Ma'in Hot Springs in Jordan, and of course the large variety of *Onsen* (hot spring) hot springs found in Japan (Seppanen, 2018; Planetyze, 2020). In addition, China is becoming one of the fastest markets in the world for hot springs (Migliaccio, 2018). Thermal/hot springs will be discussed more in a later chapter.

Table 3.3: Types of thermal/mineral springs establishments, developed from Global Wellness Institute, 2019; Yeung and Johnston, 2018

Primarily Recreational	Primarily Wellness	Primarily Therapeutic or Curative
Thermal/mineral water swimming pool facilities	Thermal/mineral water bathing facilities	Health resorts and sanatoria that use thermal/mineral waters for treatments
Thermal/mineral water-based waterparks	Thermal/mineral water-based spas	
Hotels/resorts with thermal/mineral water swimming pools	Thalassotherapy spas and resorts	
Thermal or hot springs resorts		

Discussion: Find a domestic or an international thermal/mineral spring business/location and introduce it to the class in terms of its characteristics, benefits, customer segments, etc.

Holistic tourism

Holistic tourism encompasses treatments or activities that encourage self-transformation through balancing the mind, body, and spirit. Because of the diversity required for this approach, holistic tourism is often practiced through retreats or other full-featured itineraries. Activities like yoga encourage physical, mental, and spiritual well-being; life coaching or other emotional support programs inspire psychological improvement, and artistic courses stimulate self-expression and creativity. By incorporating such a variety of behaviors into one program, participants explore the balance of their everyday life and discover what might be missing or need improvement.

Yoga and meditation

Yoga, which means union of the body, mind, and spirit, grants people who practice it stress relief through meditation, physical postures (*asana*), and breathing techniques (*pranayama*) (Dilette et al, 2019). Yoga and meditation retreats focus on the mind-body connection, with a spiritual aspect incorporated for some practitioners. Yoga and meditation retreats have long been popular in many areas of the world, for example, countries like India. Yoga has become so ingrained in society and culture in the past few decades that the United Nations Education, Scientific, and Cultural Organization (UNESCO) has named it an "intangible cultural heritage of humanity" (Sharma & Nayak, 2019). Many yoga businesses have opened in recent decades, making it more accessible for the general population and those looking for all levels of immersion and experience.

There are many forms of yoga, such as hatha, bikram/hot yoga, iyengar, restorative, anusara, vinyasa, and ashtanga, and practices often include or are supplemented by a period of meditation (Gaiam, 2020). Table 3.4 provides a brief description of the eight different types of yoga listed above.

Table 3.4: Types of yoga. Adapted from Gaiam (2020)

Type of yoga	Brief description
Hatha	Generic term used for any form of yoga that focuses on posture
Bikram	Walks through 26 yoga poses in a heated room
Hot Yoga	Similar to Bikram but this style uses different poses than Bikram, so they use a different name
Iyengar	Focuses on finding proper alignment in each pose. This type of yoga uses props like chairs or blocks to aid users in finding proper alignment.
Restorative	Use passive poses so the user can experience the benefits of a pose without physical effort
Anusara	Type of yoga that allows students to experience grace and open their hearts
Vinyasa	Known for fluid movement and smooth transitions between poses
Ashtanga	Rigorous form of yoga that connects each pose with a breath and focuses on posture. This type of yoga is completed the same way every time.

Discussion: Discuss the wellness benefits of each of the following types of yoga: hatha, bikram/hot yoga, iyengar, restorative, anusara, vinyasa, and ashtanga.

There is a subset of wellness tourism that involves yoga. **Yoga Tourism** is when a guest travels to a destination to engage in the practice of yoga and yoga-related activities to enhance their physical, mental, and spiritual well-being (Sharma & Nayak, 2019). Yoga tourists typically visit yoga retreats, seminars, conferences, and festivals when they travel for yoga. A **yoga retreat** is when the experience is planned and developed around the practice of yoga (Dilette et al, 2019). It is important to note that there is a difference between the broad idea of wellness tourism and the specific subset of yoga tourism. When guests engage in yoga tourism, it requires them to dedicate themselves to the art of yoga at that destination (Sharma & Nayak, 2019). Yoga tourists may also have different motivations than wellness tourists, such as "seeking spirituality, enhancing mental well-being, enhancing physical condition, and controlling negative emotions" (Dilette et al, 2019). This dedication, in turn, invokes more intense emotions in guests than may be seen in other forms of wellness tourism (Sharma & Nayak, 2019).

Spiritual hospitality and tourism

Spiritual hospitality and tourism can be defined as an act of visiting somewhere locally, nationally or internationally to visit spiritual places such as (1) mosques, churches, synagogues and temples and (2) natural environments such as forests, oceans, lakes, spiritual gardens, wildlife parks for birds and animals, botanical gardens, caves, and rocks, for spiritual reasons to fulfill the need for being grateful, forgiveness, and have inner peace (IGI Global, 2019). The two components of this definition align nicely with the work of Cheer, Belhassen, and Kujawa (2017), who propose that spiritual travel can be both secular and religious (see Figure 3.2). While "Wellness and Healing" are noted as specific drivers of secular spiritual tourism, it can certainly be argued that most, if not all, of the drivers in both the secular and religious categories are relevant to the wellness of the mind, body, or spirit.

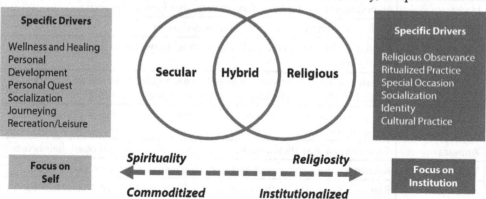

Figure 3.2: Primary drivers for spiritual tourism. (Adapted from Cheer et al., 2017)

Many visitors to religious sites may have secular motivations, such as viewing the architecture and history of a centuries-old Catholic church, admiring the architecture and history of a centuries-old mosque, or visiting the holy city of Jerusalem. Buildings and cities are not the only places travelers go to connect to the world spiritually; some find comfort and growth in nature, others through techniques such as meditating or chanting. Bathing can also be symbolic of spiritual wellness, as the mind can be purified through the body.

Medical tourism

Medical tourism is a legacy of health tourism (Amouzagar, et al., 2016). Its roots date back to the Middle Ages, and medical tourism became popular in the nineteenth century when people in the middle class traveled to towns with hot springs or thermal springs to improve their quality of life. In the 20th century, those from the upper class in lesser developed regions would travel to more developed areas for their health care (Constantin, 2015). Medical tourism, or traveling to another location or country for medical care, is generally designated as different from wellness tourism since it is often treating an existing condition rather than preventing a new one (Centers for Disease Control and Prevention, n.d). Today, the main features of medical tourism are the vast number of people traveling, people traveling to lesser developed regions due to high-quality treatments at low prices and the ability to get there and stay there for a low price, the infrastructure provided by the internet, global industrial development in private and public health care, and international health policy development (Constantin, 2015).

Medical tourism can go hand-in-hand with wellness travel. Table 3.5. describes the medical health paradigm as viewing mental and physical health as two separate entities, where the patient is generally passive and allows the medical professional to do active work. On the other hand, the wellness health paradigm promotes the partnership between mind, body, and spirit, and believes health to be separate from the disease. In this concept, the patient is required to assume some responsibility in the healing process as an active participant, a feature that is seen as empathic and empowering (Voigt, 2014). Some argue that it can be the motive of the traveler that helps distinguish between wellness and medical tourism, where wellness travelers are motivated to travel to maintain their well-being and medical travelers are motivated to travel for treatment for a medical condition. Since the motivations of travelers are never visible, this distinction may be harder to discern (Loh, 2014). Medical tourists fall into one of the four following categories: (Wongkit and McKercher, 2013: Sag & Zengul, 2019, p. 297).

- **Dedicated** – has a pre-determined treatment plan and traveling mostly for treatment;
- **Hesitant** – decides on the treatment options after arriving at the medical tourism destination yet traveling primarily for treatment;
- **Holidaying** – has a pre-determined treatment plan, however, traveling mostly for pleasure; and
- **Opportunistic** – decides about the procedure after arrival and traveling primarily for pleasure.

Two types of medical tourism are surgical travel, which involves undergoing an operation, and therapeutic tourism, which involves partaking in some sort of healing treatment. Surgical travel usually involves one or more of the following types of procedures: cosmetic surgery, dentistry, cardiology/heart surgery, orthopedic surgery, obesity surgery, fertility (in vitro or sex-reassignment operations), and transplantation of organs, tissues, or cells (Constantin, 2015). Certain countries are known for specializing in medical travel and its associated recuperation, for example, cosmetic surgery in certain South American countries. Therapeutic tourism may include a stay in a medical hotel or a sanatorium, as it often contains longer-term care or multiple check-ups. **Medical spas** are a type of facility that combines surgical and therapeutic treatments. They "operate under the full-time, on-site supervision of a licensed healthcare professional, providing comprehensive medical and/or wellness care in an environment that integrates spa services with traditional, alternative or cosmetic medical therapies and treatments" (Global Wellness Institute, 2019a and Yeung and Johnston, 2018).

The top nations in promoting medical tourism around the world include the United States of America, Mexico, Costa Rica, Turkey, Israel, India, Singapore, Malaysia, Thailand, Taiwan, and South Korea (Sag & Zengul, 2019).

Table 3.5: Comparing medical and wellness in hospitality and tourism (Adapted and developed from Voigt, 2014)

	Biomedical health paradigm	Wellness health paradigm
Definition of health	Absence of disease Separation of mind and body ('body as machine' metaphor)	Positive functioning; a balance between internal and external forces Oneness of body/mind/spirit (body as part of an integrated, multidimensional system) interlinked with an external system
Definition of disease	A biological process where pathogens damage the 'body machine'	A systemic imbalance, mostly not reducible to a single biologic cause
Relationship between health and disease	Health and disease are dichotomous opposites Health and disease are an objective, observable phenomena	Health and disease are two separate dimensions Health and disease are a subjective and perceptual phenomenon
Focus of health care	Short-term focus on curing or alleviating disease symptoms	Long-term focus on health prevention
Characteristics of health care and intervention process	Standardized care High tech/low touch Intervention focuses on invasive procedures, pharmaceutical drugs, and high-tech diagnostics Consultation is paternalistic	Individualized care Low tech/high touch Intervention emphasizes non-invasive procedures, lifestyle-based interventions, 'self-healing' and herbal medicines Consultation is participatory, empowering, and empathic
Role of patient	Patient remains mostly passive, authority is inherent in the health professional	Patient should assume self-responsibility and needs to become an active participant

Occupational wellness

Although wellness in the workplace has become more acknowledged in recent years, and it has become a $48 billion industry, occupational wellness and work-life balance are still popular topics (Global Wellness Institute, 2019a). The concept of **workplace wellness** "includes expenditures on programs, services, activities, and equipment by employers aimed at improving their employees' health and wellness. These expenditures aim to raise awareness, provide education, and offer incentives that address specific health risk factors and behaviors (e.g., lack of exercise, poor eating habits, stress, obesity, and smoking) and encourage employees to adopt healthier lifestyles" (Global Wellness Institute, 2019b and Yeung and Johnston, 2018, p. 81).

Mathis, Jackson, Valentine, and Meglich (2017) define **wellness programs** as "plans and initiatives offered to employees and managers to maintain and improve their health before issues emerge". Workplace wellness programs have been shown to have positive results for both employees and organizations – one 2010 study found a $3.27 reduction in medical costs for every dollar spent on wellness programs, and $2.73 reduction in absenteeism costs for every dollar spent (Baicker, et al., 2010). HR professionals in the workplace are tasked with making these programs fun and engaging to ensure employee participation as well as their success.

One example of a hospitality company that offers a great workplace wellness program is Toronto's Delta Hotels and Resorts. The company hosted a Mental Health Week to help highlight a large number of mental health issues and mental illnesses in Canada as well as help reduce the stigma around mental health. The campaign also showcased ways employers can help their employees reduce stress, anxiety, and depression, which are common mental health issues associated with work (Rise Staff, 2019). Another example is Canyon Ranch, discussed in the case study that opens this chapter, which offers corporate wellness programs. From a company retreat at one of its locations to bringing one of its professionals to an office to host a lecture to establishing a wellness program for the office or company, Canyon Ranch has a corporate wellness program to fit whatever a company needs (Canyon Ranch, 2020).

An individual's **work-life balance** determines how much time they spend at or thinking about work, versus how much time they dedicate to their family and personal life. Over the past decade, studies on professional "burnout" have increased, and consistently show that highly trained professionals experience depression and anxiety despite being at the top of their career in their personal and professional lives. This issue leads to burnout syndrome and contributes to absenteeism in the workplace, which can lead to suicide in its most severe form in personal lives (Ungerleider et al., 2017). Therefore, it is crucial to develop **valid and reliable instruments such as** a wellness index for workers (WIW) to systematically measure and evaluate employee wellness, and provide basic directions for developing a workplace wellness program (Choi et al., 2016).

Another job-related topic area is **workaholism** and **work engagement**. Workaholism is considered to be a "bad" type of working hard, and work engagement is a "good" type of working hard (Van Beek et al., 2012). A **workaholic** is a "work-obsessed individual who gradually becomes emotionally crippled and addicted to power and control in a compulsive drive to gain approval and public recognition of success" (Killinger, 2011). This desperate drive to work can lead to lots of unhealthy side effects, many of which can be prevented or resolved by addressing them through a wellness program. Contrasting workaholism, work engagement refers more job satisfaction and commitment to the organization. The employees show more proactivity, high performance, high life satisfaction and good health. Therefore, work engagement with positive outcomes is a good type of working hard.

> **Discussion:** If you are currently working for an organization, briefly discuss what workplace wellness activities this business is offering their employees and managers. How can they improve their workplace wellness program?

Summary

This chapter covered the spectrum of health and wellness in hospitality and tourism. We have defined spas, thermal and mineral springs, yoga, meditation, and occupational wellness. Various types of tourism were studied, and the drivers for spiritual tourism were explored. This chapter also compared medical and wellness tourism and the concept of occupational wellness.

Discussion questions

1. How can wellness tourism overcome the stressors and challenges of everyday life?
2. What can we learn from the Canyon Ranch case study?
3. What overlap exists between wellness tourism and medical tourism?
4. What are the top spa businesses in your city and country?
5. What are the leading destinations for active exploration in your country and globally?
6. What are the leading domestic and international hot spring destinations?
7. What are the different forms of yoga?
8. Why is workaholism a significant problem for some people, and how can it be treated through wellness management?
9. What types of wellness programs are common in workplaces?

Homework

Analyze the city/region you are currently living (e.g., Orlando or Central Florida) in terms of what it offers in the spectrum of health and wellness hospitality and tourism. How can it become a better medical and wellness destination?

Definition of key terms

Health tourism – Using services that improve physical or psychological health with the help of mineral water springs, climatic conditions or medical intervention in an area outside one's place of residence for more than 24 hours and less than one year (Amouzagar et al. 2016, p.88).

Holistic tourism – Encompasses treatments or activities that encourage self-transformation through balancing the mind, body, and spirit.

Hot springs – Naturally occurring thermal springs of water hotter than 98°F (37°C); the water is usually heated by emanation from or passage near hot or molten rock.

Medical Spas – Operate under the full-time, on-site supervision of a licensed healthcare professional, providing comprehensive medical and/or wellness care in an environment that integrates spa services with traditional, alternative, or cosmetic medical therapies and treatments (Yeung and Johnston, 2018).

Spa – A facility that offers professional services to offer the renewal of mind, body and spirit.

Spiritual tourism – An act of traveling domestically or overseas to visit spiritual places such as (1) mosques, churches, and temples and (2) natural environments such as forests, oceans, lakes, spiritual gardens, wildlife parks for birds and animals, botanical gardens, caves, and rocks for spiritual reasons to fulfill the need for being grateful to almighty, forgiveness, and inner peace (IGI Global, 2018).

Thalassotherapy – The therapeutic use of seawater, marine algae, and marine mud in various body treatments (Travel to Wellness, 2019).

Wellness program – Program designed to maintain or improve employee health before problems arise (Mathis et al., 2017).

Work-life balance – How much time an individual spends at or thinking about work, versus how much time they dedicate to their family and personal life.

Workaholic – A work-obsessed individual who gradually becomes emotionally crippled and addicted to power and control in a compulsive drive to gain approval and public recognition of success (Killinger, 2011).

Workplace wellness – Includes expenditures on programs, services, activities, and equipment by employers aimed at improving their employees' health and wellness. These expenditures aim to raise awareness, provide education, and offer incentives that address specific health risk factors and behaviors (e.g., lack of exercise, poor eating habits, stress, obesity, and smoking) and encourage employees to adopt healthier lifestyles (Yeung and Johnston, 2018).

Yoga tourism – Visiting a destination to participate in yoga and yoga related practices that can improve the traveler's physical, mental and spiritual well-being.

References

Amouzagar, S. et al. (2016). Qualitative Examination of Health Tourism and its challenges. *International Journal of Travel Medicine and Global Health*, 4(3). 88-91.

Azman, I., & Chan, K. L. J. (2010). Health and spa tourism business: Tourists' profiles and motivational factors. *Health, Wellness and Tourism: healthy tourists, healthy business*, 9, 24.

Baicker, K., Cutler, D., & Song, Z. (2010). Workplace wellness programs can generate savings. Health Affairs, 29(2), 304-311.

Canyon Ranch. (2019a). History. Retrieved December 21, 2019, from https://www.canyonranch.com/about-us/history/

Canyon Ranch. (2019b). Integrative Approach. Retrieved December 21, 2019, from https://www.canyonranch.com/about-us/integrative-approach/

Centers for Disease Control and Prevention. (n.d.). Medical Tourism. Retrieved December 22, 2019, from https://www.cdc.gov/features/medicaltourism/index.html

Choi, M. J., Son, C. S., Kim, J., & Ha, Y. (2016). Development of a wellness index for workers. *Journal of Korean Academy of Nursing*, 46(1), 69-78.

Constantin, A. (2015). International Health Tourism. *International Journal for Responsible Tourism*, 4(1). 59-72.

Cheer, J. M., Belhassen, Y., & Kujawa, J. (2017). The search for spirituality in tourism: Toward a conceptual framework for spiritual tourism. *Tourism Management Perspectives*, 24, 252-256.

Dictionary.com. (2019). Hot Spring. Retrieved December 23, 2019, from https://www.dictionary.com/browse/hot-spring

Dilette, A.K, Douglas, A.C., and Andrzejewski, C. (2019). Yoga tourism – a catalyst for transformation? *Annals of Leisure Research*, 22(1). 22-41. DOI: 10.1080/11745398.2018.1459195

Encyclopaedia Britannica. (2006). Mofette.Encyclopaedia Britannica. Retrieved on January 30, 2020 from https://www.britannica.com/science/mofette

Gaiam. (2020). A beginner's guide to 8 major styles of yoga. Retrieved January 5, 2020, from https://www.gaiam.com/blogs/discover/a-beginners-guide-to-8-major-styles-of-yoga

Global Wellness Institute. (2019a) What is The Wellness Economy? Retrieved December 20, 2019, from https://globalwellnessinstitute.org/what-is-wellness/what-is-the-wellness-economy/

Global Wellness Institute. (2019b). Wellness Definitions. Retrieved December 20, 2019, from https://globalwellnessinstitute.org/what-is-wellness/wellness-economy-definitions/

Han, H., Thuong, P., Kiatkawsin, K., Ryu, H., Kim, J., & Kim, W. (2019). Spa hotels: Factors promoting wellness travelers' postpurchase behavior. *Social Behavior and Personality*, 47(6). 1-13. DOI: 10.2224/sbp.7605

Hoffman Institute. (2020). The Hoffman Process. Retrieved June 2, 2020 from https://www.hoffmaninstitute.org/

IGI Global. (2019). What is Spiritual Tourism. Retrieved December 21, 2019, from www.igi-global.com/dictionary/creative-tourism-and-cultural-heritage/39292

International SPA Association. (n.d.) About ISPA. Retrieved December 21, 2019, from https://experienceispa.com/#about

Killinger, B. (2011). Understanding the dynamics of workaholism. Retrieved December 22, 2019, from https://www.psychologytoday.com/us/blog/the-workaholics/201112/understanding-the-dynamics-workaholism

Local Adventurer. (2020). 25 amazing hot springs in the US you must soak in. Retrieved January 5, 2020, from https://localadventurer.com/amazing-hot-springs-in-the-us/

Loh, C.A. (2014). Health tourism on the rise? Evidence from the Balance of payments statistics. *European Journal of Health Economics*, 15. 759-766. DOI: 10.1007/s10198-01.-0521-0

Mathis, R.L, Jackson, J.H., Valentine, S.R., and Meglich, P.A (2017). *Human Resource Management*. Cengage Learning.

Migliaccio, M. (2018). Thermal spas and their role in wellness tourism: An Italian overview. *African Journal of Hospitality, Tourism and Leisure*, 7(6).

Planetyze. (2020). Top 10 Onsen (Hot Springs) to visit in Japan. Retrieved January 5, 2020, from https://planetyze.com/en/japan/tokyo/blog/top-10-onsen-hot-springs-to-visit-in-japan

Rise Staff. (2019, July 4). List of Companies with Wellness Programs: 10 Amazing Workplaces. Retrieved on January 30, 2020 from https://risepeople.com/blog/10-companies-with-amazing-workplace-wellness-programs/

Sag, I., and Zengul, F.D. (2019). Why medical tourists choose Turkey as a medical tourism destination? *Journal of Hospitality and Tourism Insights*, 2(3). 296 – 206. DOI: 10.1108/JHTI-05-2018-0031

Seppanen, J. (2018). 9 best hot springs around the world. Retrieved January 5, 2020, from www.themanual.com/travel/best-hot-springs-around-the-world/

Sharma, P., and Nayak, J.K. (2019). Do tourists' emotional experiences influence images and intentions in yoga tourism? *Tourism Review*, 3. 646-666. DOI: 10.1108/TR-05-2018-0060

Singapore Airlines. (2018). SIA And Canyon Ranch Announce Partnership To Enhance Customer Experience And Well-Being On The World's Longest Flights. Retrieved December 24, 2019, from https://www.singaporeair.com/en_UK/us/media-centre/press-release/article/?q=en_UK/2018/July-September/jr1018-180815

3

Smith, M., & Puczkó, L. (2008). *Health and Wellness Tourism*. Routledge.

Sotiriadis, M., Van Zyl, C., and Poole, C. (2016). Suggesting a framework for innovation management in the industry of wellness tourism and spas. *African Journal of Hospitality, Tourism and Leisure*, 5(4). 1-17.

Tawil, R. F. (2011). Classifying the hotel spa tourist: A multidimensional qualitative approach. *International Journal of Humanities and Social Science*, 1(20), 155-169.

Travel to Wellness. (2019). Thalassotherapy. Retrieved December 23, 2019, from https://www.traveltowellness.com/thalassotherapy/

Ungerleider, R. M., Ungerleider, J. D., & Ungerleider, G. D. (2017). Promoting occupational wellness and combating professional burnout in the surgical workforce. *Surgical Patient Care*, 205-224.

Van Beek, I., Hu, Q., Schaufeli, W. B., Taris, T. W., & Schreurs, B. H. (2012). For fun, love, or money: What drives workaholic, engaged, and burned-out employees at work?. *Applied Psychology*, 61(1), 30-55.

Voigt, C. (2014). Towards a conceptualization of wellness tourism. In Voigt, C.& Pforr, C., *Wellness tourism from a destination perspective*, 19-44.

Vukovic, P., Cavlin, G., and Cavlin, M. (2015). Complementarity in the development of rural tourism with the development of thermal baths, spa and wellness tourism. *Economics of Agriculture*, 62(1). 259-270.

Wongkit, M. and McKercher, B. (2013), Toward a typology of medical tourists: a case study of Thailand, *Tourism Management*, 38(1). 4-12.

Yeung, O. & Johnston, K. (2018). *Global Wellness Tourism Economy Monitor October 2018*. Global Wellness Institute. Retrieved November 8, 2019, from https://globalwellnessinstitute.org/ industry-research/ global-wellness-tourism-economy/

4 Wellness Tourism Regions and Destinations

This chapter looks at some of the historically known wellness destinations and discusses the emerging regions and what they have to offer tourists. While some developing destinations are beginning to go beyond traditional spas, there is more opportunity to share their wellness offerings with visitors. This may be a way to encourage tourism while maintaining an authentic destination and preventing overtourism. This chapter also lists some of the well-known wellness destinations in the United States and globally.

Learning outcomes

By the end of this chapter, students should be able to do the following:

1. Discuss the historic town of Bath.
2. Define wellness destination.
3. List several other historical wellness destinations.
4. Identify the main wellness regions globally.
5. Identify the top wellness destinations in the USA.
6. Identify the top wellness destinations globally.

Case study: Visit Bath: Spas Ancient and Modern

The historic English town of Bath is synonymous with healing waters and spas. For over 2,000 years, dating back to 43 AD when the Roman Empire controlled the land that is now England, the region has attracted travelers in search of wellness. The water contains 42 minerals and escapes the earth at approximately 45°C (113°F), although it is then cooled to a more comfortable 33.5°C (92.3°F). The original baths are available to tour but are not used anymore due to the high levels of the dangerous micro-organism *Naegleria fowleri*. Instead, the newly constructed Thermae Bath Spa and the refurbished Cross Bath use recently drilled boreholes to offer a way for visitors to experience the same waters safely. The Grand Pump Room opened in the 1790s as a gathering space serving refreshments and water from the hot springs. It now serves as a restaurant and museum featuring artifacts from the Roman period (Bath's Historic Venues, 2019; UNESCO, 2019; Cowie, 2019; Thermae Bath Spa, 2019).

The Thermae Bath Spa opened in 2006 at the cost of approximately £40 million, ending a 30-year period in which there was no bathing experience available due to the discovery of *Naegleria fowleri*. In 2011, the local tourism bodies determined that there was a need for a more cohesive promotion of the bath experience. Out of this came the Spas Ancient and Modern Package at a 2011 price of £59, which includes a ticket to visit the original Roman Baths, a three-course lunch or Champagne after-noon tea in the Pump Room, and a two-hour spa session at Thermae Bath Spa. This package is a partnership between the Heritage Services of Bath and North East Som-erset Council, Bath Tourism Plus, the Thermae Bath Spa, and the Grand Pump Room catering team (Rollins, 2015).

The marketing budget allocated to this project was only £1,500. This included build-ing a simple website, listing the new package on partner websites, creating a paper brochure, arranging familiarization (FAM) trips, developing a PR and promotional campaign aimed at regional media, and briefing the relevant tourism board partners on the project. The efforts of this reduced budget, along with continuous monitoring and incorporating of partner and guest feedback, lead to revenues of over £600,000 in the promotion's first three years alone (Rollins, 2015).

Discussion questions

1. What does the town of Bath have to offer wellness tourists?
2. What enabled the Spas Ancient and Modern Package to be so successful?
3. What lessons can wellness tourism destinations learn from this?
4. Do you know any other similar ancient spa destinations?

Wellness regions and destinations

A **tourist destination** is a place, city or a country, which offers tourism and travel products and services to tourists so they can visit it (Beirman, 2003). Many places throughout the world are known as tourist destinations, and each has its unique selling points. Wellness is one of the ongoing trends in travel and one way for a destination to set itself apart from competitors. A **wellness destination** is a country, region, city, town, or event that tourists and residents visit to improve their holistic health.

Wellness travel has become increasingly popular, not only in established tourism destinations but also in developing markets. A **developing country**, or one with a standard of living or level of industrial production well below that which is possible with financial or technical aid, often turns to tourism as a way to build their economy. Destinations with less advanced tourism infrastructure are generally more pristine and retain more of their natural unvarnished appeal. According to the 2018 Global Wellness Economy Monitor report, "wellness tourism growth is very much a tale of developing markets, with Asia-Pacific, Latin America-Caribbean, Middle East-North Africa, and sub-Saharan Africa all clocking robust gains, and accounting for 57 percent of the increase in wellness trips [from 2015 to 2017]. Over the past five years, Asia was the number-one growth sector in both wellness tourism trips and revenues, where trips grew 33% in two years, to 258 million annually" (Yeung & Johnston, 2018).

When it comes to outbound travelers, Europeans currently lead the world with the highest pre-Covid-19 number of wellness trips (291.8 million in 2017), and travelers from North America lead with the highest expenditures ($241.7 billion in 2017). The numbers differ slightly when it comes to inbound travel; the United States ranks highest with 176.5 million trips and $226.0 billion in expenditures, followed by Germany (66.1 million trips, $65.7 billion in expenditures) and China (70.2 million trips, $31.7 billion in expenditures) (all 2017 numbers) (Yeung and Johnston, 2018).

Historical wellness tourism regions and destinations

Emerging wellness tourism destinations do have their unique selling propositions, which will be discussed in the next section. However, they can learn from the regions or destinations that have been embracing wellness tourism for decades and even centuries; other destinations have been long known as places to visit for health and relaxation. In ancient Greece and Rome, public bathhouses were considered to be social and therapeutic. Bathing complexes spread through the Roman Empire, featuring not only baths but also libraries, gyms, and entertainment spaces. Questions surrounding the morality of bathing during the Middle Ages lead to the downfall of such facilities. Still, with the rise of the Enlightenment movement in 18th century Europe and the corresponding belief that mineral water had curative properties, "cure towns" began to emerge around the continent. The trend moved quickly to the United States, where resorts opened promising improved health by bathing in cold and **hot springs** (pools formed by water that is heated by the Earth's interior, volcanic areas, or very hot rock heated by magma,) taking long walks, listening to lectures, dining on locally produced food, and enjoying spa treatments.

The Dead Sea, bordered by Jordan, Israel, and the West Bank, has been a popular wellness destination for centuries, due to its location at the lowest elevation on earth and extremely high salt content. It is believed that the minerals in its water, low rate of allergens in the atmosphere, lower exposure to UV rays due to its position below sea level which results in increased cloud cover, and higher atmospheric pressure all offer health benefits for those suffering from all kinds of ailments ranging from psoriasis to cystic fibrosis (Pletcher, 2019; Hoyt, 2019).

Another destination long renowned for its hydrotherapy is the Baden-Baden region of Germany. Twelve **thermal/mineral springs** circulate approximately 800,000 liters of water per day from 2,000 meters under the earth, reaching temperatures as high as 155 degrees F (68 degrees C). The Salina Sea Salt Grotto boasts that the salt content in its air is one of the highest in the world, and salt crystals coat the walls. Baden-Baden has capitalized on these springs for many years by also offering complementary services such as aromatherapy, yoga classes, and massage therapy (Baden-Baden Kur & Tourismus GmbH, 2019).

India also has a long-standing reputation as a spiritual healing destination. Ashrams and retreats offering various types of health treatments have been popular wellness travel locations for centuries. Yoga, meditation, and the health practices of Ayurveda are well known to relax and clear the mind and body while returning to traditional aspects of health like connecting with the earth and giving thanks for all of one's blessings (Yeung & Johnston, 2018).

For travelers looking for a combined physical, mental, and spiritual retreat, Sedona, Arizona, has long been a popular destination in the United States. Going beyond the usual offerings like yoga, spas, and hiking (which are all abundant), Sedona is also known for its spiritual tours and psychic readings. The city also has a proudly owned reputation as a vortex or "swirling [center] of energy that [is] conducive to healing, meditation, and self-exploration" (Sedona Arizona, 2019). Spa treatments using local ingredients and the historical knowledge of the earth from Native Americans incorporate the region's physical healing properties into guests.

These are only a few examples of popular wellness destinations that have emerged throughout history. Emerging tourist locations looking to promote their wellness aspects can learn from the success of these well-known destinations. However, not all historical wellness destinations have seen success, and some have even proven to be destructive to their health-seeking visitors.

Throughout history, the search for miracle cures to real or imagined ailments has drawn people to all kinds of treatments. The Battle Creek Sanitarium in Michigan was managed from 1876 to 1943 by Dr. John Harvey Kellogg, of cereal fame, drawing such notable patients as Amelia Earhart, Henry Ford, Warren G. Harding, and Mary Todd Lincoln. Kellogg described his facility as "a composite physiologic method comprising hydrotherapy, phototherapy, thermotherapy, electrotherapy, mechanotherapy, dietetics, physical culture, cold-air cure, and health training" (Kellogg, 1908).

At the McMichael Institute in Niagara Falls, New York, Dr. George H. McMichael offered "Double Chloride of Gold Remedies for the Liquor, Morphine & Tobacco

Habits," one facility of many in the late 1800s that that promised quick relief from addiction through the consumption of gold (Nickell, 2016). Edward and Elizabeth Muncie claimed to be able to diagnose and heal illness by analyzing a patient's orifices and performing subsequent surgery at their Muncie Surf Sanatorium in New York (Cellania, 2018). These are only a few examples of the lengths people have gone to in their search for wellness.

Emerging wellness tourism regions and destinations

As the world becomes more accessible and destinations develop their tourism offerings, wellness tourism, and the authenticity often associated with it is becoming a popular way to attract travelers. These destinations are viewed as unspoiled by outside visitors, and may offer new wellness approaches not found anywhere else.

Asia-Pacific region

Wellness Tourism Worldwide (2020) found that, historically, in Southeast Asia, destinations view wellness tourism concentrated on spiritual tourism and medical tourism as their most important assets. In the Far East, assets surrounding spiritual tourism were historically most important. The Pacific has also placed high importance on the natural environment in regards to wellness tourism.

Today, wellness travel offerings in Asia have begun to expand beyond the traditional yoga and spa treatments and into sound therapy, tai chi, meditation, and spiritual guidance. Each country has its traditions, and unique settings, local ingredients, and modes of healing, and travelers are looking to explore every one individually. For example, India created a National Medical and Wellness Tourism Promotion board in 2016 to coordinate efforts on behalf of this sector, and Sri Lanka also promotes its Ayurvedic strengths combined with a beautiful natural setting and spiritual heritage (Yeung & Johnston, 2018).

At the onset of Covid-19, China was the fastest-growing market for wellness tourism trips (from 2015-2017), with an increase of 21.9 million wellness trips (20.6% annual growth rate), followed by India's 17.3 million increase (20.3% annual growth rate). When it comes to spa facilities and revenues, the Asia-Pacific region rivals leader Europe, with 48,679 spas and $26.5 million in revenue in 2017. China is the second spa market in the world (behind only the United States), with 15,664 spas employing 376,576 people and bringing in $8.24 billion in revenue in 2017. The Asia-Pacific region dominates the thermal/mineral springs category, with 25,916 facilities bringing in $31.6 billion in 2017. China and Japan lead the region with 3,900 and 20,972 spas, respectively, seeing $17.5 billion and $12.8 billion in revenues (Yeung & Johnston, 2018). While the Covid-19 pandemic has altered these numbers and trends, they are important to know as a benchmark for tourism and wellness recovery.

China's massive wellness tourism market comprises mostly domestic travelers, often looking to rediscover their cultural traditions like Traditional Chinese Medicine (TCM) and herbal medicine, qigong, meditation, and martial arts. Australia is home to many well-known wellness hot springs and resorts and has also been hosting an increasing number of wellness festivals and events. Their tourism board has named wellness as one of the five key niches for tourism development and is promoting investment in the sector (Yeung & Johnston, 2018).

Although the Asia-Pacific region is not traditionally known as a medical tourism destination, some countries are promoting their advanced medical industries and wellness offerings as a place to recover from procedures or receive a medical checkup or life coaching while on vacation. Countries like Malaysia, Singapore, South Korea, Thailand, and the Philippines offer more traditional healing techniques such as TCM, Ayurveda, Tibetan, and other integrative medicines (Yeung & Johnston, 2018).

Latin America-Caribbean region

Wellness Tourism Worldwide (2020) found that historically, the most important wellness tourism asset has been the natural environment of the Latin America-Caribbean region. Medical tourism was not as prevalent in this region as a wellness tourism option previously. As of the onset of Covid-19, the top destination for wellness tourism in Latin America and the Caribbean was Mexico, with 18.7 million trips and $12.85 billion in inbound tourism receipts in 2017. Brazil and Chile followed behind, with 10.5 and 7.9 million trips respectively, and $4.07 and $2.22 billion received. Mexico also leads in the spa industry, with 3,837 spas and $1.77 billion in revenue in 2017, followed by Brazil and Argentina, both with around 2,300 spas and $800 million in revenue. Brazil and Argentina are also highest ranked in the thermal/mineral springs category, with 207 and 159 springs respectively, bringing in $718 million and $251.3 million in revenue respectively (Yeung & Johnston, 2018).

Latin America and the Caribbean boast a diverse population, many types of natural habitats, and unique cultural histories. Visitors are often attracted to the region for resting and relaxing in warm weather. The destinations also offer a range of adventure activities, eco-tourism, biodiversity and nature, and thermal/mineral springs. Although jungle/eco-spas are very popular in destinations like Costa Rica and Belize, tourism boards are recognizing that travelers want more. Many locations are moving from luxury spas to more active wellness retreats incorporating other aspects of healthy living as well (Yeung & Johnston, 2018).

Many Latin American countries are already known for their medical tourism. For example, Argentina and Brazil specialize in beauty enhancement treatments, and Mexico, Cuba, and Colombia have strong reputations for medicine and surgery. Although wellness travel is considered to be separate from medical travel, these destinations are developing complementary services for patients before and after medical visits, incorporating other healing modalities such as indigenous ingredients and treatments (Yeung & Johnston, 2018).

Middle East-North Africa region

According to Wellness Tourism Worldwide, the Middle East used to focus its wellness tourism assets on natural healing versus medical tourism. Today, though, medical tourism is growing in importance in the region. The continent of Africa, both North

Africa and Sub-Saharan Africa (discussed in the next section) believed spiritual tourism and their natural environment were their most important wellness tourism assets (Wellness Tourism Worldwide, 2020).

Although the Middle East-North Africa region is still quite young as a wellness tourist destination, wellness-oriented trips to countries like the United Arab Emirates, Morocco, and Israel are beginning to increase (pre-Covid-19). In 2017, the UAE received 1.8 million wellness visitors, with a total spend of $3.75 billion, Morocco saw 2.8 million visitors who spent $1.72 billion, and Israel received 0.9 million wellness travelers who spent $1.13 billion. Many of these visitors came for the spas; Morocco has 2,107 ($294.8 million in revenue), the UAE has 933 ($873.1 million), and Israel offers 520 ($281.8 million). Algeria leads the region in the number of thermal/mineral springs (181), but Tunisia leads in revenue from these natural features ($189.8 million). Israel ranks second on this list ($66.5 million in revenue from only six thermal/mineral springs), due primarily to their wellness tourism offerings centered on the Dead Sea (Yeung & Johnston, 2018).

Although many of the destinations in this region still focus their wellness marketing campaigns primarily on spas, a few are using the word "wellness" on their website. They are slightly expanding their message to include more diverse aspects. For example, Morocco discusses the benefits of its water through thalassotherapy, balneotherapy, and hydrotherapy, and promotes the experience of a traditional communal hammam as a complement to the more luxurious spas (Moroccan National Tourist Office, 2019). Similarly, Abu Dhabi promotes many spas on its website but also includes an Ayurvedic-oriented wellness center (Visit Abu Dhabi, 2019); Egypt discusses the healing properties of its sunny and dry climate and sulphuric springs (Egypt, 2019); and Jordan is capitalizing on its hot springs, proximity to the Dead Sea, and meditation tourism (Jordan Tourism Board, 2019). Several of the Gulf countries are also building holistic wellness retreat centers and large-scale mixed-use projects combining residential, tourism/hospitality, commercial, and health/medical components, targeting both tourists and the local population that is interested in a healthy lifestyle (Yeung & Johnston, 2018).

Sub-Saharan Africa region

Sub-Saharan Africa has long been known as a safari and beach tourism destination, including high-end "spafari" lodges that also offer spa services. Still, they are beginning to expand into a more holistic wellness focus. As one of the more developed Sub-Saharan countries, South Africa leads in wellness tourism, receiving four million inbound wellness travelers, who spent $2.25 billion in 2017 (Yeung & Johnston, 2018). Kenya is second in overall wellness tourism, with 300,000 trips and $412.3 million received. These two countries have spa revenues in the region; South Africa has 1,161 spas that brought in $715 million, and Kenya has 304 spas with receipts of $133.6 million in 2017 (Yeung & Johnston, 2018). Africa has been one of the regions most drastically affected by Covid-19, and its recovery continues to be slow, but these numbers represent the posibilities that wellness tourism can bring to the area.

Although many Sub-Saharan countries have thermal springs, South Africa is the only country of note in the region with a thermal/mineral springs market; 29 establishments received $58.2 million in revenue in 2017. Moving past safaris, beaches, and spas, these countries are offering experiences like mindfulness safaris, yoga in the wilderness, and body treatments in the bush. Wellness travelers are invited to go stargazing in Namibia, to meditate among wildlife in Zambia, and take a long beach walk in Mozambique to reconnect with nature. Traditional African wellness treatments such as calabash massage, izinyawo foot cleanse, and drumming meditation are becoming sought-after (Yeung and Johnston, 2018). These wellness-oriented activities allow travelers to interact with the local people and natural habitat unobtrusively and respectfully while allowing visitors to learn about local cultures and their approach to wellness.

The Global Wellness Institute has identified these regions as the upcoming top growth markets for wellness tourism (Yeung and Johnston, 2018). Still, it is important also to remember the thriving destinations of North America and Europe. Developing markets can observe these established destinations to learn about their successes and missteps as they grew their wellness tourism offerings and promotions throughout the years. Overtourism is a well-founded concern that is becoming all too common, and wellness tourism is both a way to make destinations more susceptible to the phenomenon, but also offers a way to prevent and overcome it.

European-West Asian region

Many countries are not yet marketing their health and wellness tourism potential or are unable to use the potential hidden in natural endowments effectively. The most significant wellness supplies and tourist movements are located in Europe (mostly in German-speaking and Mediterranean countries), North America and Southeast Asia (Csirmaz, & Pető, 2015). However, there is a significant difference between Western and Eastern health and wellness tourism in terms of products and services.

Many health and wellness traditions and practices of Eastern origin have become both accessible and popular in the West especially in Europe, the United States and England. These health and wellness practices are adapted quickly by Westerners, who have discovered that these practices share an important overlap with biomedicine. The health and wellness traditions of the East are idealized as ancient, pure and natural.

However, there are 'asymmetrical translations,' between Western and non-Western health traditions. Non-Western theories "embody a ubiquitous power imbalance in relationship to the more dominant 'Western' biomedical model" (Newcombe, 2012; Sax, 2009). Whereas the Eastern philosophy uses whole natural, religious and traditional formulas to heal the body and mind, the Western philosophy mostly excludes therapeutic methods and applies scientific methods and pharmaceuticals. As a result of the desire for more pure and natural remedies in the West, demand for Eastern treatments has been growing. Now, health care and wellness centers in Western countries offer Eastern therapies, spas, supplements, foods, drinks and herbs for medical care to their customers regularly.

Top wellness destinations

Top destinations in the USA

Although most destinations have some component of wellness that they can share with visitors, a few have long been associated with wellness tourism. Below are the top ten wellness destinations in the United States as ranked by TripAdvisor (2018).

1. **Sedona, Arizona**. As mentioned previously in this chapter, Sedona offers more than just yoga, spas, and hiking throughout the red rock formations. The beautiful desert town is also known for mental and transcendent features like spiritual tours and psychic readings, due in part to its 'vortex', or "swirling [center] of energy that [is] conducive to healing, meditation, and self-exploration" (Sedona Arizona, 2019, 2020).

2. **Hawley, Pennsylvania**. This town is home to a number of notable lakes, which makes it a nice summer location for tourist reflection. Tourists can also be one with nature by horseback riding on a trail or taking a wildlife boat tour on Lake Wallenpaupack.

3. **Ojai, California.** Ojai is located in Southern California in a valley northwest of Los Angeles. It is a picturesque small town completes with small shops, a local farmers' market, and outdoor trails that feature hiking, horseback riding, mountain biking, and rock climbing.

4. **Amelia Island, Florida.** Consistently making the top lists of wellness destinations, Amelia Island is known for its pristine nature, uncrowded beaches, and outdoor activities. A popular farmers' market supplies locals, visitors, and restaurants with fresh produce and other ingredients for healthful meals.

5. **Calistoga, California.** This wellness destination is located in wine country, complete with natural springs that are good for mud baths and thermal springs. If thermal springs do not interest the tourists, then they can hike the trails in the Napa State Park or the Petrified Forest.

6. **Lenox, Massachusetts.** Another city in the Northeast offering activities in four different seasons, Lenox, has been a popular retreat in the Berkshire region for centuries. Pleasant Valley has plenty of hiking trails and ways to interact with nature, and the city features multiple spas. Also located in Lenox is the popular Canyon Ranch resort (the case study in Chapter 3).

7. **Palm Springs, California**. With an astonishing 354 days of sunshine per year, Palm Springs embraces outdoor activities. The city has a 5.5-acre Wellness Park with walkways, a fitness course, water fountains, and beautiful landscaping. Plenty of mineral hot springs are available for soaking, and healthy eateries and spas support an active lifestyle (Palm Springs Bureau of Tourism, 2019).

8. **Park City, Utah.** This location makes the list due to its world-class spas made popular by visitors to the Sundance Film festival. The destination boasts restaurants, open venues for concerts, health clubs, and film screenings. Wellness tourists can also explore the scenic Union Pacific Rail Trail.

4

9. **Stowe, Vermont.** Vermont is more than skiing and winter sports, and destinations like Stowe embrace this. Home to Mount Mansfield, Vermont's highest peak, Stowe has world-class winter terrain, but the idyllic New England village has plenty to do in the other three seasons too. Shopping, dining, zip-lining, climbing, and hiking and, of course, spas, bring wellness to visitors all year long (Vail Resorts Management Company, n.d.).

10. **Wailea, Hawaii.** This location has one of the best beaches on the island of Maui that lets visitors paddleboard and snorkel. It also has high rated spas where visitors can relax and experience serenity.

Top wellness destinations globally

The United States is not the only country with popular wellness destinations; many regions around the world have been welcoming health-seeking travelers for decades or centuries. Building on the locations mentioned earlier in this chapter, here are the top nine non-USA wellness destinations according to TripAdvisor (2018):

1. **Bali, Indonesia.** Bali offers spa services ranging from traditional Balinese treatments to technologically advanced hydro and chromo therapies. Energy healers also abound for those seeking healing methods such as reiki, craniosacral, theta, and shamanic sound. Tarot readers, spiritual counselors, and more supplement the well-known yoga and healthy food options for wellness travelers (Bali Spirit, 2020).

2. **Rishikesh, India.** This holy city in the foothills of the Himalayas and on the banks of the Ganges River is known as the yoga capital of the world. This destination was popularized by the Beatles and their 1968 trip to study transcendental meditation with the Maharishi Mahesh Yogi; local ashrams are available to visitors. Holy rituals are performed nightly near the river, musical ceremonies are common, and the area is surrounded by beautiful hiking and adventure activities (Bishara, 2019).

3. **Hepburn Springs, Australia.** In the state of Victoria, this town has been known for its spas for centuries. Surrounded by mineral springs, bathhouses and spas are prevalent in the area. The local community of healers, artists, writers, musicians, and gardeners welcomes travelers, and restored historical buildings bring guests back to the past to reconnect with a simpler time. Hepburn Regional Park and other parks and gardens make the beautiful and relaxing land and water features accessible to visitors, while seasonal fare and local wines fuel travelers for their journey (Visit Victoria, 2020).

4. **Ko (or Koh) Samui, Thailand.** More than simply a beach destination (although there is plenty of sun, sand, and relaxation available), Koh Samui has a wide range of budget and luxury offerings. Natural and human-made attractions are common, from waterfalls to mummified monks. The Ang Thong National Marine Park comprises 42 islands in the Gulf of Thailand rich with waterfalls and hidden coves to explore. The abundance of buddhas and shrines also make this island a spiritual haven (Hotels.com, 2020).

5. **Costa Rica**. An entire country dedicated to wellness and environmental sustainability, Costa Rica is truly a paradise. Throughout the destination, there is a multitude of opportunities to get close to nature, such as trekking, being immersed in the fresh air of the forest, barefoot walks, high-quality, healthy food, and lots of healing opportunities. Local products like volcanic mud, tropical fruits, chocolate, and coffee are used in spa treatments, and hydrotherapy and hot springs are prevalent (Costa Rica Tourism Board, 2020).

6. **Goa, India**. India's smallest state is host to dozens of wellness centers and many yoga retreats. With more than 80 miles of coastline, plenty of water-related activities are available, making Goa an ideal location to learn to scuba dive or relax on the beaches. Vegetarian and pescetarian restaurants and dishes are widely available, and meals generally include locally sourced ingredients. Bhagwan Mahavir Wildlife Sanctuary is one of four protected wildlife areas in Goa, rounding out both land and sea activities (Russell & Calder, 2009).

7. **Zermatt, Switzerland**. Zermatt is located at the base of the famous Matterhorn peak. After a long day on the mountain, partaking in either winter or summer activities, dozens of spas and relaxing wellness treatments are available. Lakes, hiking, biking, beauty and health services, and top-notch medical services bring plenty of benefits to wellness travelers (Zermatt Tourism, 2020).

8. **The Maldives**. Home to the gorgeous over-water bungalows shown all over social media, the Maldives has lots of wellness features too. Luxury retreats, in particular, abound throughout the country, giving wellness travelers a comfortable place to stay and offerings like signature spa treatments, healthy cuisine, chakra alignment, sound healing, and mindfulness training (Maldives-Magazine.com, 2019).

9. **Ibiza, Spain**. Although Ibiza has long been known for its party atmosphere, the island has recently been turning itself into a wellness destination. Organic food regimes, daily yoga or tai chi, and healing treatments varying from reflexology, to internal organ massages, to trampolining sessions are replacing nightclubbing in popularity. Still an island where variety and individuality is encouraged, Ibiza offers something for many different types of wellness seekers (Conde Nast Traveller, 2020).

10. **Turkey**. Turkey is very famous for its hot springs and mineral waters. A total of 230 geothermal fields have been discovered in Turkey and the country is ranked as the first country in the world in terms of geothermal power capacity increase from 2010–2015 (Simsek, 2017). The geothermal facilities are also used for health purposes offering various services. For example, hot springs and mineral waters, also known by the Turkish name **Ilıca**, are used for bathing as a form of spa treatment. According to experts, these waters are formed in two ways. First, "the surface waters leaking from the cracks melt the minerals on its way, reach the heated layers in the deep, and evaporate and condense with the effect of the heat here and return to the earth," or "the waters, which have melted some minerals in the layers close to the magma, evaporated and condensed and came to

the surface with tectonic events". The waters are in three forms: very hot, hot and cold temperatures. Because of the therapeutic effects of hot, mineral underground waters, they are used in a bath or a partial bath, called **Spa Treatment or Balneotherapy.** The chemical properties of these waters consist of bicarbonate, sulphate, salty, sulphurous, carbon dioxide, ferrous, arsenic, iodized, mixed and radioactive mineral waters. They are used for many physical health problems such as inflammatory rheumatism, sports injuries, neurological damage, mechanical back and neck problems and more. In addition to bathing, there are open-top mineral healing waters available for drinking that contains various mineral salts, chemical compounds and gases. **Mud baths** are another natural healing sources for physical therapy, fracture-dislocation, skin disorders and hemorrhoids and **caves** are used for respiratory diseases using different minerals and salts located in Anatolia. Locals and health professionals have used and recommended those natural therapeutic sources for healing purposes for a very long time. (Turkiyedeki kaplicalar ve termal oteller, 2021).

Summary

This chapter reviewed some of the historically known wellness destinations and discussed the emerging regions throughout the world and what they can offer wellness visitors. Many countries in the Asia-Pacific, Latin America-Caribbean, Middle East-North Africa, and Sub-Saharan Africa areas can benefit from sharing their unique wellness features with the world. This chapter also listed some of the well-known wellness destinations in the United States and globally.

Definition of key terms

Developing country – A country having a standard of living or level of industrial production well below that possible with financial or technical aid (Dictionary.com, n.d).

Hot spring – A pool formed by water that is heated by the Earth's interior, volcanic areas, or very hot rock heated by magma.

Thermal/mineral springs – Encompasses the revenue-earning business establishments associated with the wellness, recreational, and therapeutic uses of water with special properties, including thermal water, mineral water, and seawater (Yeung and Johnston, 2018).

Tourist destination – A place, city or a country, which offers tourism and travel products and services to tourists.

Wellness destination – A country, state, region, city, town, or event that tourists and local residents visit to improve their holistic health.

Discussion questions

1. What are the historical wellness regions and destinations?
2. What natural wellness features do each of the regions of the world offer tourists?
3. What benefits does wellness tourism offer to a country, developed or developing?
4. What cautions do developing countries need to take when promoting their wellness tourism?
5. What are the top wellness destinations in the USA?
6. What are the top wellness destinations globally?

4

Homework

Choose an emerging wellness destination either in the United States or globally, which is not discussed in this text and research how it is promoting wellness tourism. What product offerings does it have? How does it market these offerings to potential visitors? How could it capitalize more on its unique attributes?

References

Baden-Baden Kur & Tourismus GmbH. (2019). The Thermal Baths. Retrieved November 29, 2019, from https://visit.baden-baden.de/en/health-wellness/thermal-baths

Bath's Historic Venues. (2019). Roman Baths History. Retrieved November 28, 2019, from https://www.bathvenues.co.uk/roman-baths-history

Bali Spirit. (2020). Your Guide to Holistic Bali. Retrieved January 22, 2020, from https://www.balispirit.com/

Beirman, D. (2003). *Restoring Tourism Destinations in Crisis: A Strategic Marketing Approach.* Crows Nest, NSW: Allen & Unwin.

Bishara, M. (2019). 9 things to do in the yoga capital of the world. Retrieved January 22, 2020, from https://www.cnn.com/travel/article/rishikesh-india-yoga-capital-and-much-more/index.html

Canyon Ranch. 2020). Canyon Ranch Lenox. Retrieved January 22, 2020, from https://www.canyonranch.com/lenox/

Cellania, M. (2018). The 19th-century sham medicine that saw oracles in orifices. Retrieved November 28, 2019, from www.neatorama.com/2018/01/17/The-19th-Century-Sham-Medicine-That-Saw-Oracles-in-Orifices/

Conde Nast Traveller. (2020). Retrieved January 22, 2020, from https://www.cntraveller.com/gallery/ibiza-health-retreats

Costa Rica Tourism Board. (2020). Wellness. Retrieved January 22, 2020, from https://www.visitcostarica.com/en/costa-rica/things-to-do/wellness

Cowie, A. (2019). Woman risks brain eating disease to take a 3-hour swim in Roman Baths. Retrieved November 28, 2019, from https://www.ancient-origins.net/news-general/roman-baths-0012370

Csirmaz, É., & Pető, K. (2015). International trends in recreational and wellness tourism. *Procedia Economics and Finance, 32*, 755-762.

Dictionary.com. (2019). Definition of developing country. Retrieved November 29, 2019, from https://www.dictionary.com/browse/developing-country

Egypt. (2019) Spa & Wellness. Retrieved November 30, 2019, from http://www.egypt.travel/en/products/spa/spa-and-wellness

Global Wellness Institute. (2018). Global Wellness Tourism Economy Report. Retrieved November 28, 2019, from https://globalwellnessinstitute.org/industry-research/global-wellness-tourism-economy/

Hotels.com. (2020). Koh Samui – Thailand: Everything You Need to Know About Samui. Retrieved January 22, 2020, from http://www.kosamui.com/

Hoyt, A. (2019). Is the Dead Sea really dead? Retrieved November 29, 2019, from https://science.howstuffworks.com/environmental/earth/oceanography/dead-sea-dead2.htm

Jordan Tourism Board. (2019). Leisure & Wellness. Retrieved November 30, 2019, from http://na.visitjordan.com/Whattodo/LeisureWellness.aspx

Kellogg, J.H., M.D. (1908). *The Battle Creek Sanitarium System. History, Organisation, Methods.* Michigan: Battle Creek. p. 13. Retrieved November 29, 2019, from https://archive.org/details/battlecreeksani00kellgoog

Maldives-Magazine.com. (2019). 10 best luxury wellness retreats in Maldives. Retrieved January 22, 2020, from https://maldives-magazine.com/top-10/10-best-wellness-retreats.htm

Moroccan National Tourist Office. (2019). Thermalisme, hammam & spa, thalasso, balnéo. Retrieved November 30, 2019, from https://www.visitmorocco.com/en/experiences/wellness

National Park Service. (n.d.). Retrieved May 28, 2022, from https://www.nps.gov/subjects/geology/hot-springs.htm

Newcombe, S. (2012). Global hybrids?'Eastern traditions' of health and wellness in the West. In Nair-Venugopal, S. (ed.) *The Gaze of the West and Framings of the East.* Palgrave Macmillan, London, pp. 202-217.

Nickell, J. (2016). Historic "gold cure" for addiction. Retrieved November 28, 2019, from https://centerforinquiry.org/blog/historic_gold_cure_for_addiction/

Pletcher, K. (2019). Dead Sea. Retrieved November 29, 2019, from https://www.britannica.com/place/Dead-Sea

Palm Springs Bureau of Tourism. (2019). Your 4-day wellness reboot. Retrieved January 22, 2020, from https://www.visitpalmsprings.com/health-and-wellness-reboot/

Rollins, P. (2015). Bath: Spas, Ancient and Modern, in Dvorak,D., Saari, S. & Tuominen, T. (eds) *Developing a Competitive Health and Well-being Destination*, Retrieved November 28, 2019, from https://globalwellnesssummit.com/wp-content/uploads/Industry-Research/Global/2015-developing-a-competitive-health-and-well-being-destination.pdf

Russell, H. & Calder, S. (2009). The Complete Guide to: Goa. Retrieved January 22, 2020, from https://www.independent.co.uk/travel/asia/the-complete-guide-to-goa-1720996.html

Sax, W. (2009) Introductory Speech at '*The Magic of Yoga: Conceptualizing Body and Self in Transcultural Perspective*' an International and Interdisciplinary Workshop/Symposium, 11–12 Dec Karl Jaspers Centre, University of Heidelberg.

Sedona Arizona. (2019). What is a Vortex? Retrieved November 29, 2019, from https://visitsedona.com/spiritual-wellness/what-is-a-vortex/

Sedona Arizona. (2020). Welcome to Red Rock Country. Retrieved January 22, 2020, from https://visitsedona.com/

Simsek, S. (2017). The Turkish Geothermal Experience. In Bertani, R. (ed) *Perspectives for Geothermal Energy in Europe*, World Scientific Publishing Europe Ltd, pp. 157-186.

Thermae Bath Spa. (2019). The Waters of Bath. Retrieved November 28, 2019, from https://www.thermaebathspa.com/news-info/about-the-spa/the-waters-of-bath/

TripAdvisor. (2018). TripAdvisor names most blissful destinations for wellness travel. Retrieved January 22, 2020, from http://ir.tripadvisor.com/news-releases/news-release-details/tripadvisor-names-most-blissful-destinations-wellness-travel

Turkiyedeki kaplicalar ve termal oteller (2021). Retrieved March 16, 2021, from https://www-kaplicalar-org.translate.goog/kaplica-nedir?_x_tr_sch=http&_x_tr_sl=tr&_x_tr_tl=en&_x_tr_hl=en&_x_tr_pto=op,sc

UNESCO. (2019). City of Bath. Retrieved November 28, 2019, from https://whc.unesco.org/en/list/428/

Vail Resorts Management Company. (n.d.). Stowe, Vermont. Retrieved January 22, 2020, from https://www.stowe.com/

Visit Abu Dhabi. (2019). Wellness & Spa. Retrieved November 30, 2019, from https://visitabudhabi.ae/en/see.and.do/leisure/wellness.and.spa.aspx

Visit Victoria. (2020). Hepburn Springs. Retrieved January 22, 2020, from https://www.visitvictoria.com/regions/daylesford-and-the-macedon-ranges/destinations/hepburn-springs

Wellness Tourism Worldwide. (2020). Wellness for Whom, Where and What? Retrieved June 8, 2020, from https://www.globalwellnesssummit.com/wp-content/uploads/Industry-Research/Global/2011-wellness-tourism-worldwide-wellness-for-whom.pdf

Yeung, O. and Johnston, K. (2018). Global Wellness Tourism Economy Monitor October 2018. Global Wellness Institute. Retrieved November 8, 2019, from https://globalwellnessinstitute.org/ industry-research/global-wellness-tourism-economy/

Zermatt Tourism. (2020). Wellness. Retrieved January 22, 2020, from https://www.zermatt.ch/en/wellness

5 Segmentation in Wellness in Foodservice, Hospitality and Tourism

This chapter discusses the concept of segmentation in wellness in foodservice, hospitality, and tourism. First, it defines segmentation and offers discussions on some common ways to divide a wellness market into smaller groups. Each type of segmentation is then detailed further, and examples of how these methods apply to wellness in foodservice, hospitality, and tourism are given.

Learning outcomes

By the end of this chapter, students should be able to do the following:

1. Discuss the case study of Big Sky Yoga Retreats.
2. Define segmentation and explain different types of segmentation as applied to wellness.
3. Discuss the scope and segments of wellness in foodservice, hospitality, and tourism.
4. Explain whether and how wellness travelers are different from other segments.
5. Offer suggestions on how foodservice, hospitality, and tourism businesses can segment their wellness customers.

Case study: Big Sky Yoga Retreats

Originally started in Montana, Big Sky Yoga Retreats now offers luxury yoga retreats for women around the world. Their signature LUXE Cowgirl Yoga™ retreat focuses on yoga and the human-horse connection, demonstrated by its slogan, "Where Yeehaw Meets Namaste." This three-night retreat in Clyde Park, Montana, is offered twice a year and sells out quickly. They also offer a selection of other packages such as body empowerment retreats for moms and their teenage daughters, cowgirl yoga and hiking in Patagonia; Luxe Yoga, hiking, and spa treatments in the French Alps; yoga and vineyards in Tuscany and Sicily, "yogatography" (yoga + photography), and other various yoga outdoor retreats (Big Sky Yoga Retreats, 2019).

The 2022 rates are approximately $2,500 (depending on the retreat chosen and room type booked) for three days and nights. All packages include rustic-chic accommodation, daily yoga classes, gourmet meals and wines, meditation and journaling guidance, and other activities depending on the type of retreat a guest chooses (wildlife watching, photography courses, vineyard tours, etc.). Optional features such as a portrait photography session with a favorite horse are an additional cost.

Big Sky Yoga Retreats has a distinct segment or target audience. They appeal to women looking for a women-only retreat, with enough disposable income to be able to afford a $750-$900 per night wellness experience. There are some differences between programs, for example, the body empowerment retreat attracts mother-daughter pairs, the yogatography retreat is specifically for women looking to improve their photography skills while riding horses and doing yoga. Their guests are affluent women seeking a wellness retreat in a remote and relaxing destination.

Discussion questions

1. What does Big Sky Yoga Retreat offer to their guests?
2. What is their segmentation strategy, and how effective is it?
3. Beyond the factors of being affluent and female, what other characteristics do Big Sky Yoga Retreat's guests have?
4. What can we learn from Big Sky Yoga Retreat?

Scope and segments of wellness in foodservice, hospitality and tourism

The wellness market is vast, worth an estimated $4.2 trillion in 2017 (pre-Covid-19), and growing (Global Wellness Institute, 2019). Although Covid-19 affected the tourism industry in a huge way, including wellness travel, it is expected that the sector will recover around 2024 and continue to grow from there (World Economic Forum, 2022). Therefore, numbers from 2017 will be used in this chapter to best illustrate the potential of this market.

The wellness market as a whole encompasses much more than tourism, but the combined value of categories affecting the foodservice, hospitality, and tourism industries reach into the trillions. With billions of people worldwide joining the wellness movement, it is important to consider how to divide them into reachable audience segments.

Table 5.1: Value of the global wellness economy in 2017 (Adapted from Global Wellness Institute, 2019).

Segment	Value (in USD billions)
Personal care, beauty, and anti-aging	$108.3
Healthy eating, nutrition, and weight loss	$702
Wellness tourism	$639
Fitness and mind-body	$595
Preventive and personalized medicine and public health	$575
Traditional and complementary medicine	$360
Wellness real estate	$134
Spa economy	$119
Thermal/mineral hot springs	$56
Workplace wellness	$48
Total	$4.2 Trillion

Understanding segmentation in wellness

Segmentation is "the process of defining and subdividing a large homogenous market into clearly identifiable segments having similar needs, wants, or demand characteristics" (BusinessDictionary, 2020). These individual clusters are then called **segments**; the process of segmentation offers a way to optimize offerings and communications to different customer groups. According to Konu (2010), "segmentation can combine different customer information to get a wider picture of different (well-being) tourist segments." The primary segmentation methods in business-to-consumer (B2C) marketing are demographic, psychographic, and behavioral (see Table 5.2). In wellness tourism, there is a connection between the wellness tourists' lifestyle and their affinity for wellness and wellness tourism.

Demographic segmentation of wellness

Demographic variables concerning wellness include such features as location (geographic segmentation), gender, age, ethnicity, education level, and income level. Wellness tourists are not homogenous and these elements are often considered to be the simplest to recognize, as they are generally observable in current and past customers, clients themselves can self-identify their factors, and secondary data like census bureau figures are often free and publically available for further research to understand each segment better (Voigt et al., 2011).

Table 5.2: Types of segmentation (Adapted and developed from Qualtrics, 2020; Kotler & Keller, 2016).

	Demographic	Psychographic	Behavioral
Definition	Classification based on individual attributes	Classification based on attitudes, aspirations, values, etc.	Classification based on actual behavior
Examples	Geography City or metro size Density (urban, suburban, or rural) Climate Gender Nationality Social class Age Ethnicity Education level Occupation Income level Family lifecycle (young & single v. married with children) Family size Religion Generation (Millennials/Generation Y, Generation X, Baby Boomers, or the Silent Generation)	Psychographic lifestyle (i.e., culture-oriented, sports-oriented, or outdoor-oriented) Personality Traits (i.e., compulsive, gregarious, authoritarian, or ambitious) Values Opinions Interests	User Status (i.e., non-user, ex-user, potential user, first-time user, or regular user) Usage Rate (i.e., light user, medium user, heavy user) Benefits Sought (i.e., quality, service, benefit, speed) Occasion (regular occasion versus special occasion) Purchase Decision Loyalty Status Attitude Readiness stage (i.e., unaware, aware, informed, interested, desirous, or intending to buy)
Decision criteria	Target customers on home country, age, gender, wealth, or family status	Target customers based on values or lifestyle	Target customers based on purchase behavior, usage behavior, or benefits sought
Difficulty	Simple	More advanced	More advanced

A potential wellness customer's location will affect many factors, for example, how long it takes to travel to a destination, their weather and chosen seasons to visit a destination, any visa or travel requirements, and more. Their age can affect their choices of wellness activity, expected freedom, amount of disposable income, and the ability to travel. An individual's education level may be correlated with their job type or income level, which helps to determine the size of their budget, freedom to travel, and free time for wellness activities. Family status is also an important factor; single wellness travelers may have more flexibility in their schedules and may be more likely to travel with a group of friends, and married couples without children will have different wellness needs than those with children. It is essential to carefully consider the most likely wellness customers, adjust health and wellness offerings as needed, and market them most appropriately. For example, research on European wellness and treatment seekers indicates that health and wellness clients are mostly middle-income, relatively young, females with higher education and a high level of awareness on prevention related to spiritual and physical improvement (Dryglas &

Salamaga, 2018). These descriptors may be different from global segments, but they provide insights into the demographics of wellness/spa resort tourists to medical European spa resorts.

Psychographic segmentation of wellness

Psychographic variables are more difficult to use for wellness segmentation, as they are generally not readily observable, and wellness customers cannot always describe or explain these factors about themselves. Factors like attitudes, aspirations, values, opinions, lifestyle, interests, and personality traits are often difficult to define and identify segments (Qualtrics, 2020). Relative to wellness in hospitality and tourism, psychographic variables could include a wide variety of things, such as dietary preferences, previously held beliefs or opinions about a destination, aspirations to change one's lifestyle such as becoming a yoga instructor or beginning a new wellness routine, taking an in-depth trip to learn more about an interest such as sustainable farming, and more. One important psychographic variable is personality. Although this is defined in many different ways and incorporates lots of factors, one common framework for understanding personality is the Big Five personality traits, also known as the Five-Factor Model (Cherry, 2019): The five traits in this model are:

1. Openness.
2. Conscientiousness.
3. Extraversion.
4. Agreeableness.
5. Neuroticism.

Each of these five variables represents a scale with two extremes. For example, the opposite end of the "extraversion" variable scale is "introversion." As people typically fall at some point along the scale rather than at one of the extremes, these variables can be difficult to define. Still, the model offers one foundational way to think about personality. Wellness travelers may be segmented and analyzed along with these five categories (see Table 5.3):

- *Openness* incorporates characteristics like imagination and insight. People ranked high on the openness scale are very curious about other people, have many interests, and want to try new wellness experiences.

- People who are high in *conscientiousness* like to have a set wellness schedule, are organized and pay attention to detail in wellness activities they participate and receive. They have reasonable impulse control, are goal-oriented, and are mindful of how their behavior affects others while they participate in wellness activities.

- *Extraversion* determines how outgoing a person is. Highly extraverted people are sociable, talkative, excitable, assertive, and expressive. Being around other people brings energy to an extravert, whereas introverts tend to feel depleted by social situations and need time to recharge.

Table 5.3: Big five segmentation scale applied to wellness (Adapted and developed from Cherry, 2019)

High	Low
Openness	
Very creative Open to trying new wellness activities Enjoys new wellness challenges Likes abstract wellness concepts	Not very imaginative Dislikes change and new wellness activities Resists new wellness ideas Dislikes abstract/theoretical wellness concepts
Conscientiousness	
Spends time preparing for wellness activities Finishes important wellness tasks right away Pays attention to detail in wellness activities Likes having a set schedule in wellness activities	Procrastinates important wellness tasks or does not complete them at all Makes messes and does not take care of things in wellness activities Fails to return things or put them back where they belong Dislikes structures and schedules in wellness activities
Extraversion	
Likes being the center of attention in wellness activities Enjoys meeting new people and starting new conversations in wellness activities Has a full social circle and finds it easy to make new friends during wellness activities Feels energized when around other people Says things before thinking about them while participating in wellness activities	Dislikes being the center of attention activities Dislikes making small talk Prefers solitude in wellness activities Finds it difficult to start conversations Feels exhausted when having to socialize a lot in wellness activities Carefully thinks things through before speaking while in participating in wellness activities
Agreeableness	
Very interested in other people and others' wellness Cares about others Feels empathy and concern for others Enjoys helping and contributing to the happiness of other people in wellness activities Assists others who require help to improve their wellness	Takes little interest in others and their problems Does not care about how other people feel Insults and belittles others Manipulates others to get what they want
Neuroticism	
Experiences a lot of stress while participating in wellness activities Worries about many different things Gets upset easily Has dramatic shifts in mood Feels anxious Struggles to bounce back after stressful events	Emotionally stable Deals well with stress Rarely feels sad or depressed Does not worry much Is very relaxed while participating in wellness activities

- Highly *agreeable* people demonstrate a lot of kindness, affection, altruism, and other prosocial behaviors in developing, participating, and consuming wellness products and services. They tend to cooperate well with others, whereas those low in agreeableness are more competitive and take little interest in others.

- The *neuroticism* trait determines an individual's emotional stability and reaction to stress. Highly neurotic people worry and feel anxious a lot if they may experience a wellness product and service for the first time, can be susceptible to sadness and mood shifts, and find it hard to relax.

Personality
Openness
Conscientiousness
Extraversion
Agreeable
Neuroticism

Figure 5.1: Five-Factor Model. Adapted from Tunikova (2018)

These five traits have been found to be relatively universal and are shaped by both biological (genetic) and nurture (environmental) factors (McCrae & Terracciano, 2005; Power & Pluess, 2015; Jang et al., 1996). Although an individual's personality is generally considered to be stable by the time they are five years old, as people age, the five factors may shift slightly. For example, research has demonstrated that as people get older, they tend to become less extraverted, less neurotic, and less open to new experiences. On the other hand, agreeableness and conscientiousness tend to increase as people grow older (Jang et al., 1996; Marsh et al. 2013). The key for foodservice, hospitality, and tourism businesses is to understand these traits, segment their potential customers, and offer unique wellness products and services to their targeted customer segments.

Discussion: Think about the Big Five personality traits. Where do you fall on the spectrum for each trait? How would it affect your preferences in wellness activities?

How can understanding the Big Five personality traits (openness, conscientiousness, extraversion, agreeableness and neuroticism) help foodservice, hospitality, and tourism businesses in developing and offering wellness products and services? Give specific suggestions for product development, service delivery, and marketing strategies.

Similar to the Five-Factor Model, another popular model for psychographic segmentation is the Strategic Business Insight's VALS framework (Kotler & Keller, 2016; Strategic Business Insights, 2020). This model separates users into eight different groups (innovators, thinkers, achievers, experiencers, believers, strivers, makers, and survivors) based on their psychological traits. The two main elements of this model are consumer motivation and consumer resources. Users are motivated by ideals, achievements, and self-expression.

Innovators display motivations in all three groups in various degrees. Users in this group (Strategic Business Insights, 2020):

- Are always taking in information (antennae up) in regards to wellness.
- Are confident enough to experiment by trying new wellness activities.
- Make the highest number of financial transactions in regards to wellness tourism.
- Are skeptical about wellness and wellness tourism advertising.
- Have international exposure (they like to venture outside of their home country for wellness activities).
- Are future-oriented in regards to their health and wellness.
- Are self-directed wellness consumers.
- Believe science and research and development are credible and rely on information to make wellness decisions.
- Are most receptive to new ideas and technologies in the realm of wellness tourism.
- Enjoy the challenge of problem-solving in wellness.
- Have the most extensive variety of wellness interests and activities.

Thinkers are motivated by their ideals and have access to more resources. Users in this group (Strategic Business Insights, 2020):

- Have "ought" and "should" benchmarks for social conduct which can affect participation in wellness activities.
- Tend toward analysis paralysis which can affect decisions related to wellness and participation in wellness activities.
- Plan, research, and consider before they act.
- Enjoy a historical perspective.
- Are financially established.
- Are not influenced by what's hot, so they may visit wellness destinations that are not as trendy.
- Use technology in functional ways.
- Prefer traditional intellectual pursuits.
- Buy proven wellness products.

Believers are also motivated by their ideals, but they have less access to resources. Users in this group (Strategic Business Insights, 2020):

- Believe in basic rights and wrongs to lead a good life.
- Rely on spirituality and faith for inspiration which may lead them to participate in more spiritual-related wellness activities over other wellness activities.
- Want friendly wellness communities.
- Watch TV and read romance novels to find an escape.

- Want to know where things stand; have no tolerance for ambiguity.
- Are not looking to change society.
- Find advertising a legitimate source of information.
- Value constancy and stability (can appear to be loyal).
- Have strong me-too attitudes.

Achievers are motivated by achievement and have access to more resources. Users in this group (Strategic Business Insights, 2020):

- Have a "me first, my family first" attitude.
- Believe money is the source of authority.
- Are committed to family and job.
- Are fully scheduled.
- Are goal-oriented and will work towards their wellness goals.
- Are hardworking.
- Are moderate.
- Act as anchors of the status quo.
- Are peer conscious in wellness activities.
- Are private.
- Are professional.
- Value technology that provides a productivity boost.

Strivers are motivated by achievement as well, but they do not have access to a lot of resources. Users in this group (Strategic Business Insights, 2020):

- Have revolving employment; high temporary unemployment can affect their wellness and participation in wellness activities.
- Use video and video games as a form of fantasy.
- Are fun-loving.
- Are imitative.
- Rely heavily on public transportation.
- Are the center of low-status street culture.
- Desire to better their lives but have difficulty in realizing their desire which may affect their participation in wellness activities.
- Wear their wealth.

Experiencers are motivated by self-expression, and have access to a lot of resources. Users in this group may react in the following way in wellness settings (Strategic Business Insights, 2020):

- Want everything.
- Are first in and first out of wellness trend adoption.
- Go against the current mainstream.
- Are up on the latest fashions.

- Love physical activity (are sensation seeking) which affects the wellness activities they choose.
- See themselves as very friendly.
- Believe that friends are extremely important.
- Are spontaneous.
- Have a heightened sense of visual stimulation.

Makers are motivated by self-expression as well but have access to fewer resources. Users in this group (Strategic Business Insights, 2020):

- Are distrustful of government.
- Have a strong interest in all things automotive.
- Have strong outdoor interests (hunting and fishing).
- Believe in sharp gender roles.
- Want to protect what they perceive to be theirs.
- See themselves as straightforward; appear to others as anti-intellectual.
- Want to own land.

It is important to note that this group is one of the least likely to participate in wellness activities and wellness tourism based on their characteristics and behaviors.

Survivors do not have any motivation and have the least access to resources out of all of the groups. Users in this group (Strategic Business Insights, 2020):

- Are cautious and risk-averse.
- Are the oldest consumers.
- Are thrifty.
- Are not concerned about appearing traditional or trendy.
- Take comfort in routine, familiar people, and places.
- Are heavy TV viewers.
- Are loyal to brands and products.
- Spend most of their time alone.
- Are the least likely use the internet.
- Are the most likely to have a landline-only household.

Like the makers, this group is also less likely to participate in wellness activities and tourism due to their characteristics and behaviors.

> **Discussion:** Take the Strategic Business Insights VALS Survey at http://www.strategicbusinessinsights.com/vals/presurvey.shtml.
> What is your VALS type? How would that affect your wellness activity preferences?
>
> How can understanding the eight different VALS types (innovators, thinkers, achievers, experiencers, believers, strivers, makers, and survivors) help foodservice, hospitality, and tourism businesses to develop and offer wellness products and services? Give specific suggestions for product development, delivery, and marketing strategies.

Behavioral segmentation of wellness

Similar to psychographic variables, behavioral variables are challenging to use in segmenting wellness customers, mainly because they can vary by situation. For example, remember from Chapter 1 that the primary wellness traveler is a tourist whose trip or destination is primarily motivated by wellness. In contrast, the secondary wellness traveler seeks to maintain wellness while traveling or participates in wellness experiences while taking any trip for leisure or business. The same customer falls into two different segments depending on the occasion and benefits sought from a specific trip.

Two of the primary ways to segment by the behavior of wellness customers are **purchase** and **usage behavior** (Middleton et al., 2009). Purchase behavior will determine who, what, when, why, how, and where the wellness customer acquires a wellness product, and usage behavior is affected by how the customer plans to use the wellness product and service. Variables affecting purchase behavior include:

1. Who is purchasing the wellness trip (a travel agent or an individual) and who is taking the trip (solo, family, or friend group).
2. What kind of wellness trip they are purchasing and what products and services they want included, when they make the purchase (far in advance for a family reunion or annual vacation, or a last-minute weekend trip).
3. How often they make a similar wellness purchase (is this a monthly work trip or an annual family trip).
4. Why they are making the wellness purchase.

How and where the customer makes the wellness purchase are important determinants of where a wellness service needs to be marketed and bookable (e.g., on online travel agencies, instant booking widget on a company's own website, etc.) and what payment methods they accept and what payment schedule is required.

Other behavioral factors that can influence how customers are segmented are the **occasion** and **benefits sought** from the purchase (Middleton et al., 2009). For example, a traveler looking for a relaxing beach and spa destination for their honeymoon will likely have different requirements than someone searching for a weekend hiking getaway to a nearby town. There are three main types of occasions:

1. Universal (purchases that apply to the majority of a segment or target audience).
2. Recurring (purchases that one individual customer makes consistently over a period of time).
3. Rare (purchases that an individual customer makes only once or very infrequently).

For example, if a special event happens for only one weekend at a destination, all travelers to that event will be coming at the same time and will have similar needs (universal). A business traveler that goes to the same destination for one week a month is a recurring purchase made consistently over time. A honeymoon trip or high-end bucket list trip may only be made once in a traveler's lifetime (rare).

There are additional behavioral factors that could be considered when it comes to segmenting wellness travelers, many of which differ by the individual business. For example, a customer that has a high level of loyalty to one hotel chain is a much easier target for a hotel within that brand than for a competitive brand. A user's status can also affect how they need to be approached. A first-time wellness traveler may need more information on a resort's benefits and offerings than a guest on their fifth visit to the location. The stage a potential customer is in the purchase process also affects the communication message they should receive – a person doing initial research will need different information and calls to action than a shopper comparing prices and searching for specific date availability to accommodate their schedule. The decision roles (initiator, influencer, decider, buyer, and user) of the user play an important part in segmenting wellness travelers (Kotler & Keller, 2016). A wife may initiate the conversation of visiting a yoga retreat for vacation while the husband researches options. Then a joint decision is ultimately made between the two of them since both of them will be attending the retreat for vacation.

Segmentation by activities, interests, and opinions

Health and wellness tourism is now promoted by many destinations, and recent studies show that well-planned customer service increases competitive advantage. Since wellness tourism relates heavily to well-being and living a healthy life, one can also segment wellness tourists based on their activities, interests, and opinions. This method is defined as focusing specifically on lifestyle features as they relate to a product or service (Konu, 2010). Activities would include work, social events, vacations, and hobbies; interests include topics like family, food, community, and recreation, and opinions are beliefs surrounding issues like education, culture, and social issues. Besides "health promotion treatments," "mental learning," "experience of unique tourism resources," "complementary treatments," "relaxation," "healthy eating" and "social activities" are also effective in the marketing of health and wellness tourism (Chen et al., 2013). This type of segmentation gives a more all-encompassing look at wellness tourists and can predict wellness tourist behavior more accurately than segmentation based on demographic data alone (Konu, 2010).

Discussion: How does the Activities, Interests, and Opinions segmentation differ from demographic, psychographic, and behavioral segmentation? In what ways is it the same as demographic, psychographic, and behavioral segmentation?

What can activities, interests, and opinions segmentation discover about wellness tourists that demographic, psychographic, and behavioral segmentation cannot?

Practical use of segmentation of wellness customers

To qualify as a wellness segment, a group of customers should be **measurable**, **accessible**, **substantial**, and **actionable** – some researchers also include defensible, durable, competitive, homogenous, and compatible in their qualifications of a wellness segment (Qualtrics, 2020; Suresh et al., 2017). *Measurable* signifies that the size of a wellness segment can be measured in terms of the number of individuals and their purchasing power. *Accessible* indicates that the wellness segment can be reached by the organization with promotional tools (social media, newspaper ads, television commercials, email newsletters, etc.). *Substantial* refers to a segment that is large enough to warrant receiving a different product or marketing message, and it is worth the investment to target them differently from other segments. To be *actionable*, a segment must be able to act on a marketing message by purchasing a product.

The above requirements suggest that it is possible to estimate the size of a segment, and that it is large enough to make it worth customizing a product or marketing campaign to that group. The members of these wellness segments should be accessible by the communication styles available to the company, and they need to be able to take action on the product offered (for example, segment members must be able to travel to the destination being marketed). If a potential group does not have all of these qualities, it does not warrant its own segment. It can be combined with another segment, or perhaps it is not a good target at all.

It is important to note that the same traveler can fall into multiple segments depending on various factors. For example, a traveler may be on a business trip and choose to eat healthily, go for a run each morning, and visit the spa once during their trip, categorizing them as a secondary wellness traveler in this situation. Alternatively, that same traveler could be on a personal vacation focused primarily on yoga and detoxing, labeling them a primary wellness travelers in that scenario. A traveler could bring their family on a weekend exploration of a nearby park but might go with a group of friends on a rock-climbing expedition into the mountains.

In wellness foodservice, hospitality, and tourism, all of these factors affect how customers should be segmented and targeted. For example, a secondary wellness traveler may reserve a business trip through an online travel agency (OTA) and will request a spa appointment in the booking notes. This person may not do any research beyond filtering and sorting on their preferred OTA, and making a reservation at the hotel closest to their business meeting that also has a spa. In this situation, it is essential to ensure that all OTA listings are complete and current with information and attractive professional photographs about the spa.

A primary wellness traveler may be looking for a weeklong all-inclusive yoga and wellness retreat within driving distance, that offers locally grown organic meals, a minimum of two yoga sessions per day, and activities to disconnect from technology and reconnect with nature. In this scenario, a retreat that would fit their needs must have a complete and optimized website that ranks high in search engine results (i.e., has high search engine optimization (SEO)), listings and partnerships with organizations that promote such retreats and where customers may turn for information, etc.

Segmentation is essential to discuss concerning wellness tourism as it relates to the idea of "packaging." **Packaging** is combining related services into a single offer for the tourist (Suresh et al., 2017). By identifying segments of wellness tourists, resorts and destinations can package similar activities together to better appeal to those tourists, which increases the likelihood that they will visit that resort or destination.

How are wellness travelers different?

Although any traveler can look for a wellness component in their trip (including secondary wellness travelers incorporating only one or two aspects), primary wellness travelers do share some commonalities. They often look beyond having an engaging experience and into the realm of self-improvement. This may mean wanting an authentic and sustainable travel experience like a bicycle ride through a village and having lunch with local people while learning about their traditional crafts. This shows a higher degree of openness and agreeableness in these situations, rather than a desire for a strictly planned schedule of visiting popular tourist destinations and eating at familiar restaurants.

While the budget and destinations of wellness travelers vary, as well as the specific activities chosen on a trip, wellness travelers may require more emotional attention than more traditional guests. Wellness practices like yoga, meditation, journaling, acupuncture, and even walking through nature can release deep emotions that have been blocked and boxed away mentally for months or years. This is an important component for staff to be trained in, in addition to the more obvious and expected needs of any traveler looking for a healthy and self-fulfilling experience.

Examples of segmenting in wellness tourism research

Various studies and authors discover different ways to segment wellness tourists by the way they seem to form clusters or groups based on similarities in behavior, motivations, the benefits they want to gain from wellness tourism, etc. This section discusses some of these ways to give readers a better understanding of segmentation for this niche form of tourism.

Damijanic (2009), in her study on "the concept of wellness as a form of a healthy lifestyle in tourism settings" found that wellness tourists fall into four distinct clusters. These four clusters are "high-level wellness," "diet and health-oriented," "fitness-oriented," and "low-level wellness" and were segmented based on the importance of "diet, social interactions, cultural diversity, fitness, health awareness, and personal development" during stays at wellness hotels. The high-level segment rated the six factors as very important, whereas the low-level segment did not rate those factors as important. The diet and health segment rated the diet and health factors high, and the fitness-oriented segment rated fitness as high, hence their segment names.

In a 2010 study on Finnish wellness tourists, Konu (2010) found six segments of wellness tourists. They are (1) sport and nature segment, (2) home appreciating segment, (3) family and health-oriented sport and nature segment, (4) culture appreciative self developers segment, (5) material wellbeing appreciators segment and (6) indifferent about traveling and social issues segment. This study used the activities, interests, and opinions method to segment and found that there may be a connection between lifestyles and wellness tourism in regards to the segmentation of tourists. These segments were based on activities, interests, and opinions on items like indoor group exercises, jogging, fishing, taking different treatments, etc.

Hritz, Sidman, and D'Abundo in their 2014 study looked at segmenting college-educated members of Generation Y (aka Millennials) who are health and wellness travelers. They found five distinct groups in their study: "escapers," "after hours," "amenity seekers," "most unwell," and "most well." The "escaper" group is characterized by people who feel emotionally, spiritually, and psychologically well but may not feel well physically; they also seek travel as an escape from everyday life and are more likely to travel by themselves. The "after hours" group feels well spiritually and physically but may seem unwell in their psychological or emotional health; this group is the least active, least likely to engage in wellness tourism, and prefers social activities and nightlife when they vacation over wellness. The "amenity seekers" segment perceive themselves to be relatively healthy in all aspects of health and wellness, and they look for various amenities like outdoor activities or tours to push them to travel to a specific location rather than having the innate need or want to visit that destination. The "most unwell" group perceived themselves as the least healthy but are motivated by physical activity to overcome that perception and fit in with others. Lastly, the "most well" segment viewed themselves as having high levels of wellness when compared to others and want to learn new things and chase adventure in their wellness travels (Hritz et al., 2014).

In their 2017 study, Suresh, Ganesan, and Ravichandran grouped wellness tourists based on their behavior, specifically their usage. In their study, they found three different groups of tourists: "occupational ailment prevention seekers and regular clients," "heredity ailment prevention seekers and new clients," and " anti-aging spirituality seekers and strong review." This study grouped wellness tourists based on their behaviors and their usage occasion in regards to wellness products (Suresh et al., 2017).

Chen, Liu and Chang in their 2013 study looked at essential customer services to older adults in Asian wellness tourism, segmenting them into three sub-groups: "Holistic group," "Physiotherapy group," and "Leisure and recreation group." (Chen et al., 2013). Studies like these help segment wellness travelers based on the benefits they seek from a tourism destination. For example, segmentation provides guidance on how to manage and market local wellness products and facilities. Although each segment is different in terms of what they look for in products and services, the end goal is to meet their needs and wants, resulting in a high level of satisfaction. This then leads to repeat business and referrals, demonstrating the benefit of segmentation in tourism (Pesonen et al., 2011).

Summary

This chapter discussed the concept of segmentation in wellness in foodservice, hospitality, and tourism. It defined segmentation and provided discussions on some common ways to segment a market into smaller groups. The chapter also detailed each type of segmentation further and provided examples of how these methods can be applied to segment wellness customers in foodservice, hospitality, and tourism.

Definition of key terms

Accessible – It must be possible to reach a segment with the promotional tools (social media, newspaper ads, television commercials, email newsletters, etc.) available to the marketer).

Actionable – A segment must be able to act on a marketing message by purchasing a product.

Measurable – It must be possible to measure the size of a segment in terms of the number of individuals and their purchasing power.

Packaging – Combining related and complimentary services together into a single offer for the tourists.

Purchase behavior – Who, what, when, why, how, and where the customer acquires a product.

Segment – A cluster of similar customers grouped based on shared characteristics.

Segmentation – The process of defining and subdividing a large homogenous market into clearly identifiable segments having similar needs, wants, or demand characteristics (BusinessDictionary, n.d.).

Substantial – A segment must be large enough to warrant receiving a different product or marketing message, and it must be worth the investment to target them differently from other segments (Qualtric, n.d.).

Usage behavior – If and how a consumer plans to purchase a product or service and how this customer will use this product and service.

Discussion questions

1. What is segmentation?
2. What are the three primary methods of segmentation?
3. How can we apply segmentation in wellness?
4. How can a foodservice, hospitality, and tourism business find out more details about their wellness customers and how to segment them?
5. What qualities should a wellness segment have to qualify it as a separate group worthy of a different product or marketing message?
6. What different wellness segments might you personally fit into? What kind of wellness products and services would you want from a wellness business? How could they best reach you for marketing purposes?

Homework

Choose a business that you are familiar with that has a wellness aspect. Discuss the following: What offerings do they have? To whom do their wellness products and services appeal? What different marketing messages do they have, and how does it seem they are using segmentation to reach their varying audiences?

References

Big Sky Yoga Retreats. (2019). Yoga Retreat Styles. Retrieved December 6, 2019, from https://bigskyyogaretreats.com/

BusinessDictionary. (2020). Market Segmentation. Retrieved January 29, 2020, from /www.businessdictionary.com/definition/market-segmentation.html

Chen, K. H., Liu, H. H. & Chang, F. H. (2013). Essential customer service factors and the segmentation of older visitors within wellness tourism based on hot springs hotels. *International Journal of Hospitality Management*, 35, 122-132.

Cherry, K. (2019). The Big Five personality traits. Retrieved January 29, 2020, from www.verywellmind.com/the-big-five-personality-dimensions-2795422

Cobb-Clark, D.A. & Schurer, S. (2012). The stability of big-five personality traits. *Economics Letters*, 115(2), 11-15.

Damijanic, A. (2019). Wellness and healthy lifestyle in tourism settings. *Tourism Review*, 74(4). 978-989. DOI: 10.1108/TR-02-2019-0046.

Dryglas, D. & Salamaga, M. (2018). Segmentation by push motives in health tourism destinations: A case study of Polish spa resorts. *Journal of Destination Marketing & Management*, 9, 234-246.

Global Wellness Institute. (2019) What is the wellness economy? Retrieved December 5, 2019, from https://globalwellnessinstitute.org/what-is-wellness/what-is-the-wellness-economy/

Hritz, N.M., Sidman, C.L. & D'Abundo, M. (2014). Segmenting the college educated Generation Y health and wellness traveler. *Journal of Travel & Tourism*, 31(1). 132-146. DOI: 10.1080/10548408.2014.861727.

Jang, K.L., Livesley, W.J. & Vernon P.A. (1996). Heritability of the big five personality dimensions and their facets: a twin study. *Journal of Personality*. 64(3), 577-91.

Konu, H. (2010) Identifying potential well-being tourism segments in Finland. *Tourism Review*, 65(2). 41-51. DOI: 10.1108/166605371011061615.

Kotler, P. & Keller, K.L (2016). *A Framework for Marketing Management*. Pearson: Boston, US.

5

Marsh, H.W., Nagengast, B. & Morin, A.J.S. (2013). Measurement invariance of big-five factors over the lifespan: ESEM tests of gender, age, plasticity, maturity, and la dolce vita effects. *Developmental Psychology*. 49(6), 1194-1218.

McCrae, R. R. & Terracciano, A., (2005). Universal features of personality traits from the observer's perspective: Data from 50 different cultures. *Journal of Personality and Social Psychology*. 88, 547-561.

Middleton, V. T., Fyall, A., Morgan, M. & Ranchhod, A. (2009). *Marketing in Travel and Tourism*. Elsevier: Oxford, UK.

Pesonen, J., Laukkanen, T., & Komppula, R. (2011). Benefit segmentation of potential well-being tourists. *Journal of Vacation Marketing*, 17(4), 303-314.

Power, R.A. & Pluess, M. (2015). Heritability estimates of the Big Five personality traits based on common genetic variants. *Translational Psychiatry*. 5: e604.

Qualtrics. (2020). What is Market Segmentation? Retrieved January 29, 2020, from https://www.qualtrics.com/experience-management/brand/what-is-market-segmentation/

Strategic Business Insights. (2020). US Framework and VALS Types. Retrieved January 31,2020 from www.strategicbusinessinsights.com/vals/ustypes.shtml

Suresh, S., Ganesan, P., and Ravichandran, S. (2017). Behavioral segmentation of wellness clients. *Journal of Travel and Tourism Research*, 131 – 150.

Voigt, C., Brown, G., & Howat, G. (2011). Wellness tourists: in search of transformation. *Tourism Review*, 66(1/2), 16-30. https://doi.org/10.1108/16605371111127206

World Economic Forum (2022). This is the impact of Covid-19 on the travel sector. Retrieved May 29, 2022, from https://www.weforum.org/agenda/2022/01/global-travel-tourism-pandemic-covid-19/

6 Health and Wellness Food and Beverage Trends

This chapter discusses the concept of health and wellness food and beverages as well as health and wellness food trends in foodservice, hospitality, and tourism. First, it defines health and wellness food and beverages. Then, it discusses the value of the health and wellness food and beverage market in the USA and globally. Next, it identifies and discusses several health and wellness food and beverage trends. Finally, it outlines how health and wellness food and beverage offerings can be combined with other wellness activities.

Learning outcomes

By the end of this chapter, students should be able to do the following:

1. Discuss the case study of The Smoothie Industry.
2. Define the concept of health and wellness food and beverages.
3. Explain the market value of health and wellness food and beverage market in the U.S. and globally.
4. Identify and explain several healthy food and beverage trends.
5. Discuss how health and wellness food and beverages can be combined with other wellness activities.
6. Offer suggestions on how foodservice, hospitality, and tourism businesses can utilize health and wellness food and beverage trends in their business operations.

Case study: The smoothie industry

The smoothie industry will grow in size from $12.10 billion in 2021 to an estimated $17 billion by 2027, a compound annual growth rate (CAGR) of 10.1%. Due to the typically high amount of raw vegetables and fruits in each drink, along with other additives like dairy or plant-based milk and nutritional supplements, smoothies are often seen as a good source of fiber and other nutrients. The global market for smoothies is highly fragmented, with many different regional and domestic companies. The largest market for smoothies is currently North America, and the fastest-growing market is the Asia-Pacific region (Market Data Forecast, 2022).

Independent outlets and franchises (such as Smoothie King and Planet Smoothie) alike are capitalizing on the current market desire for smoothies, as outlets open throughout the world. The growing trend of healthy eating, especially raw and organic food products, is only one of the reasons for this increase in the popularity of smoothies; some of the others include (technavio, 2019):

- The increasing awareness of gluten sensitivity and intolerance, as well as the growing incidence rate of celiac disease, a serious autoimmune disease where digesting gluten can lead to small intestine damage (Celiac Disease Foundation, 2020), are leading consumers to seek out gluten-free food products like smoothies.

- The growing amount of digestive health problems, weight management issues, and demand for healthy food, is driving the demand for more nutritious food.

- Consumers are becoming more concerned about the origin and quality of their food sources, including fruits and vegetables. The availability of organic produce for smoothie production is key.

- Vendors are creating new and innovative products, such as smoothie bowls, to increase the diversity of their offerings. Ingredient combinations are also virtually endless, which offers limitless options for consumers with different tastes and needs. Also, some smoothie companies are innovating by modifying ingredients, for example, using Greek yogurt for more protein and fewer calories or substituting high-calorie chocolate syrup with cocoa powder (Planet Smoothie, 2020).

It is clear that the smoothie industry, along with related products like cold-pressed juices, is rapidly growing. This aligns well with the goals and growth of the wellness travel industry.

Discussion questions

1. How is the smoothie industry innovating?
2. What are the primary factors contributing to the growth of the smoothie industry?
3. How can smoothie vendors cater to the needs and desires of wellness travelers?

The concept and scope of health and wellness food and beverages

Food and beverages in the health and wellness industry are specially formulated to provide nutritional, health, and functional benefits to consumers. Consumers' concerns about the quality of ingredients in their diet, along with generally increasing health awareness, are leading to a desire for healthier food and beverage offerings (PRNewswire, 2018). The health and wellness food market was valued at $733 billion in 2020 and is estimated to be worth $1 trillion in 2026 (Statista, 2021). Food is a vital part of local economies and destinations where the food originates. Food authenticity especially is a key factor in place attachment (Chang et al., 2021; Shi et al., 2022). Therefore, wellness destinations should combine their unique culinary resources and health and wellness facilities to market and promote the region.

Health and wellness food and beverage trends

Special diets have long been promoted as wellness cures, and eating trends are continuing in that path. The Millennial generation, those born between 1981 and 1996, in particular, has specific requirements for their purchases: 49% expect all products to be Genetically Modified Organism/GMO-free, 43% expect organic, 53% natural, 64% sustainable, and 56% are looking for all products to be recyclable (Innovation Group, 2017). Consumers are looking for locally sourced, organic, healthy foods that match their diet of choice and offer more than physical sustenance. A few health and wellness food and beverage trends are discussed below.

Farm-to-table / locally sourced

Consumers, in general, are becoming more distrustful of the industrial food system, and are seeking real, local, sustainable alternatives like locally grown produce. One term for this is farm-to-table, which describes the process of local products (produce, meat, flowers, etc.) being grown on a local farm, then brought straight to a market where the community (including local restaurants and other establishments) can purchase them and bring them home to their table (UnityPoint Health, 2018). Another popular term for this is farm-to-fork, defined by Rutgers (2020) as "a food system in which food production, processing, distribution, and consumption are integrated to enhance the environmental, economic, social and nutritional health of a particular place." This process helps consumers to diversify their food and eat more nutritious options, help the environment, support the local community and economy, reduce the amount of packaged food consumption, educate their children, simplify their lives, and other benefits often associated with the wellness movement.

The buzzwords "farm-to-table" now are commonly seen in restaurant promotional marketing as a way to attract consumers looking for organic just-picked fruits and vegetables, fresh fish, and locally raised meats sourced from nearby suppliers. In rural and suburban areas, this might come from traditional farms with an organic and sustainable focus, like free-range chickens, cows, and pigs, and crops grown without pesticides. In urban areas, especially in regions known as "food deserts," where no fresh produce is available, the focus is on innovations like urban farms. These are becoming viable due to advances like vertical farming, which allows for a much higher production level per square foot than traditional farming methods (Innovation Group, 2017). There are four principles, or pillars, of the farm-to-table concept (Rutgers, 2020):

1. **Food security.** Community food systems are concerned with not only the needs of individuals or families but also with those of the entire community, including low-income households.

2. **Proximity.** The components of a local food system (or restaurant) should be as close to each other as possible. This allows relationships to form between producers, retailers, and consumers, and it reduces the environmental impact of transportation.

3. **Self-reliance.** A community that can meet its own food needs reduces the reliance on outside resources, as well as eliminating long-distance food transportation.

4. **Sustainability.** Locally oriented food systems are more likely to be sustainable over generations, as they do not destroy resources in the process of production.

5. This idea of buying locally grown fresh food is a return to shopping habits of past centuries, where consumers would visit local farms or vendors to purchase whatever was in season at the time. There are over 8,000 farmers' markets in the United States alone, and they are a popular destination for shopping, dining, and socializing with other consumers and getting to know the farmers themselves. For those who may not have the budget for farmer's produce or organic produce, there are websites like Imperfect Foods that allow consumers to get sustainably sourced less-than-perfect produce while also helping to cut back on consumer food waste (Imperfect Foods, 2020). For time-pressed consumers or those without a convenient farmer's market, dozens of organizations offering home delivery of organic produce are available. Taking farm-to-table and locally sourced ingredients a step beyond a farmer's market visit or food delivery service, many people (35% of all households in America in 2014) are also growing their food at home or in community gardens. Millennials, in particular, are embracing this trend, up 63% to 13 million since 2008. (Yeung & Johnston, 2018).

Organic

Organic food is grown without toxic or synthetic pesticides or fertilizers, GMO ingredients, antibiotics or synthetic growth hormones, artificial flavors, colors, or preservatives, sewage sludge or irradiation (Organic Trade Association, 2019). In the last decade, the demand for organic food has risen quickly, continually showing double-digit growth year over year. Mainstream consumers are looking for organic food due to concerns over their health, the environment, and animal welfare, and they do not mind paying the additional price over conventional foods grown with chemicals, hormones, and fertilizers (Yeung & Johnston, 2018).

Organic sales in the United States reached a record of $61.9 billion in 2020, $56.5 billion of which was organic food, an increase of 12.4% over 2019. This accounts for almost 6% of all food sold in the U.S. Fresh fruits and vegetables lead the organic food sales, accounting for $20.4 billion, and reaching more than 15% of all fruit and vegetable sales in the U.S. During 2020 (much of which was during the Covid-19 pandemic lockdown), sales in the U.S. of organic flours and baked goods grew by 30%, sauces and spices reached $2.4 billion, and meat, poultry, and fish grew by 25%, as consumers look for products that are free of antibiotics, synthetic hormones, and chemicals (Organic Trade Association, 2021).

Limited-ingredient diets

Wellness consumers are embracing a variety of limited-ingredient diets, from vegetarianism to pescetarianism to paleo. Three diets similar in nature are **vegetarians**, who do not eat meat, **vegans**, who do not consume any animal products at all (including meat, eggs, milk, honey, etc.), **plant-based eaters** (eat primarily non-animal products, but may consume a limited amount), and **pescetarians**, who will not consume meat from any land animals, but will eat fish and other seafood (Healthline, 2022). Proponents of these diets often claim three primary reasons for their choices: being kind to animals, reducing the environmental footprint of factory meat farming, and the possible adverse effects of eating animal products (especially meat) on a person's health (Innovation Group, 2017).

Veganism and plant-based diets, in particular, are growing at a rapid rate. Vegans frequently justify their lack of any animal product consumption by the belief that animals should not be treated as a commodity, often leading to further choices not even to purchase products made from wool, silk, and other materials that do not cause physical harm to an animal to harvest. Britain alone has seen an increase in the number of men and women who identify as a vegan of over 360% in the past decade. This is mainly reflected in the younger generation, as 42% of vegans are between ages 15-34, and only 14% are over 65. This trend is often seen as a glamorous and sexy choice, promoted by Instagram influencers, social media celebrities, and other popular celebrities (Yeung & Johnston, 2018).

To satisfy this group of consumers, high levels of investment have been made in plant-based food alternatives. While some critics argue that food technology innovations such as lab-produced meat alternatives are counterintuitive to the trend toward traditional, locally grown, GMO-free foods, venture capitalists and others invested $350 million into food tech companies and projects in 2012 alone. Startups are working on developing meat alternatives beyond corn- and black bean-based veggie burgers that offer flavors and textures almost identical to their meat counterparts. For example, Impossible Foods has developed a burger that includes a plant-derived version of heme, a component of hemoglobin that contributes to the characteristic color and taste of meat, and San Francisco-based Memphis Meats says it has made the world's first lab-grown chicken strips from animal cells. Beyond Meat's Beyond Burger was backed by Bill Gates and Twitter co-founder Biz Stone. Fast food restaurants have even invested in plant-based food alternatives as seen in Burger King's Impossible Whopper and Dunkin's Beyond Sausage Breakfast sandwich (Impossible Foods, 2020; King, 2019). However, this trend may need some time to catch on, as 36% of Millennials are embracing meat alternatives, compared to only 14% of Baby Boomers (Innovation Group, 2017).

Another limited-ingredient trend on the opposite end of the spectrum when it involves meat is the **Paleo** diet. Derived from the word "Paleolithic," this plan is based on foods that could be obtained through hunting and gathering during the Paleolithic era (2.5 million to 10,000 years ago), such as fruits, vegetables, fish, lean meats, nuts, and seeds. Supporters claim that changes brought with farming, such as dairy, grains, and legumes, happened too quickly for the human body to adapt. Therefore, Paleo diet followers typically avoid grains, legumes, potatoes, dairy products, refined sugars, salt, and highly processed foods in general (Mayo Clinic, 2017).

Plant-based diets

While similar to limited-ingredient diets, plant-based diets have become a trend in their own right. Plant-based proteins are more sustainable to the earth and kinder to animals and can reduce the risk of type 2 diabetes, heart disease, certain types of cancer, and other significant illnesses (Imatome-Yun, 2019). While some strict plant-based diets are similar to veganism, with no consumption of any animal products allowed, others are centered around plants but focus on whole foods and healthy fats and allow animal products such as fish, limited dairy, and poultry. Some examples of popular plant-based diets are Mediterranean diet, the Dietary Approaches to Stop Hypertension (DASH) diet, and the Mediterranean-DASH Intervention for Neurodegenerative Delay (MIND) diet, all rich in fiber, minerals, and vitamins (Harvard Medical School, 2020).

Immersive and sensory food experiences

Tourism is an experiential product, and culinary travel experiences are becoming an important factor in the decision-making process. More than two-thirds (71%) of U.S. Millennials will recommend a destination based solely on its food offerings, and 82% of U.S. respondents say they are most excited about trying local restaurants and food when they travel. Festivals of all types are a popular reason to travel. Food festivals, in particular, are becoming trendier than ever, often with celebrity chefs in attendance and plenty of live music. The four-day London Coffee Festival in 2017 attracted over 30,000 people, and music festival Coachella 2017 hosted vendors like San Diego vegan-friendly restaurant Kindred, Tin Vuong's popular Southeast Asian-inspired Little Sister and Brooke Williamson's Playa Provisions. Non-festival events centered on food are also becoming popular, such as New York City's 2017 15-day exhibition at Boba Room that focused on bubble tea. The fusion of art and cuisine is being celebrated around the world, with contemporary artists and dining establishments partnering to offer distinctive and unique events. From the atmosphere to cutlery and other dining elements, even the accompaniments to the food are being modified to craft a unique experience.

One of the best ways to obtain an immersive and sensory experience is through virtual reality (V.R.) and augmented reality (A.R.). In foodservice, the Italian restaurant chain Carluccio's has used V.R. video footage to supplement their dining experience by showing scenes of Italy linked to the dishes being consumed. Similarly, London's One Aldwych hotel allows customers to order a whiskey cocktail, then virtually travel to the distillery in the Scottish Highlands where the liquid is aged, and return to London to drink their beverage. Holographic illusions can make food appear that seems realistic to help diners make better food choices.

These trends are likely to become more popular in wellness-specific foodservice, hospitality, and tourism soon. V.R. and A.R. could be used to support experiences for people who are not able to travel or physically participate in such wellness activities as yoga or hiking, as this technology may still provide some of the mental benefits. Similarly, individuals with eating disorders or those lacking confidence in social settings may be able to improve their overall wellness through these virtual tools. (Innovation Group, 2017).

Eating for happiness

As scientists learn more about the health benefits of individual foods, those filled with antioxidants and others that boost serotonin and other "happiness hormones" are becoming more popular (Yeung & Johnston, 2018). Serotonin is synthesized from the amino acid tryptophan, found in such foods as eggs, cheese, pineapples, tofu, salmon, nuts and seeds, and turkey (Jenkins, 2014). Research has found that an anti-inflammatory diet high in vegetables, fish, olive oil, and nuts, similar to a Mediterranean diet, reduced symptoms of depression in 32% of one sample (National Health Service, 2018). Additional ongoing research suggests that introducing specific bacteria into the gut may reduce stress and anxiety associated with post-traumatic stress disorder (Lamb, 2017). J. Walter Thompson named "Mood Food" one of its top trends for 2018, citing evidence of airlines, airports, restaurants, and other service businesses going beyond the idea of food as physical fuel and into the realm of mental health benefits as well (Innovation Group, 2017).

In practice, wellness travelers will look for menus that include such items as blueberries, blackberries, spinach, green tea, tuna, salmon, bananas, nuts, seeds, and of course, dark chocolate and red wine. Foods high in fiber have earned a reputation for their healthfulness, with health-oriented individuals choosing brown and wheat bread over white, and snacking on nuts and seeds. Fermented foods have also long been touted for their probiotic benefits. As research and awareness increase about the gut-brain-happiness axis (a field called *psychobiotics*, [Sarkar et al., 2016]), foods like yogurt, kefir, kimchi, sauerkraut, and kombucha will continue their rise in popularity (Yeung & Johnston, 2018). Many food establishments are joining this trend, like

Honeybrains, a New York City-based café with a neurologist-designed menu to promote brain wellness. The café incorporates ingredients such as avocado, quinoa, and raw honey that the brand claims lower the risk of Alzheimer's disease and offer other brain-healthy benefits (Innovation Group, 2017).

Healthy beverages

Fruit smoothies and vegetable juices have long been favorites of the wellness consumer, with their nutritional density, convenience, and ability to incorporate supplements. However, today's healthy beverages are going far beyond simple smoothies and cold-pressed juices. Non-alcoholic "wellness bars" are popping up around the world, promoting health elixirs in unique flavor and ingredient combinations. Dirty Lemon's 2017 pop-up in New York City's trendy Nolita neighborhood was themed to look like a vintage drugstore and sold $10 variations of their detox drinks that are traditionally only sold online. Local mixologists contributed to the flavor combinations with non-traditional ingredients like collagen and activated charcoal, and the experience was designed to feel more "craft cocktail bar" than "healthy drink center" (Innovation Group, 2017).

More traditional cocktail bars are also embracing the wellness beverage movement. Seedlip, a non-alcoholic "spirit" distilled from herbs and based on non-alcoholic remedies from *The Art of Distillation* written in 1651, has become common in many trendy cocktail bars around the world. Although it does not contain any alcohol, Seedlip tastes like liquor, giving mocktails a more genuine flavor. Even alcoholic beverage manufacturers are using vegetables such as carrots and beets to give their distilled products a unique twist, and mixologists more often are incorporating vegetable juices into their signature cocktails. Colorful food and drinks like yellow turmeric and beetroot lattes will continue to expand in popularity. They will receive competition from other colorful ingredients like sea greens, peas, absinthe, spirulina, butterfly pea, and purple variations of other common vegetables like carrots and basil (Newhart, 2019).

Other beverages are capitalizing on the demand for healthy drinks as well, including one of the oldest of all, tea. Michelin-starred Fera restaurant at London's Claridge's hotel now offers a tea-pairing menu, serving tea matched with restaurant courses as is often seen with wine. These specialty teas are rare, elevating the meal beyond simply pairing flavor profiles, and into a more immersive and sensory experience (Innovation Group, 2017).

Use of technology

Technological devices such as fitness wearables (i.e., Fitbit) are already common ways to measure activity levels throughout the day, and many smartphone apps allow for diet and nutrition tracking. However, technology will be continuing to advance in the area of food and beverages in health and wellness. The "smart diet" concept will enable consumers to not only track their activity and calorie intake but also completely customize and individualize their approach to physical and mental health. Innovations like increased personal data collection, personal health testing kits, and artificial intelligence-enabled apps will help individuals reach their own unique health goals.Technology will also be used to shorten production time, create new products, and confirm trustworthiness. Agricultural innovations such as floating farms and super crops will emerge in food-insecure locations like Africa and India. (Mintel, 2019). Vertical farming, or crops that are grown to maximize space in indoor locations like warehouses, will benefit from innovations to reduce their currently high energy needs and become a more viable option in food-insecure places like cities (Gifford, 2019). Food waste will be converted into new products, like rejected cereal pieces being turned into beer, or organic mushroom waste transforming into containers (Mintel, 2019).

Many other uses of technology will be seen in the upcoming years as well. Lab-grown meat will be a reality, and improvements to packaging will be completed to make it more biodegradable and less harmful to the environment. Ghost or cloud kitchens that only produce food for delivery, and are not customer facing and therefore have lower overhead, will rise in popularity (Gifford, 2019). Technology has endless potential for food and beverage services in health and wellness.

The kitchen: Reimagined

Another exciting trend in wellness food choices is a reimagining of the traditional kitchen (See Table 6.1). Applicable to restaurants and other service providers, but also the home kitchen (an indirect competitor to foodservice providers), this trend will affect how consumers source, store, and prepare their meals. Food will be grown in-house or delivered conveniently with minimal packaging and local ingredients, cabinets and pantries will be transformed from dark long-term food storage to environments suitable for sustaining living food, meals will be prepared using a range of temperatures from a variety of sources, and excess will be composted or recycled. Perhaps most important from a foodservice perspective, the kitchen will serve not as a traditional isolated food preparation location, but instead as a community gathering location designed to nourish not only the body but also the mind and spirit (Yeung & Johnston, 2018).

Slow food restaurants

Slow food is a counter-movement that wants people to be less reliant on fast food like McDonald's or processed foods and beverages like Coca-Cola. This movement has its roots in Mediterranean culture that celebrates the tastes of food and enjoys cooking versus eating quickly just to be done with it. Slow food restaurants are becoming increasingly popular across the world as more people begin to jump on this trend. In these types of restaurants, it takes longer to prepare and cook food (the restaurants often use fresh ingredients), and guests are encouraged to eat slowly and enjoy the food and company around them (Batinic, 2013).

Table 6.1: Comparing wellness kitchen with conventional kitchen

CONVENTIONAL	WELLNESS
Delivery	
Ingredients and prepared food come in paper, aluminum, and plastic bags, jugs, boxes, and cans. These can leach into food that is full of preservatives and additive ingredients.	Fresh food is harvested from in-home gardens, and unprocessed local ingredients and bulk items are available, and delivery may be automated.
Storage	
'Dead' food stored in freezing/near-freezing or at room temperatures behind doors and easily forgotten about for long periods.	'Living' food kept alive or dormant in a range of temperature and humidity controlled environments with transparent display doors.
Preparation	
Packaging from pre-made and pre-mixed food is recycled or thrown away.	Fresh food reduces the need for packaging. Preparation spaces have multiple work stations and allow for easy cleanup.
Cooking	
Microwaves thaw, cook, and reheat main dishes. Stoves and ovens are meant to cook food quickly at high temperatures.	Food is cooked using a range of temperatures and a variety of sources to maintain nutrients and enhance natural flavors.
Disposal	
A lot of bulky packaging is needed, and only some of it is recyclable. The rest is sent to landfills.	Unpackaged, fresh food and reusable containers reduce trash, and compost collection returns organic matter to the soil.
Consumption	
Fast, unconscious eating habits increase food proportions. Food is lacking in nutrients, and unhealthy additives allow for convenience and long shelf life.	Visible storage of healthy and fresh food is tempting, food preparation is conscious, and mindful consumption helps regulate proportions.
Social Activity	
Food is prepared in isolation before serving the dishes in a separate space.	The kitchen is the heart of the home, designed for gathering, entertaining, and nourishing.

Adapted and developed from: www.globalwellnesssummit.com/2018-global-wellness-trends/

Functional foods

There is no concise agreed-upon definition of what a functional food is, but researchers and officials agree that functional foods have the following traits (Nazir et al., 2019) :

- Health benefits – should enhance the target function or help to prevent the disease occurrence.
- Nature of food – remain as a traditional food.
- Level of function – beyond its basic nutritional function.
- Consumption pattern – per normal routine diet.

Consumers prefer functional foods to help reduce the chances of developing chronic illnesses like cardiovascular disease, Alzheimer's disease, and osteoporosis, or to increase their overall health like "boost their immune system" or "increase energy" (Nazir et al., 2019). Functional beverages are the most popular functional food item at the moment because they are easy to deliver and store, it is easier to include all the desired ingredients for all the desired benefits, and it has a high level of convenience of meeting consumer ideals in regards to container design and contents. These beverages can address the needs of various different market segments, whether it is members of an older generation looking for anti-aging beverages or a segment looking to compensate for lack of a well-rounded diet. The following are the most popular types of functional beverages: dairy-based, vegetable and fruit-based, sports drinks, energy drinks, tea and tea-based, and whey and soy protein-based (Nazir et al., 2019). The functional foods market was estimated to be $281.14 billion in 2021 and is anticipated to grow to over $529.66 billion by the year 2028 (Fortune Business Insights, 2022). The United States, Japan, and Europe are the top three markets in the world for functional foods (Nazir et al., 2019).

Fermented foods can be discussed in this functional foods section since they have various health benefits. They are defined as "foods or beverages produced through controlled microbial growth, and the conversion of food components through enzymatic action" (Dimidi et al., 2019). They offer various health benefits such as "anti-oxidant, anti-microbial, anti-fungal, anti-inflammatory, anti-diabetic and anti-atherosclerotic activity" (Şanlier et al., 2019). A significant portion of the current global food market is represented by fermented food and beverages (e.g., kefir, yogurt, kimchi, sauerkraut, kombucha) and the largest and fastest growing market is Asia Pacific. The global fermented food market is "projected to grow at a CAGR 4.6% during the period 2021-2026" (Mordor Intelligens, 2022) since the fermentation technologies have improved rapidly with the development of microbial and enzyme-based processes (Xiang et al., 2019). Although the health importance of fermented foods is known by many cultures, they are just becoming widespread in many Western societies.

Combining health and wellness foods and beverages with other wellness activities

People are beginning to think of foods and beverages as not only sustenance, but also as part of an overall health and wellness lifestyle. They want to consume ingredients and products that align with their overall health and fitness goals; beyond merely losing weight and looking good, they want to embrace personal responsibility and *feel good* (Berry, 2018). Wellness practices like traditional Chinese medicine and yoga are also beginning to influence consumers' diets. Chinese and Ayurvedic herbs like Ashwagandha, which is claimed to reduce stress and improve concentration, are being incorporated into food and beverage products (Crawford, 2016). Food movements like farm-to-table are re-centering the focus on local communities, which is another recognized component of wellness.

Activities like wellness retreats also often integrate a healthy diet as part of their program. For example, weeklong yoga retreats may be inclusive of meals, generally vegetarian, to match the traditional principles of yoga. Spas often serve healthy food and beverages on-site to complement the overall benefits of a day of wellness.

Summary

This chapter focused on the concept of health and wellness food and beverages and discussed health and wellness food trends in foodservice, hospitality, and tourism. First, it defined health and wellness food and beverages and discussed the value of that market in the USA. Next, it identified and discussed a few health and wellness food trends. This chapter also discussed how health and wellness food and beverage offerings could be combined with other wellness activities.

Definition of key terms

Fermented foods – Foods or beverages produced through controlled microbial growth, and the conversion of food components through enzymatic action (Dimidi et. al., 2019).

Organic – Food grown without toxic and synthetic pesticides or fertilizers; GMO ingredients; antibiotics or synthetic growth hormones; artificial flavors, colors, or preservatives; and sewage sludge or irradiation (Organic Trade Association, 2019).

Paleo – A diet based on foods that in the past could be obtained through hunting and gathering during the Paleolithic era (2.5 million to 10,000 years ago), such as fruits, vegetables, fish, lean meats, nuts, and seeds (Mayo Clinic, 2017).

Pescetarianism – A diet consisting of no meat other than seafood.

Plant-based – A diet of primarily non-animal products, but some followers may consume a limited amount.

Veganism – A diet consisting of no animal products.

Vegetarianism – A diet consisting of no meat.

Discussion questions

1. How do you define the concept of health and wellness food and beverage?

2. What are the key health and wellness food and beverages trends covered in this chapter?

3. Are there any other health and wellness of food and beverage trends that are not covered in this chapter?

4. How can a small independent restaurant incorporate some of these wellness food and beverage trends into their menu, operations, and marketing?

5. For food-based tourism, what popular regions or destinations around the world are associated with health and wellness food and beverages?

6. How can Virtual Reality (V.R.) and Artificial Reality (A.R.) assist in boosting food and beverage wellness among consumers?

Homework

1 Find a foodservice business that promotes wellness as one of its core goals and principles. In 500 words, describe what they offer, what benefits their customers receive, how they communicate the benefits to their target audience, and how they could improve.

2 What are the health benefits of fermented foods and beverages and how can you use them as a part of wellness facilities?

References

Batinic, I. (2013). Current trends in hospitality industry. *Journal of Process Management – New Technologies, International*, 1(4). 91-96.

Berry, D. (2018). Redefining health and wellness for 2019 and beyond. Retrieved February 5, 2020, from https://www.foodbusinessnews.net/articles/12805-redefining-health-and-wellness-for-2019-and-beyond

Celiac Disease Foundation. (2020). What is Celiac disease? Retrieved February 8, 2020 from https://celiac.org/about-celiac-disease/what-is-celiac-disease/

Chang, J., Okumus, B., Li, Z. W., & Lin, H. H. (2021). What serves as the best bridge in food consumption: experiential value or place attachment?. *Asia Pacific Journal of Tourism Research*, 26(12), 1302-1317.

Crawford, E. (2016). 7 trends influencing the evolution of health, wellness and consumers' views of food. Retrieved February 5, 2020, from https://www.foodnavigator-usa.com/Article/2016/01/15/7-trends-influencing-health-wellness-and-consumers-views-of-food

Dimidi, E., Cox, S. R., Rossi, M., & Whelan, K. (2019). Fermented foods: definitions and characteristics, impact on the gut microbiota and effects on gastrointestinal health and disease. *Nutrients*, 11(8), 1806.

Fortune Business Insights. (2022). The functional foods market. Retrieved May 29, 2022, from www.fortunebusinessinsights.com/functional-foods-market-102269

Gifford, C. (2019). Top 5 food tech innovations. Retrieved February 5, 2020, from https://www.theneweconomy.com/technology/top-5-food-tech-innovations

Global Wellness Summit. (2018). 2018 Global Wellness Trends Report. Retrieved December 7, 2019, from https://www.globalwellnesssummit.com/2018-global-wellness-trends/

Harvard Medical School. (2020). The right plant-based diet for you. Retrieved February 5, 2020, from https://www.health.harvard.edu/staying-healthy/the-right-plant-based-diet-for-you

Healthline. (2022). What's the difference between a plant-based and vegan diet? Retrieved May 29, 2022, from https://www.healthline.com/nutrition/plant-based-diet-vs-vegan

6

Imatome-Yun, N. (2019). Plant-based primer: the beginner's guide to a plant-based diet. Retrieved February 5, 2020, from https://www.forksoverknives.com/plant-based-primer-beginners-guide-starting-plant-based-diet/

Imperfect Foods. (2020). Our sourcing. Retrieved February 8, 2020 from https://www.imperfectfoods.com/sourcing

Impossible Foods. (2020). Impossible Whopper. Retrieved February 8, 2020 from https://impossiblefoods.com/burgerking/

Innovation Group. (2017). The Future 100: 2018. Retrieved December 7, 2019, from https://www.jwtintelligence.com/trend-reports/the-future-100-2018/

Jenkins, T. A., Nguyen, J. C., Polglaze, K. E., & Bertrand, P. P. (2016). Influence of tryptophan and serotonin on mood and cognition with a possible role of the gut-brain axis. *Nutrients*, *8*(1), 56.

King. M. (2019, July 2014). Great taste, plant-based: Dunkin' Partners with Beyond Meat to introduce new beyond sausage breakfast sandwich in Manhattan. Retrieved February 8, 2020 from https://news.dunkindonuts.com/news/beyond-meat-dunkin

Lamb, S. (2017). A shot against Post-Traumatic Stress Disorder. Retrieved December 7, 2019, from https://www.scientificamerican.com/article/a-shot-against-post-traumatic-stress-disorder/

Market Data Forecast. (2022). Global Smoothies Market Analysis. Retrieved May 29, 2022, from https://www.marketdataforecast.com/market-reports/smoothies-market

Mayo Clinic. (2017). Paleo diet: What is it and why is it so popular? Retrieved December 7, 2019, from https://www.mayoclinic.org/healthy-lifestyle/nutrition-and-healthy-eating/in-depth/paleo-diet/art-20111182

Mintel. (2019). Mintel announces global food and drink trends for 2030. Retrieved February 5, 2020, from https://www.mintel.com/press-centre/food-and-drink/mintel-announces-global-food-and-drink-trends-for-2030

Mordor Intelligens (2022). Fermented foods and beverages growth, trends, Covid-19 impact and forecasts (2022 - 2027). Retrieved March 31, 2022 from https://www.mordorintelligence.com/industry-reports/fermented-foods-beverages-market

National Health Service. (2018). Eating a Mediterranean diet 'may lower your risk of depression'. Retrieved December 7, 2019, from https://www.nhs.uk/news/food-and-diet/eating-mediterranean-diet-may-lower-your-risk-depression/

Nazir, M., Arif, S., Khan, R. S., Nazir, W., Khalid, N., & Maqsood, S. (2019). Opportunities and challenges for functional and medicinal beverages: Current and future trends. *Trends in Food Science & Technology*, *88*. 513-526.

Newhart, B. (2019). Veggie cocktails and cheese tea. Retrieved February 5, 2020, from www.beveragedaily.com/Article/2019/11/18/Veggie-cocktails-and-cheese-tea-An-early-look-at -2020-beverage-trends

Organic Trade Association. (2019). U.S. organic sales break through $50 billion mark in 2018. Retrieved December 7, 2019, from https://ota.com/news/press-releases/20699

Organic Trade Association. (2021). U.S. organic sales soar to new high of nearly $62 billion in 2020. Retrieved May 29, 2022, from https://ota.com/news/press-releases/21755

Planet Smoothie. (2020). How big is the smoothie industry? Retrieved February 5, 2020, from https://planetsmoothiefranchise.com/research/how-big-is-smoothie-industry/

PRNewswire. (2018). The health and wellness food and beverages market in Americas is forecasted to grow at a CAGR of 6.99% during the period 2017-2021. Retrieved February 5, 2020, from www.prnewswire.com/news-releases/the-health-and-wellness-food-and-beverages-market-in-americas-is-forecasted-to-grow-at-a-cagr-of-699-during-the-period-2017-2021-300576914.html

Rutgers. (2020). From Farm to Fork. Retrieved February 5, 2020, from https://njaes.rutgers.edu/food-nutrition-health/farm-to-fork.php

Şanlier, N., Gökcen, B. B., & Sezgin, A. C. (2019). Health benefits of fermented foods. *Critical reviews in food science and nutrition, 59*(3), 506-527.

Sarkar, A., Lehto, S.M., Harty, S., Dinan, T.G., Cryan, J.F. & Burnet, P.W.J. (2016). Psychobiotics and the manipulation of bacteria – gut-brain signals. *Trends Neuroscience, 39*(11). 763-781. Doi:10.1016/j.tins.2016.09.002

Shi, F., Dedeoğlu, B. B., & Okumus, B. (2022). Will diners be enticed to be travelers? The role of ethnic food consumption and its antecedents. *Journal of Destination Marketing & Management, 23*, 100685.

Statista. (2021). Health and wellness food market value worldwide in 2020 and 2026. Retrieved May 29, 2022, from https://www.statista.com/statistics/502267/global-health-and-wellness-food-market-value/

technavio. (2019). Smoothies market by product, consumption pattern, and geography - forecast and analysis 2020-2024. Retrieved February 5, 2020, from https://www.technavio.com/report/smoothies-market-industry-analysis

UnityPoint Health(2018). How the farm to table trend can create a healthier lifestyle. Retrieved February 5, 2020, from https://www.unitypoint.org/desmoines/article.aspx?id=cf426bcc-5b52-4109-9a16-e53bf37ddf8a

Xiang, H., Sun-Waterhouse, D., Waterhouse, G. I., Cui, C., & Ruan, Z. (2019). Fermentation-enabled wellness foods: A fresh perspective. *Food Science and Human Wellness, 8*(3), 203-243.

Yeung, O. & Johnston, K. (2018). Global Wellness Tourism Economy Monitor October 2018. Global Wellness Institute. Retrieved November 8, 2019, from https://globalwellnessinstitute.org/ industry-research/global-wellness-tourism-economy/

6

7 | Spa and Hot Spring Development and Management

This chapter discusses spa and hot spring development and management. The chapter first introduces the case study of Hévíz, Hungary. Next, it explains the concepts of spas and hot springs and discusses key issues when developing these facilities. The chapter also explains the economic impact of spas and hot springs. Then, it discusses the determinants of customers' satisfaction with these amenities, and finally offers information about managing spas and hot springs.

Learning outcomes

By the end of this chapter, students should be able to do the following:

1. Explain the Thermal Lake of Hévíz in terms of its offerings and economic impact.
2. Explain the difference between a spa and a hot spring.
3. Discuss key issues when developing spas and hot springs.
4. Highlight the economic impact of spas and hot springs.
5. Discuss the determinants of customer satisfaction with spas and hot springs.
6. Discuss the management of spas and hot springs.

Case study: Hévíz, Hungary

Hévíz, Hungary is home to the second-largest biologically active natural thermal lake in the world, and the largest in Europe, known as the Thermal Lake of Hévíz. The lake was formed through volcanic activity 22,000 years ago (Tourism Observatory, 2014). Its healing powers are said to be most beneficial for those who have musculoskeletal disorders. The lake water supports the prevention of illness as well as offers recreation and leisure opportunities. Spanning 4.4 hectares, the 38-meter deep lake is fed by both hot and cold mineral-rich springs, and the water is completely replaced every three days. This constant evaporation clears the air, water lilies blanket the surface, and the surrounding forest provides a natural shelter from the wind (Hotel Spa Hévíz, 2018a). The lake offers the beneficial properties of carbonated, sulfuric, calcium, magnesium, and bicarbonate medicinal waters, and its temperatures average 23-25°C (73–77°F) in winter and 33-36°C (91–97°F) in summer (Hévíz City Council, 2019).

Two extensive facilities are available to help visitors maximize the healing powers of the lake. Spa Hévíz and its accompanying hotel dates back to the 18th century and offers nine indoor pools and very modern amenities (Fuller, 2018). The full portfolio of wellness-oriented services available includes saunas, a salt cave, steam and ice baths, cosmetics, massages, and hand and foot treatments, in addition to healthy meals and recreational activities. Therapy treatments include Ayurvedic massages, wave massage therapy, vibration training, shockwave therapy, deep oscillation therapy, mudpacks, ultrasounds, and thermal water cream massage, among others (Hotel Spa Hévíz, 2018b). For those looking toward the medical tourism end of the spectrum, Szent András (Saint Andrew's) Hospital specializes in healing chronic musculoskeletal and rheumatic disorders and disease (Hotel Spa Hévíz, 2018c). The Spa and Hospital partner together to give guests the advantages of advanced medical healing, spa treatments, and the curative powers of the thermal waters, all in one location.

The city of Hévíz was one of the top 20 nominees for the European Commission's European Best Destination 2020 award, among esteemed competitors like Paris, Rome, Amsterdam, Athens, Milan, London, and Prague. The CEO of European Best Destinations, Maximilien Lejeune, stated "the beauty of the city center of Hévíz combined with a great offer of wellness care around the thermal water, therapeutic massage, sauna, sports, without forgetting our taste buds with the delicious wines and the Hungarian gastronomy, the specialties of Zala County, Egregy wines. Hévíz offers a complete experience to travelers. After a day at the spa, they can relax in Hévíz's restaurants, listen to live music, taste local products." (Municipality of Hévíz, 2019) In 2012, the number of annual visitors to Hévíz reached 224,645 (113,802 of which were international visitors). These guests brought in revenues to the local area of approximately $50 million per year, and in 2012 the tourism industry in the city employed 2,459 people, out of a population of only 4,663 (53% of the population was employed in tourism) (Tourism Observatory, 2014).

Discussion questions

1. What makes the Thermal Lake of Hévíz unique for visitors?
2. What do Spa Hévíz and its accompanying facilities offer wellness travelers?
3. What is the economic impact of the Thermal Lake of Hévíz?
4. Do you know of similar thermal lakes?

Spa and hot spring resort development

Spas and hot springs differ in one key area. A spa can be built virtually anywhere, whereas the location of a hot spring is dependent on the natural phenomena that cause them to occur. Tourist interest in hot springs is expected to continue to grow due to an increased interest in experiencing cultural traditions, connecting with nature, and seeking alternative wellness treatments (Yeung & Johnston, 2018). Tourism surrounding spas and hot springs affects not only these facilities, but also accommodation and foodservice providers, retailers, transportation businesses, and other operators of activities and attraction facilities. Destination management organizations (DMOs), local governments, and residents benefit through tax revenues, increased employment, and more. There are four primary types of spas (Mill, 2011):

1. **Resort spa** – Located on the property of a hotel, usually as part of a resort that also offers other activities as well. Hotel and spa guests intermingle, and the resort spa is generally an important profit center for the property.

2. **Amenity spa** – Also typically located on the property of a hotel, the amenity spa is treated as an added facility and is not an important profit center.

3. **Destination spa** – The spa is the main focus of the property, which offers specific health and fitness programs, and additional activities, to guests only.

4. **Medical spa** – Offers a variety of health practices and treatments, and is supervised full-time by a licensed medical professional.

As discussed in a previous chapter, the International Spa Association also recognizes the below as other types of spas (Vukovic et al., 2015):

1. **Club Spa** – "The primary use is fitness, but it also offers a wide array of professionally-led spa services on a daily basis."

2. **Cruise Ship Spa** – "A spa center on a cruise ship that offers professionally led spa services, fitness services and wellness components, as well as a spa menu with carefully chosen meals."

3. **Day Spa** – "A spa center that offers professional spa services on a daily basis. This kind of spa is best developed in western Europe."

4. **Mineral Springs Spa** – "A spa that offers natural minerals, thermal or other springs used for hydrotherapeutic treatments. This kind of spa center is the more typical of the European spa/wellness sector."

An on-site spa also often provides additional revenue to a resort; it has been shown to increase revenue per available room (RevPAR) and average daily room rate (ADR) (Tabacchi, 2010). Resort general managers also indicate that having a spa enhances their occupancy, perceived value for money, length of stay, and marketing advantage (Tabacchi, 2010). A spa can also be useful in the following ways (Mill, 2011):

- Attracting more visitors in the off and shoulder (season between peak and non-peak seasons) seasons.

- Lengthening the shoulder season, thereby shortening the off-season.

- Being more competitive than other spa resorts.
- Giving business guests a reason to extend their stay.
- Giving leisure guests to book and return the resort.
- Positioning the resort as a destination for incentive travel.
- Enriching spouse/companion programs for business travelers.
- Providing an indoor activity option during poor weather.

Discussion: In what other ways can having on-site spas be beneficial for resorts and business hotels?

Although they can offer many benefits to the local area, caution should be taken when developing spa and hot spring facilities, to protect the natural resources and enhance rather than drain them. Hot spring resorts present a different challenge to hoteliers, as the springs are naturally occurring, and therefore, location opportunities are more limited. Additionally, hot springs are generally considered public amenities regulated by a local government or organization and are not often able to serve as proprietary resources for one business. A resort built around a hot spring may see many of the same positive results noted above for spas. Still, their facilities must be competitive with others in the area, and they must deliver a desirable product to the marketplace. Managing spas and hot spring resorts will be discussed further in a later section of this chapter.

7

Hot springs

Hot springs, also called geothermal or thermal springs, have been used as healing centers since as far back as 3000 BC on all continents, including Antarctica. Although their popularity has waxed and waned over the centuries, the wellness movement has given them new life. The terms "hot springs" and "thermal springs" are being used throughout this book, but it is useful to note that there are multiple types of hot springs. For example, mineral springs have curative properties when ingested or bathed in, and saline springs have a very high salt content and are useful for treating skin conditions and joint problems (Erfurt-Cooper, 2010). These springs can be seen as a "pull factor" in tourism as their benefits attract tourists to them (Milenkovski et al., 2018). Wellness tourists favor hot springs and thermal baths because they (1) help improve their overall health and wellness, (2) allow them to relax and rest, and (3) can spend time outside of their hotel or accommodation at their wellness destination (Vukovic et al., 2015).

Wellness tourists can find simple hot springs for general ailments, and chloride springs, sulfur springs, and radioactive springs for all kinds of unique healing properties. As explained in Table 7.1, chloride bonds easily with other elements to form compounds such as salt, and it is a major electrolyte found throughout the body's blood, lymph (a colorless fluid that contains white blood cells and helps to clean body tissue) and fluids (Iron Mountain Hot Springs, 2020). Sulfur hot spring water feels silky, and its components soften the keratin found in skin, making it more pliable and elastic (Bathclin, 2020). Radioactive hot springs contain a high concentration of radon, a weak radioactive substance produced when radium decays. Low doses of exposure to radon may improve the body's metabolism, immunity, antioxidant functions, and natural healing capabilities (Misasa Onsen Ryokan Cooperative, 2020).

Table 7.1: Benefits of the different types of hot springs

Chloride: Chloride bonds easily with other elements to form compounds such as salt, and it is a major electrolyte found throughout the body's blood, lymph and fluids.	**Sulfur:** Its components soften the keratin found in skin, making it more pliable and elastic.	**Radioactive:** Low doses of exposure to radon may improve the body's metabolism, immunity, antioxidant functions, and natural healing capabilities.

Proponents of health springs claim that the warmth and high mineral content of the water are good for a person's health. Those afflicted with joint pain, muscular problems, and skin conditions can especially benefit from the enriched warm water. However, caution should be used, as some springs have water hotter than boiling point, which can cause burns or even death. Some also contain naturally occurring chemicals that can hurt humans (World of Phenomena, 2019).

Hot springs often form near areas of volcanic activity, when water deep below the surface of the Earth is heated by rocks or other means. This water often reaches 98°F (36.7°C) or higher. Sometimes this water mixes with dirt and clay on its way to the surface, causing a **mud pot**. These mud pots are often highly acidic, bubbling pools; when minerals are present that turn the mud brightly colored, it is called a **paint pot**. Tiny single-celled organisms called **extremophiles**, or **thermophiles**, are similar to bacteria and thrive in a hot spring environment. These microscopic organisms can also cause the water to be stained in bright colors (World of Phenomena, 2019).

Research from Clark-Kennedy & Cohen (2017) indicated that "relaxation," "peace and tranquility," "tolerance" and "escape" are the main hot springs motivations for clients. They believe that hot springs have significant benefits for fainting/dizziness, back pain, arthritis, stress/anxiety, depression and insomnia. Therefore, while relaxation is currently the main driver of spa and hot spring visits, *balneotherapy* is considered as a complementary therapy. Matz et al. (2003, p. 132) state, "balneotherapy involves immersion of the patient in mineral water baths or pools. Today, water therapy is being practiced in many countries. Examples of unique and special places for balneotherapy are the Dead Sea in Israel, the Kangal hot spring in Turkey, and the Blue Lagoon in Iceland. Bathing in water with a high salt concentration is safe, effective, and pleasant for healing and recovery."

Hot springs: economic impact and destinations

Hot springs are a $50 billion+ global industry and a growing segment of health and wellness tourism (Clark-Kennedy & Cohen, 2017). There are approximately 34,000 thermal/mineral hot springs located in 109 countries around the world, for a total economic impact of $56.16 billion, employing approximately 1.8 million people worldwide, and the industry is projected to grow by 4.8% annually (Milenkovski et al., 2018). The vast majority of these establishments, over 90% of the market, are in the Asia-Pacific region (25,916 establishments and economic value of $31.60 billion) and Europe (5,967 establishments and revenues of $21.73 billion). China and Japan ranked the top two hot spring destinations in the world, with 3,900 establishments and $18 billion in revenue and 20,972 establishments and $12.8 billion in revenue, respectively. Germany, Russia, and Italy complete the top five, with all other countries receiving less than one billion dollars in revenue in 2017 (Yeung & Johnston, 2018). Table 7.2 lists the top 20 thermal springs markets in 2015.

Many traditional hot springs cater to a domestic clientele and offer only basic facilities, to match their low admission fees. For example, hot springs in Japan, known as *onsen*, can be categorized into three tiers. A local public onsen is typically for residents, and ranges in cost from free to $5 to visit. Day onsen is found in big cities and operates similarly to a day spa, with added amenities bringing the average daily cost to $15-20. The third primary type is onsen ryokan or traditional lodges that are located far from cities and also provide additional facilities, for a higher daily cost (including food and accommodation) of approximately $200. More and more, governments around the world recognize the high value of wellness travelers, including those interested in thermal/hot springs, and countries are investing in new facilities and renovating and improving existing services (Yeung & Johnston, 2018).

Table 7.2: Top 20 thermal springs markets in 2015 (Adapted and developed from Milenkovski et al., 2018)

Rank	Country	Number of Spas	Revenues (in billions)
1	China	2,200	$15,721.6
2	Japan	17,326	$12,493.4
3	Germany	1,265	$6,823.7
4	Russia	823	$3,075.9
5	Italy	760	$1,674.5
6	Austria	181	$905.1
7	Turkey	267	$691.5
8	Hungary	546	$665.9
9	Spain	247	$658.8
10	Poland	185	$620.6
11	France	175	$582.4
12	Brazil	147	$526.1
13	Czech Republic	90	$513.0
14	United States	217	$487.7
15	Switzerland	71	$479.6
16	Slovenia	74	$426.8
17	Slovakia	97	$371.0
18	Portugal	84	$308.2
19	Iceland	139	$301.1
20	South Korea	96	$293.2

Perhaps the most famous hot springs in the world are the onsen in Japan. Spas are built around many of the onsen for year-round visitors to relax in the warm water, even in the winter. In unusually cold weather, troops of snow monkeys, or macaques, are known to bathe in the warm natural springs, even when humans are present, to help them survive the cold winter temperatures. The most famous spring that is also home to bathing snow monkeys is *jigokudani*, found in Japan's Nagano Prefecture. Also located in Japan, the famous *blood pond* spring has high concentrations of iron in the water, causing the water to turn bright red and resemble blood (World of Phenomena, 2019). Each hot spring has its own "Onsen ID Card," which provides information such as the origin of the hot spring water, the mineral composition and pH, therapeutic and curative effects, temperature, osmotic pressure, and any contraindications and cautions. (DSM Wellness Management, 2016).

Other countries famous for their hot springs are Turkey and Algeria. In Turkey, *Pamukkale* (meaning "cotton castle") boasts cascading white deposits of travertine. Water at the *Hammam Debagh* in Algeria is hot enough to boil an egg. It cascades over a cliff, leaving white mineral deposits along the cliff face that look like waterfalls (World of Phenomena, 2019).

A few of the western states in the United States are also known for their hot springs. The *Grand Prismatic Spring* in Yellowstone National Park is the largest hot spring in the world, at 300 feet (91 meters) wide and 160 feet (49 meters) deep. It earns its name because of the presence of algae and thermophile bacteria, which causes the water to appear all the colors of the rainbow, from dark blue in the center to red near its banks. The city of Hot Springs, Arkansas, was built around natural hot springs in the area because of the perceived health benefits of the springs. Eight of the bathhouses in Hot Springs are still open to this day (World of Phenomena, 2019).

Famous hot spring resorts

While there are scores of resorts around the world that take advantage of the local hot springs, especially in the geographic areas mentioned previously in this chapter, a few are consistently cited as outstanding accommodations to visit (Schlichter, 2018):

1. *Tabacon Thermal Resort & Spa.* In Arenal, Costa Rica, an array of flowing waterfalls and steaming hot springs sits at the base of the Arenal Volcano. While these hot springs are open to the public, the luxurious Shangri-La Gardens section is reserved for guests of the resort.

2. *Puyuhuapi Lodge & Spa.* Near the serene Dorita Bay in Chilean Patagonia, this ecolodge is a great central location for exploring the region. The lodge offers meals created from locally sourced ingredients, and the hot springs are known for their thalassotherapy algae.

3. *Indian Springs Calistoga.* Three different pools are filled with naturally heated mineral water from four geysers at this full-service resort in California's Napa Valley. Accommodation options range from rooms to cottages, bungalows, and houses, and the spa itself is famous for its Calistoga mud bath treatment.

4. *San Giovanni Terme Rapolano.* Situated in a different wine country, Tuscany, Italy, this hot spring resort features five thermal pools overlooking the Tuscan countryside. The on-site spa offers treatments with specialized ingredients like healing thermal mud and mango butter.

5. *Takinoya.* On the island of Hokkaido, Japan, the Takinoya resort takes advantage of the many onsen of the region, complete with rocky pools and infinity-style pools with views of the wilderness. Traditional meals, gardens, and bedding options round out this experience.

6. *Thermal Springs in Pamukkale.* Pamukkale is one of Turkey's spa tourism centers, famous for its white cloud-like rock formations (travertine) and thermal healing waters. Another place with beneficial waters is the ancient city of *Hierapolis*, whose history goes back 2800 years; visitors who endure heart, vascular, paralysis and nervous diseases frequently visit the thermal springs. In the same region, another important spa tourism center is the Karahayıt thermal which offers unique red healing hot water and thermal mud for the treatment of orthopedics, neurological, rheumatic, stomach and skin diseases (Turkish Airlines, 2022).

Discussion: Apart from the above, can you find some other famous hot spring resorts globally?

7

Determinants of hot spring visitor satisfaction

Thermal/hot spring establishments with value-added spa services (e.g., facials, massage, and hydrotherapy) comprise barely 25% of facilities around the world but account for 66% of annual industry revenues. This speaks to the benefits of supplementing naturally occurring thermal/hot springs with human-made hotels and spa facilities to bring in high-value travelers.

A group of researchers in China identified nine factors, which affected customer satisfaction of Chinese hot spring tourists: environmental quality, specialized resources, convenience, food, service quality, facilities, consumption emotion, perceived value, and targeted consumers (Mi et al., 2019). Environmental quality includes cleanliness, ecology, cultural features, and recreational activities. Specialized resources comprise the chemical composition, microelements, and mineral concentration, and water temperature. Hot spring facility managers can address these two categories through monitoring and communicating the composition and stability of the water's health benefits to guests. Similarly, the categories of convenience, food, service quality, and the facility can be measured through guest satisfaction surveys, and feedback should be taken into account to make improvements.

The two psychological factors of consumption emotion and perceived value are more difficult to manage, as they can vary drastically by traveler group. These are very important components, as they have been shown to affect consumer satisfaction, complaint behavior, and word-of-mouth intentions, and therefore measuring these factors is essential for evaluating service. Comment cards and on-site evaluations can be useful for measuring satisfaction immediately, and follow-up requests for feedback can be sent shortly after the visit via social media, email, or other distance communication techniques. Consumers can be selected for targeting based on various types of segmentation, including psychological factors. Because of the variation in traveler segments, hot spring facility managers can offer different services, and guest satisfaction with each should be measured individually to influence future product planning.

Spas

Many spa facilities and hotels have been built around hot springs to promote natural features and provide supplemental amenities. In addition to the city of Hévíz as discussed earlier in this chapter, the AQUA DOME Hotel in Oberlängenfeld, Austria has increased access and amenities around the Längenfelder Baths, a day spa has been built at the Peninsula Hot Springs in Fingal, Australia, and the Terme di Saturnia hotel provides visitors to the hot springs of the same name in Saturnia, Italy (Fuller, 2018). These are just a few examples of how spas can supplement the natural powers of hot springs, but spas are frequently built in many other locations as well to serve a wide variety of wellness travelers.

Wellness travelers "expect fitness, weight loss, self-discovery, and experience that other people will envy, and/or self-pampering" while visiting spas. On a similar note, their motives can fall into five categories: "friendship and kinship, relaxation and relief, escape, self-reward and indulgence, and health and beauty"(Koskinen & Wilska, 2019). This is why spas and spa tourism, in particular, are a part of the "experience economy," which, as defined by Pine and Gilmore (1998), is "an economy in which many goods and services are sold by emphasizing the effect they can have on people's lives." Tourists go to spas for the experience of it all and to reap the benefits listed above. This service economy idea as it relates to spas ties into the idea of the "servicescape" which is the physical aspects of a place as well as the amenities provided to a guest. In a spa, this includes the active area (the lobby and check-in area), the buffer area (space in between active and quiet area), and the quiet area (area where guests are receiving relaxing treatments). (Sotiriadis et al., 2016) Each guest will perceive the servicescape differently based on how they subjectively interpret the ambiance (physical aspects, sounds, smells, etc.) of each location. But nevertheless, it is important for spas to still try their best to meet (and possibly) beat the expectations of their guests when it comes to the perceptions of the servicescape.

Spa economic impact and destinations

In 2017 (pre-Covid-19), the Asia-Pacific region boasted the highest number of spa facilities (48,679 facilities and $26.5 billion in revenue), but Europe reached the highest revenues ($33.3 billion from 46,282 spa facilities). North America was a close third (30,394 facilities and $22.9 billion in revenue), followed distantly by Latin America-

Caribbean, Middle East-North Africa, and Sub-Saharan Africa. However, when it comes to individual countries, the United States is number one, with 26,317 spa facilities employing 395,707 people and achieving revenues of $20.83 billion. The U.S. and the other four top countries (China, Germany, Japan, and France) account for 48 percent ($45.04 billion) of the total global revenues of $93.6 billion. In addition to spa facility operations, additional peripheral industries like spa capital investments; spa education; spa media, associations, and events; and spa consulting added up to a total $118.8 billion spa economy in 2017 (Yeung & Johnston, 2018). As discussed in previous chapters, the true financial effect of Covid-19 on the wellness travel industry has yet to be seen.

Complementing its hot springs, Budapest, Hungary is known as the Spa Capital of the World due to its 123 natural thermal springs and drilled wells delivering 18 million gallons of healing waters per day to their visitors. Throughout its history of being colonized by the Romans and Turks, lots of bathhouses and other facilities were built to take advantage of this water. Budapest is famous for both its natural waters and human-made spas that are available to supplement the naturally occurring springs (Budapest Gyógyfürdői És Hévizei Zrt, 2012).

Bali is a popular spa destination due to its wide variety of incredible and unique human-made spas. Visitors to the Spa on the Rocks at AYANA spa resort can receive treatments like the ultra-lavish Diamond Miracle, which incorporates a foot soak and massage, rose petal bath, massage using silk and pearl fragments and facial using sea quartz and diamond dust, all while enjoying 360-degree views of the Indian Ocean from rocks extending out over the water. Wellness travelers looking for pure relaxation can try the Sacred Nap created by the Sacred River Spa at the Four Seasons Sayan, which involves resting in a silk hammock over the jungle and listening to bedtime stories of the Buddha murmured by a resident Buddhist nun. Plenty of energy cleansing and chakra balancing ceremonies and treatments are available on the island, with or without accompaniment by a Tibetan singing bowl (Oltuski & Ladd, 2018).

When it comes to massage, Thailand's traditional Thai massage treatments are very popular. Unlike well-known practices like Swedish massage, where the client lays passively on a bed or table, Thai therapists actively move and stretch the recipient's body into multiple positions for maximum rewards. This type of active massage can provide benefits such as lowered stress, increased energy, headache relief, circulation stimulation, and improved range of motion (MedicalNewsToday, 2019). Although the concept of Thai massage is relatively well known, the quality and level of the spa facility can vary greatly, challenging spa managers in that country to maintain visitor satisfaction.

Famous luxury spa resorts

With hundreds of top-notch luxury spa resorts found around the globe, in both emerging and developed tourism destinations, the choices are endless. Beyond the locations mentioned above, a few others are setting themselves apart with unique treatments that encompass various aspects of wellness (Adamiyatt & Murphy, 2017).

1. *La Reserve Geneve*. In Switzerland, visitors can obtain a customized "Better Aging" program developed by a team of doctors, nutritionists, osteopaths, and acupuncturists to fit their specific detoxification and anti-aging goals. A 4-to-7-night stay is encouraged to allow for time to visit the 20,000 square foot lakefront Nescens spa.

2. *Villa Stephanie*. The Baden-Baden region of Germany has long been associated with its hot springs, and this resort is known for individualized medical programs for detoxing, skin rejuvenation, mental vigor, and more. As a bonus, a digital detox switch is available that blocks WiFi and encourages disconnection from the outside world.

3. *Schloss Elmau*. Another resort in Germany, this one in the Bavarian Alps, has hosted artists and authors for over 100 years. The property offers five spas, six restaurants, three libraries, a concert hall, and a yoga center for a full mental, physical, and creative reset.

4. *The Ranch*. In the Santa Monica Mountains area of Malibu, wellness travelers seeking guaranteed results are attracted to this resort and spa. A one-week stay coupled with daily routines of a 5:30 a.m. wake-up call, four-hour hike and four hours of low-impact exercise rewards guests with an average weight loss of 3 to 7% of their body weight.

5. *Vana*. For wellness travelers seeking an intense detox, this resort in India offers a signature 21-night Pancha-karma program. Located near Rishikesh, the yoga capital of the world, guests to the five-star ashram receive a customized Ayurvedic diet plan, organic cuisine, beauty treatments, and cultural outings. Traditional yoga, meditation, and Ayurvedic medicine complete the experience.

Discussion: Apart from the above, can you find some other famous luxury spa resorts?

Determinants of spa visitor satisfaction

According to Chen, Chang, and Wu (2013), in a study on wellness tourism factors in hot spring hotel customer service, the "global expansion of the spa industry necessitates service quality as an essential element of wellness tourism strategies and practices." For this reason, it is essential to focus on the experience of the guest because it can change the perception the guest has on the spa, hotel, brand, destination, etc. Chen, Chang, and Wu in that same 2013 study, found that the factors of "customer service personnel have a knowledge of first-aid," the "external environment of a hotel," the "use of toxic-free or detox food ingredients," "provides a relaxing environment," "provides instructions for hot spring therapies," "combines local cultural festivals," "provides parent-child activities," and "provides do-it-yourself group activities" ranked the highest as factors that provide guests with the best experience.

A common framework for measuring consumer satisfaction with services is the SERVQUAL model initially developed in 1985 (Parasuraman et al., 1985). One research study found that visitors to Malaysian spas were influenced by four of the five SERVQUAL dimensions: tangibility (physical environment of the service), empathy (providing care and individualized attention), reliability (providing the service dependably and accurately), and responsiveness (promptness and willingness to help). The only dimension found to be insignificant in their study was assurance (knowledge and confidence of providers) (Awad, 2012).

The SERVQUAL model proved useful in another research study at the Hévíz Spa and St. Andrew Hospital, as discussed at the beginning of this chapter, but with different findings from the Malaysian study. In this Hévíz study, researchers also found differing results based on whether the guest's visit was funded by the national hospital insurance fund (NHIF). For the NHIF-supported guests, reliability was the most important factor impacting visitor satisfaction, followed by assurance, empathy, responsiveness, and tangibility. For non-NHIF-supported guests, the components ranked as assurance, empathy, reliability, responsiveness, and tangibility. The differing results between this study and the Malaysian study, along with the comparison between the NHIF-supported and non-NHIF-supported guests, demonstrates the importance of each spa manager understanding their target visitors and their needs and wants (Lőke et al., 2018).

In a 2019 study, Han et al. also used the SERVQUAL model to analyze the post purchase behaviors of wellness tourists. They found that tangibility, assurance, and empathy play an essential role in spa visitor's satisfaction, and quality factors do not contribute to their excitement (Han et al., 2019). These conflicting findings mean spa managers can use the model as a framework for conducting their own client and market research, but each destination and product needs customization.

Management of spas and hot spring resorts

A spa or hot spring resort can be very expensive to build and operate; a turnkey, four-star quality spa can cost over $650 per square foot to construct. Buildings and amenities need to be carefully planned, implemented, and monitored, the staff needs to be specially trained, and the local area must be maintained and coordinated to provide a supportive environment for the wellness offering. Wellness travelers are often motivated by eco-tourism friendly accommodation and attractions, and these must be available in conjunction with the spa or hot spring to complement the visit.

A spa also puts heavy demands on existing hotel infrastructures such as the laundry, housekeeping, and maintenance departments. Spas are also highly labor-intensive, and staff costs are often very high, due in part to concerns like inefficient scheduling and low productivity (Mill, 2011). A selection of suggested key performance indicators (KPIs) that spas can collect and analyze follows (Singer, 2009):

- Hotel capture rate (the percentage of hotel guests who use spa services).
- Average treatment rate.
- Treatment room utilization.

- Therapist productivity.
- Revenue per available treatment room.
- Revenue per guest.
- Revenue per square foot.
- Revenue per occupied guest room.
- Number of services per guest.
- Retail sales as a percentage of treatment revenue.
- Market segmentation.
- Revenue per available treatment hour (RevPATH) (Mill, 2011).

While the above will all provide beneficial information to a spa manager, the revenue per available treatment hour (RevPATH) metric may be the most useful. This is calculated either by multiplying the treatment room occupancy by the average expenditure per person or by dividing the revenue received in a set time by the number of treatment-hours during that period (e.g., day, week, or month). This ratio can be controlled by the spa if desired; for example, a luxury spa may wish to increase treatment rates and lower occupancy to keep a quiet and selective guest experience, whereas a spa targeting budget-conscious travelers may lower rates and increase occupancy to bring in as many clients as capacity allows (Mill, 2011).

Another component to keep in mind when managing spas and hot springs is the very nature of services; they are intangible, inseparable from the production process, variable (heterogeneous), and perishable. Pure service is intangible, as it cannot be seen, tasted, felt, heard, or smelled before it is purchased, and it does not result in the customer's ownership of anything. Services are also typically produced and consumed simultaneously; the massage therapist gives the massage at the same time the client receives it, meaning the guest is participating in the production process. Because there is a high human component to services, the resulting end product may differ between providers and may even vary for the same provider on different days. For example, massage therapists often have different styles, which will result in slightly different treatments. The same therapist may also give different results on different days, depending on their circumstances. Services are perishable because they cannot be stored. If a massage therapist's appointment for one hour is canceled, they cannot merely double-book themselves in the next hour to make up for it.

Due to all of these factors, managing spas and hot springs require extra attention to customer wellness and satisfaction. Cleanliness, safety, facility quality, employee training, and other details must be carefully assessed and performed. When done correctly, these amenities can provide many benefits to a resort and local area.

Summary

This chapter discussed spa and hot spring development and management. The chapter introduced the case study of Hévíz, Hungary. It then explained the types and benefits of spas and hot springs, their economic impacts, and the popularity of different destinations. Next, the chapter discussed some determinants of customers' satisfaction with spas and hot springs. Finally, it offered information around managing spas and hot springs.

Discussion questions

1. How do you define a spa and a hot spring?
2. What are the key issues in the development of spas and hot springs?
3. What are the economic impacts of spas and hot springs?
4. What are the key determinants of customer satisfaction with spas and hot springs?
5. How different are managing spas and hot springs from managing business hotels?
6. What career opportunities may be available for you in spas and hot springs?.
7. What skills/competencies do you need for your desired position in spas and hot springs?

7

Definition of key terms

Amenity spa – Typically located on the property of a hotel, and treated as an added facility to a hotel, but not an important profit center (Mill, 2011).

Balneotherapy –The use of water for medical treatment.

Destination spa – The spa is the main focus of the property, which offers specific health and fitness programs, and additional activities to guests only (Mill, 2011).

Extremophile (or **thermophile**) – Tiny single-celled organism similar to bacteria that thrives in a hot spring environment.

Medical spa – Offers a variety of health practices and treatments, and is supervised full-time by a licensed medical professional (Mill, 2011).

Mud pot – Area on the Earth where a hot spring has mixed with dirt or clay on its way to the surface; often a highly acidic, bubbling pool.

Paint pot – A mud pot with minerals that cause the mud to be brightly colored.

Resort spa – Located on the property of a hotel, usually as part of a resort that also offers other activities as well. Hotel and spa guests intermingle, and the resort spa is generally an important profit center for the property (Mill, 2011).

Homework

1. Using the internet, find a leading hot spring resort or spa, and explain how it was developed and what it offers in particular. How can this specific resort measure and improve the satisfaction of its guests?
2. Identify a dream position in a spa or hot spring resort and discuss what skills and competencies you would need to have to reach your goal.

References

Adamiyatt, R. & Murphy, J. (2017). These are the best luxury spas in the World. Retrieved February 12, 2020, from https://www.townandcountrymag.com/leisure/travel-guide/g13797039/best-luxury-spas-in-the-world/

Awad, B. A. A. G. (2012). The relationships between service quality, satisfaction, and behavioral intentions of Malaysian spa center customers. *International Journal of Business and Social Science, 3*(1).

Bathclin. (2020). The sensations of onsen water. Retrieved February 12, 2020, from www.bathclin.co.jp/en/happybath/hot-springs/the-sensations-of-onsen-water/

Bender, T., Karagülle, Z., Bálint, G. P., Gutenbrunner, C., Bálint, P. V., & Sukenik, S. (2005). Hydrotherapy, balneotherapy, and spa treatment in pain management. *Rheumatology International, 25*(3), 220-224.

Budapest Gyógyfürdői És Hévizei Zrt. (2012). Budapest City of Spas. Retrieved December 27, 2019, from http://www.spasbudapest.com/budapest-city-of-spas

Chen, K.H, Chang, F.H., & Wu, C. (2013). Investigating the wellness tourism factors in hot spring hotel customer service. *International Journal of Contemporary Hospitality Management, 25*(7). 1092-1114. DOI: 10.1108/IJCHM-06-2012-0086.

Clark-Kennedy, J., & Cohen, M. (2017). Indulgence or therapy? Exploring the characteristics, motivations and experiences of hot springs bathers in Victoria, Australia. *Asia Pacific Journal of Tourism Research, 22*(5), 501-511.

DSM Wellness Management. (2016). Asia hotspring industry overview. Retrieved December 27, 2019, from globalwellnessinstitute.org/wp-content/uploads/2018/12/2016-Asia-Hot-Spring-Industry-overview-Sam-Foster.pdf

Erfurt-Cooper, P. (2010). The importance of natural geothermal resources in tourism. In *Indonesia: Proceedings World Geothermal Congress Bali*. pp. 25-29.

Fuller, M. (2018). 11 of the World's dreamiest, steamiest hot springs. Retrieved December 28, 2019, from www.afar.com/magazine/11-of-the-worlds-dreamiest-steamiest-hot-springs?id=11-of-the-world-s-dreamiest-steamiest-hot-springs

Han, H., Thuong, P.T.M., Kiatkawsin, K., Ryu, H.S. & Kim, J, & Kim, W, (2019). Spa hotels: Factors promoting wellness travelers' postpurchase behavior.

Social Behavior and Personality: An international journal, 47(6). 1-13. DOI: 10.2224/sbp.7605.

Hévíz City Council. (2019). Interesting things About Lake Hévíz. Retrieved December 28, 2019, from https://www.heviz.hu/hu/hevizi-to/hevizi-tofurdo/erdekessegek-a-hevizi-torol

Hotel Spa Hévíz. (2018a). Thermal Lake of Hévíz. Retrieved December 28, 2019, from https://hotelspaheviz.hu/en/thermal-lake-heviz

Hotel Spa Hévíz. (2018b). Wellness. Retrieved December 28, 2019, from https://hotelspaheviz.hu/en/wellness

Hotel Spa Hévíz. (2018c). Introduction on the hospital. Retrieved December 28, 2019, from https://hotelspaheviz.hu/en/saint-andrews-rheumatology-hospital

Iron Mountain Hot Springs. (2020). Mineral Spotlight: Chloride. Retrieved February 12, 2020, from https://www.ironmountainhotsprings.com/mineral-spotlight-chloride/

Koskinen, V., & Wilska, T.A. (2019). Identifying and understanding spa tourists' wellness attitudes. *Scandinavian Journal of Hospitality and Tourism, 19*(3). 259-277. DOI: 10.1080/15022250.2018.1467276.

Lőke, Z., Kovács, E., & Bacsi, Z. (2018). Assessment of service quality and consumer satisfaction in a Hungarian spa. *Deturope, 10*(2), 124-146.

Matz, H., Orion, E. & Wolf, R. (2003). Balneotherapy in dermatology. *Dermatologic Therapy*, 16(2), 132-140.

MedicalNewsToday. (2019). What are the health benefits of Thai massage? Retrieved December 27, 2019, from https://www.medicalnewstoday.com/articles/323687.php

Milenkovski, A., Gjorgievski, M. & Nakovski, D. (2018). Termal/Mineral Springs Industry: Need for transformation in function of tourism. *UTMS Journal of Economics, 9*(2). 181 – 187.

Mill, R.C. (2011). *Resorts: Management and Operation, 3rd Edition*. Hoboken, New Jersey: John Wiley & Sons.

Misasa Onsen Ryokan Cooperative. (2020). One of the world's richest radium springs. Retrieved February 12, 2020, from https://spa-misasa.jp/eng/radium/

Municipality of Hévíz. (2019). Hévíz is competing for the title of 'European Best Destination 2020.' Retrieved December 28, 2019, from https://www.heviz.hu/en/news/news/european-best-destination-2020

Oltuski, R. & Ladd, K. (2018). 8 over-the-top spa experiences you'll only find in Bali. Retrieved December 27, 2019, from https://www.harpersbazaar.com/culture/travel-dining/g19153578/best-spa-bali/

Parasuraman, A., Zeithaml, V. A. & Berry, L. L. (1985). A conceptual model of service quality and its implications for future research. *Journal of Marketing*, 49(4), 41-50.

7

Pine, B. J., & Gilmore, J. H. (1998). Welcome to the Experience Economy. *Harvard Business Review*, 76, 97-105.

Schlichter, S. (2018). 10 incredible hot spring resorts. Retrieved February 12, 2020, from https://www.smartertravel.com/hot-spring-resorts/

Singer, J. L. (2009). Spas & hotels: compatible, marketable & profitable. Retrieved February 12, 2020, from https://www.hospitalitynet.org/opinion/4040816.html

Sotiriadis, M., Van Zyl, C. & Poole, C. (2016). Suggesting a framework for innovation management in the industry of wellness tourism and spas. *African Journal of Hospitality, Tourism and Leisure*, 5(4). 1-17.

Tabacchi, M. H. (2010). Current research and events in the spa industry. *Cornell Hospitality Quarterly*, 51(1), 102-117.

Tourism Observatory. (2014). Hot springs, tourism & economic impacts: the case of Hévíz (Hungary). Retrieved December 27, 2019, from https://globalwellnesssummit.com/wp-content/uploads/Industry-Research/Europe/2014-Tourism-Observatory-Hot-Springs-Tourism-Hungary.pdf

Turkish Airlines (2022). Türkiye's best thermal centers warm you up in winter. Retrieved March 31, 2022 from https://blog.turkishairlines.com/en/the-best-touristic-thermal-centers-in-turkey/

Vukovic, P., Cavlin, G. & Cavlin, M. (2015). Complementarity in the development of rural tourism with the development of thermal baths, spa and wellness tourism. *Economic of Agriculture*, 62(1). 259-270.

Yeung, O. and Johnston, K. (2018). Global Wellness Tourism Economy Monitor October 2018. Global Wellness Institute. Retrieved November 8, 2019, from https://globalwellnessinstitute.org/ industry-research/global-wellness-tourism-economy

8 Wellness Events, Festivals and Activities

This chapter covers health and wellness events, festivals, and activities in food service, hospitality, and tourism. It first presents the MindBodySpirit Festival case study. Second, the chapter defines events, festivals, wellness events, and wellness festivals. Next, it categorizes health and wellness events, festivals, and activities into three distinct classes: primary, secondary, and corporate, followed by specific examples of primary, secondary, and corporate wellness activities. Then, the chapter discusses how to incorporate wellness activities in regular events and festivals. The chapter ends with a summary and discussion questions to help the reader better understand the topic.

Learning outcomes

By the end of this chapter, students should be able to do the following:

1. Explain the case study of MindBodySpirit Festival.
2. Define event, festival, wellness event, and wellness festival.
3. Categorize wellness events and define primary wellness events, secondary wellness events, and corporate and industry wellness events.
4. Provide real examples of primary, secondary, and corporate wellness events and festivals.
5. Offer suggestions on how to incorporate wellness elements into regular events.
6. Discuss the various ways the impact of an event can be measured.

Case study: The MindBodySpirit Festival

The MindBodySpirit Festival is Australia's largest health, well-being and natural therapies event. Four 3-day festival events were held in 2022: two in Melbourne, one in Sydney, and one in Brisbane. Free entrance gives attendees access to over 200 exhibitors, inspirational seminars, stage performances, and a marketplace of wellness-related vendors selling products like jewelry, cosmetics, music, books, giftware, clothing, crystals, body treatments and more.

The events also host lots of educational courses, many of which are free, on topics like cooking with spices, foods that fight inflammation and reduce autoimmune responses, merging spirituality and business, healing through Past Life Regression, and more. Psychic readings and healthy food are also available for purchase at all of the events. MindBodySpirit festivals pride themselves on bringing visitors the best in health, wellness, and spiritual guidance (MindBodySpirit Festival, 2022a).

The Melbourne festival is trying a new feature in 2022—EveryWoman, which is offering a fun girls day out with friends and family. Booths center around wine, jewelry, natural body products, candles, and lots more (MindBodySpirit Festival, 2022b).

To complement their in-person festivals, the MindBodySpirit festival organization also has an online Healthy Living Hub. This website has blog-style articles on nutrition, beauty, parenting, mental health, dream journaling, astrology, and other related wellness topics. The group is also active on many social media channels, such as Facebook, Instagram, YouTube, Pinterest, and Twitter (MindBodySpirit Festival, 2022c).

Discussion questions

1. What categories does each of the activities offered at the MindBodySpirit event fall into?

2. What additional activities could be incorporated into the MindBodySpirit event to benefit the local community?

3. What kinds of tools and habits do attendees receive from an event like this?

4. How do the Healthy Living Hub and the MindBodySpirit social media pages complement the in-person events?

Events, festivals and wellness events definitions

- An **event** is "a public assembly for the purpose of celebration, education, marketing, or reunion. Events can be classified on the basis of their size, type, and context." Some possible types of events include social/lifecycle, education and career, sports, entertainment, political, corporate, religious, and fundraising/ cause-related (EventEducation.com, 2020).

- A **wellness event** is a type of event that focuses on spiritual, social, physical, and/or emotional well-being. It may incorporate physical exercise, mindfulness education, holistic therapies, environmental awareness and engagement programs, and other activities to improve the overall well-being of attendees.

■ A **festival** is a time of celebration, with an organized series of social events. Festivals can celebrate many things, for example, religious occasions or a harvest.

■ A **wellness festival** is a festival that brings people together to celebrate overall well-being and has a focus on one or more aspects of wellness.

Categorizing health and wellness events, festivals and activities

With the growing wellness movement, different types of health and wellness events and activities abound in foodservice, hospitality, and tourism. **Primary wellness events** can be categorized as events that cater to primary wellness travelers. In contrast, **secondary wellness events** target secondary wellness travelers with add-ons to their primary travel itinerary or incorporating healthy elements into a larger event. **Corporate and industry wellness events** encompass activities sponsored by a corporation or industry association, such as a workplace wellness event hosted by a company for its employees, or a wellness tradeshow organized by a wellness industry association. Each of these categories is explained below. The Covid-19 pandemic caused many events to become virtual and accessible only online, to decrease the risk of spreading the disease. As the world recovers from the pandemic and vaccines become widely available, some people are excited and willing to meet in-person again, while others prefer to attend virtual events due to travel restrictions or personal preference. Because of this, many events are operating on a hybrid model, with in-person functions and meals, and classes and/or speakers being streamed online (Eventtia, 2022).

Primary wellness events

Primary wellness-oriented accommodations and facilities are available around the globe for all types of travelers seeking improvement in various areas of their lives. Primary wellness travelers are often looking for a way to immerse themselves in wellness for a few days, or at least a couple of hours. There are many existing wellness retreats, many of which are focused on yoga, clean living, physical fitness, recovering from a divorce or other traumatic experiences, connecting to a destination in a truly authentic way, and other activities. MindBodySpirit Festival is one example of what attendees seek out and travel to immerse themselves in a wellness experience.

Facilities also exist that focus solely on providing wellness-focused activities and programs to their visitors. Since its original location in Tucson, Arizona opened in 1979, Canyon Ranch has been a well-known health and wellness destination where visitors go to unify the mind, body, and spirit. Their wellness resorts in Tucson and Lenox, Massachusetts, have experts on staff to guide guests through improving their overall health through fitness and movement, nutrition and food, health and healing, mind and spirit, and spa and beauty. One category of offerings is called "life management" activities, and it includes consultations and programs like hypnotherapy, sleep enhancement, creative expression, and biofeedback on physiological responses to stress (Canyon Ranch, 2019a). A minimum three-night all-inclusive stay means guests spend at least two full days immersed in the healing environment and enjoying the healthy food and wellness-oriented programs and activities. Specific events and workshops offer a wide range of activities for guests from improving athletic performance with star runners, a post-divorce boot camp, practicing mindfulness in the modern world, embracing the aging process, boosting brainpower, overall living one's best life, and more (Canyon Ranch, 2019b).

More specific wellness events are also available; for example, anyone affected by any cancer can find resources at the Smith Center for Healing and the Arts in Washington, DC. The Smith Center is not a medical facility; it is a non-profit organization whose mission is to provide physical, emotional, and mental resources to help participants make life-changing decisions. The center focuses on promoting creativity and how it can lead to healing in its visitors. Workshops are held on medical topics, but yoga, cooking, and creative programs are also available for a rounded wellness experience. One-day and three-day retreats bring like-minded travelers together to grow, heal, and support each other (Smith Center for Healing and the Arts, 2020). There are many other retreat centers focused on specific activities and lifestyles like yoga, painting, and other artistic endeavors, cooking classes, hiking, horseback riding, and more designed to improve the overall wellness of their guests.

Examples of primary wellness events and festivals

There are many examples of primary wellness events and festivals all over the world. Here are a few of the most popular or unique ones:

- *National Wellness Conference* – Put on by the National Wellness Institute, this event brings together wellness professionals to learn, connect, and grow through "research-based best practices, wellness immersion, education, collaboration, networking, skill-building, professional growth and personal renewal." Certified Wellness Practitioner (CWP) credentialing and Continuing Education Credits (CECs) are available. The 2022 hybrid event was held in Orlando, Florida. While some components of the conference were only available for in-person attendees, the virtual ticket price was discounted by $200 to reflect the difference (National Wellness Institute, 2022).

- *Wanderlust* – Wanderlust has hosted wellness events around the world for over a decade. Multiple times a year, the Wanderlust Festivals combine the pillars of practice, listen, explore, learn, and taste, to help attendees incorporate wellness into their lives. Prior to the Covid-19 pandemic, their annual three-day Wellspring event in Palm Springs attracted thought-leaders, teachers, and socially conscious companies. Their 108 events are marketed as a "full day of celebration in support of the mindful movement" and boast a 5K, yoga, and meditation at "your local favorite park." As a reaction to the Covid-19 pandemic, Wanderlust closed their four stationary yoga studios in California, Texas, and Montreal, and switched their focus to online classes. The 108 events are returning in 2023, and the Wellspring event future is unknown as of May 2022 (Wanderlust, 2022).

- *Envision Festival* – Each February or March from 2011 to 2020, the Costa Rican rainforest accommodated artists, yogis, and wellness enthusiasts for the Envision Festival, which is set to return in 2023 (after a 2-year hiatus due to Covid-19). During the seven day festival, guests gather to "awaken their human potential and positive energy" while listening to popular international musicians and speakers. The festival focuses on seven pillars: sustainability, music, spirituality, movement, health, art, and education, to promote wellness. The line-up of events resembles that of popular music festivals like Coachella or Lollapalooza, where different instructors teach different things like creative drawing or the 360 movement experience at different stages or venues during the festival. (Envision Festival, 2022).

- *IRIS* – Twice a year in Hong Kong, the city's largest fitness and wellness festival brings in thousands of attendees. Eighty plus of Hong Kong's top fitness stars and instructors meld with a meditation area, Zen garden, fit district, silent disco, discovery zone, dance and workshops, and a place to shop and eat, offering something for everyone. With the Covid-19 pandemic sweeping the globe in 2020, the last IRIS festival took place in September of 2019, and the official festival website does not indicate when the festival may return. (Hybrid Group, 2020).

- *Soul Circus* – This wellness festival occurs in the United Kingdom and mixes virtue and vice. During the day, festival-goers participate in hot yoga, gong baths, aerial classes, sunset meditation, light therapy, clean eating, and spa treatments, and at night, the wellness events are balanced by live music and glittery after parties. Soul Circus markets this event as the UK's "most exciting wellness festival, celebrating movement, music, and food." (Soul Circus, 2020).

- *Balance Festival* – Another UK festival that is based in London, the Balance Festival is a three-day event nicknamed "the feel-good festival," and it celebrates the "live fit, happy, and healthy revolution." It brings wellness seekers together with global fitness experts, top wellness gurus, mindful yogis, and forward-thinking brands. This event also heavily incorporates nutritious and delicious healthy foods. The Covid-19 pandemic canceled the 2020 festival, but Balance welcomed guests back in 2021 and 2022 at reduced capacity to accommodate better social distancing. (Balance Festival, 2020).

- *MindBodySpirit Wellbeing Festival* – Not to be confused with the Australian festival in the case study, this is the third popular festival in the UK, and also takes place in London. The Festival has exhibitors, workshops, and free experiences. In the well-being market, attendees will find companies offering activation and galactic healing, colloidal silver and gold, crystal vibrations, personality analysis, henna, spiritual healing, and many others. What is unique about this festival is that they also offer free experiences to the public like the alchemy of sound or aspects of healing, so not everyone has to purchase tickets to the festival to enjoy its wellness offerings. (Mind Body Spirit, 2020).

- *Bali Spirit Festival* – In one of the world's most popular wellness destinations, this event celebrates the global community through yoga, world music, and well-being. The festival epitomizes the core mantra of Balinese Hinduism, "to live in harmony with our spiritual, social, and natural environments." The festival brings dance, martial arts, breath work, and personal development together with music, and a Dharma Fair brings the local culture into this festival. The goal of this festival is to "awaken and nourish each individual's potential for positive change within, leading to positive changes in our homes, in our communities, and around the world." The 2020 festival was postponed to 2021 due to the Covid-19 pandemic, and the 2022 festival continued as planned. (BaliSpirit Festival, 2020, 2022).

- *Telluride Yoga Festival* – The quiet community of Telluride, Colorado, hosts attendees in the pure air of the Rocky Mountains. The festival aims to "foster health and wellness in our community by creating an intimate, authentic, world-class yoga festival filled with yoga, music, meditation, hikes, dinners, wellness vendors, and more." This inspirational four-day event has over 100 offerings ranging from hiking to stand-up paddleboard, yoga to social gatherings. Attendees can also take the gondola to visit the local galleries and shops, have a coffee or a massage, listen to one of the 40 plus presenters, or enjoy a healthy dinner at a farm-to-table restaurant. This festival also offers community classes, book signings, and dharma and inspirational talks free to the community. (Telluride Yoga Festival, 2020).

- *Wellness by Design* – This is an example of a wellness mini-conference. Set near Orlando, FL, its attendees are given tools to improve their physical, social, emotional, spiritual, and financial health. This one-day event includes lunch and multiple presentations from wellness experts. (AIGA Orlando, 2020)

Secondary wellness events

Wellness-oriented attendees are concerned about details like travel time and the impact on their bodies (jetlag) and the environment (carbon emissions), and opportunities to embrace their wellness goals and learn something new. Large and small venues, both domestic and around the world, offer possibilities that will please these guests. For example, SAVOR, the caterer at the huge McCormick Place convention center in Chicago, sources some of its produce from its 2.5-acre rooftop gardens and uses meat from animals raised without antibiotics whenever possible. Smaller facilities like locally-owned retreat centers often obtain as many ingredients as they can locally, and have many connections to local wellness practitioners like yoga instructors, speakers, and other ways to incorporate wellness into a larger event. Attendees may also appreciate the chance to give back to the local community through a volunteering session or being encouraged to bring donations of clothing or toys, especially in smaller or developing destinations. (Event MB/Maritz Global Events, 2018).

When it comes to incorporating wellness-oriented details, food and beverage (F&B) service at events is one place to start. While event planners and caterers have long been offering salad and vegetable choices on a buffet or a vegetarian option for a plated dinner, this is no longer enough. Offering healthy meal options throughout the day will appeal to travelers with a wellness orientation. Instead of the typical event buffets full of fried foods and desserts, event planners need to plan healthier options like an omelet bar with egg whites and vegetables available for breakfast, a variety of salads for lunch, fruit for an afternoon snack, or dessert, and a selection of healthy proteins and vegetables for dinner. Calories are not the central concern of attendees anymore; they are also looking for local farm-to-table dishes, multiple creative selections to suit vegetarians and vegans, gluten-free options, low-carb choices, and more. Gone are the days when special dietary requests must be given far in advance to ensure they are catered to; the special requests are now the norm. Beyond mealtimes, standard break-time pastry platters are being replaced by healthy high-protein, low-sugar healthy snack options that keep attendees alert and focused throughout sessions. Smoothies, juice bars, and hydration stations (especially those that promote the refilling of reusable BPA-free water bottles) are everywhere (Event MB/Maritz Global Events, 2018).

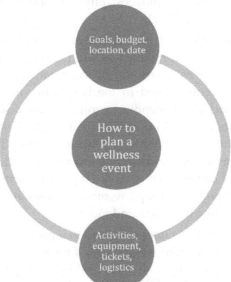

Figure 8.1: Wellness event checklist (Adapted from Mortier, 2019)

Making what seems like minor adjustments to details like seating can elevate an attendee's experience. People come in all shapes and sizes, and one type of seating does not suit all. When people are comfortable, they will pay more attention and are less likely to be distracted. While basics like choosing a room with an appropriate capacity for the session still apply, event planners must consider the types of seating available and the configuration of the space. A theater-style set up with chairs in rows facing the front is one type of default setup. Still, the height and spacing of these chairs are not comfortable for everyone, and attendees also often require table space for laptops, beverages, notepads, phones, and other conference essentials. One alternative is to offer Open Space Seating, with a variety of sofas, comfortable chairs, rockers, classroom-style seating, standing tables, and even floor pillows or bean bag pillows, to allow every attendee to choose a seating style and position that is most comfortable to them. They will likely also comment on and appreciate the attention to detail, increasing their satisfaction with the event, and encouraging word-of-mouth communication with others in their industry (Shock, 2018).

Corporate and industry wellness events

The high level of hospitalization and increased mortality rate during the pandemic have caused panic and fear among employees, specifically those who have underlying conditions such as chronic diseases. For that reason, employees are more focused than ever on their own health and safety in workplaces and expect permanent strategies from companies to protect their health and wellness. It is clear that if companies do not have a solid safety strategy to protect their staff, they will face frequent employee turnover. As business activities return to a central workplace, human resource (HR) managers and company leaders need to find workplace wellness initiatives to infuse wellness into work for their employees' physical and psychological well-being (Corporate Wellness Magazine, 2022).

The workplace wellness market is smaller than most other areas in the wellness hospitality industry, but it is still valued at $48 billion (Yeung & Johnston, 2018). Workplace wellness initiatives sponsored by corporations do not always include travel, but many host events related to the hospitality industry. The concept of **workplace wellness** "includes expenditures on programs, services, activities, and equipment by employers aimed at improving their employees' health and wellness" (Global Wellness Institute, 2019; Yeung & Johnston, 2018). This can mean raising awareness, educating employees, and offering incentives to adopt a healthier lifestyle by reducing risk factors and behaviors. These types of events can address physical and mental wellness through screenings, webinars and seminars, other informational presentations, team-building exercises, and more.

The growing popularity of wellness has lead to a proliferation of industry events like conferences and seminars. Expos exist around the globe for experts in the fitness, spa, salon, healthy lifestyle, yoga, self-love, healthy eating, energy healing, and so many more. The annual two-day WELL Summit, hosted by the organization WELL Insiders, focuses on wellness, empowerment, learning, and luxury. It attracts 500-plus wellness enthusiasts, bloggers, professionals, and entrepreneurs looking for networking opportunities and knowledge to grow their contribution to the industry (Well Insiders, 2019). Wanderlust, which sponsors the Wanderlust festivals discussed previously, hosts multi-day festivals; a unique triathlon of running, yoga, and meditation; master courses in yoga and other topical workshops; and three-day retreats specializing in the three pillars of wellness – nutrition, exercise, and rest (Wanderlust, 2019).

Incorporating wellness elements into regular events

In addition to the ideas for adding a secondary wellness focus into regular events as discussed above, wellness activities can be incorporated into almost any travel plan or event itinerary. At organized gatherings, wellness activities can be scheduled as breaks throughout a day of meetings or speakers, or can be offered before or after the day's itinerary. There are many more ways to do this than to just provide salads on the buffet; event attendees are looking for opportunities throughout the day to incorporate aspects of their daily wellness routine as well as learning new skills to bring home with them. Each piece of the itinerary must be carefully considered to see how it could be improved to promote a healthy mind, body, and spirit (Event MB/ Maritz Global Events, 2018). This can be as simple as choosing a hotel with an on-site spa, and offering attendees discounted treatments (or picking up the tab), or suggesting they take advantage of leisure time slots to receive a salon or spa treatment at a convenient location. Activities like early morning yoga classes and organized group walks or runs can bring attendees together to share common interests before or after a busy day of scheduled meetings.

Other small details can make a difference, as well. Event organizers can send daily tweets, texts, or emails to attendees with a healthy tip of the day, and health magazines and journals can be strategically placed around common break spaces to encourage browsing. Electronic versions of takeaway materials can be provided to encourage an environmentally friendly and clutter-free workspace. If weather permits, walking can be encouraged over shuttling, and elements of the event can be held outside instead of in a stuffy conference room (Alvarez, 2018).

Impact of wellness events

While it is useful to the event organizers and location hosts to understand the financial result of their events, it is also helpful to measure the environmental, social, and media effects of the event. Although the unique impact of the wellness component of events is difficult to calculate, there are methods of measuring the economic impact of traditional events. There are five key areas of event impact (eventIMPACTS, 2020):

1. **Attendance** – One of the fundamental measures of an event's impact, and other measurements often use the overall event attendance numbers. It is important to differentiate between attendees and understand the demographic profile of attendees as much as possible.
2. **Economic** – "The total amount of additional expenditure generated within a defined area, as a direct consequence of staging the event." The **direct economic impact** of an event is the spending that can be directly attributed to staging an event, and the **total economic impact** also includes the subsequent 'secondary impacts' of this additional monetary influx (eventIMPACTS, 2020).
3. **Environmental** – This area includes both explicit and hidden effects of the event on the environment, for example, land use and carbon emissions.

4. **Social** – The social impacts of an event have "almost always been observed anecdotally but rarely captured through a structured approach to impact measurement." They may include anything from creating an enjoyable or pleasurable experience to positively changing attendees' long-term behavior.

5. **Media** – This area includes evaluating the exposure of the event by estimating the number of people engaged with media coverage.

More information on measuring the economic impact of wellness events will be provided in the following chapter. The above techniques can be applied to measuring the economic impact of wellness events, but additional benefits must also be considered. For example, the reduced costs of healthcare for attendees who make beneficial changes to their lifestyles and therefore improve their long-term overall health. Wellness travelers also tend to be higher value travelers that spend more money and are more concerned about their impact on the destination (see Chapter 1). These and other considerations should be kept in mind when developing a method for measuring the specific economic impact of wellness events.

Summary

This chapter covered wellness events, festivals, and activities in foodservice, hospitality, and tourism. It first introduced the case of the MindBodySpirit Festival. Second, the chapter defined events, festivals, wellness events, and wellness festivals. Following this, the chapter categorized wellness events, festivals, and activities under three classes: primary, secondary, and corporate. Specific examples of primary, secondary, and corporate wellness activities are also explained. The chapter further discussed how to incorporate wellness activities in regular events and festivals and how to measure the economic impact of events.

Definition of key terms

Attendance impact – One of the fundamental measures of an event's impact, and other measurements often use the overall event attendance numbers. It is important to differentiate between attendances and unique attendees and understand the demographic profile of attendees as much as possible (eventIMPACTS, 2020).

Corporate and industry wellness event – An event sponsored by a corporation or industry association.

Direct Economic impact – Spend that can be directly attributed to staging an event (eventIMPACTS, 2020).

Economic impact – The total amount of additional expenditure generated within a defined area, as a direct consequence of staging the event.

Environmental impact – Both explicit and hidden effects of an event on the environment, for example, land use and carbon emissions (eventIMPACTS, 2020).

Event – "A public assembly for celebration, education, marketing, or reunion. Events can be classified based on their size, type, and context" (EventEducation.com, 2020).

Festival – A time of celebration, with an organized series of social events.

Media impact – Evaluating exposure of the event by estimating the number of people engaged with media coverage (eventIMPACTS, 2020).

Primary Wellness Event – An event that caters to primary wellness travelers.

Secondary Wellness Event – An activity that targets secondary wellness travelers with add-ons to their primary travel itinerary.

Social impact – May include anything from creating an enjoyable or pleasurable experience to positively changing attendees' long-term behavior (eventIMPACTS, 2020).

Total economic impact – Includes the direct economic impact of an event and subsequent 'secondary impacts' of this additional monetary influx (eventIMPACTS, 2020).

Wellness event – A type of event that focuses on spiritual, social, physical, and/or emotional well-being.

Wellness festival – A festival that brings people together to celebrate overall well-being, and has a focus on one or more aspects of wellness.

Workplace wellness – "Includes expenditures on programs, services, activities, and equipment by employers aimed at improving their employees' health and wellness" (Global Wellness Institute, 2019).

8

Discussion questions

1. How do we define wellness event?
2. How can we categorize wellness events?
3. Provide examples of a primary and a secondary wellness event.
4. How can be incorporate wellness elements even in regular events?
5. In what ways could the economic impact of events be measured?

Homework

1. Find a wellness event that takes place annually. Introduce its background, focus, number of attendees, and explain why people attend.
2. Find a regular event that takes place annually and discuss what wellness elements that can be included as part of this event.
3. Discuss the ways that an event impacts its host destination, in both positive and negative ways.

References

AIGA Orlando. (2020). Wellness by Design. Retrieved February 21, 2020, from https://orlando.aiga.org/event/wellness-by-design-2020/

Alvarez, D. (2018). 10 ways to incorporate wellness at your event. Retrieved February 20, 2020, from https://www.visitdallas.com/meeting-planners/blog/2018/10-ways-to-incorporate-wellness-at-your-event.html

Balance Festival. (2020). Balance Festival. Retrieved February 21, 2020, from https://www.balance-festival.com/

BaliSpirit Festival. (2020). Experience BaliSpirit Yoga Festival. Retrieved July 8, 2020, from https://www.balispiritfestival.com/experience-bali-spirit-festival

BaliSpirit Festival. (2022). Bali Spirit Festival. Retrieved May 30, 2022, from https://www.balispiritfestival.com/

Canyon Ranch. (2019). Explore Experiences. Retrieved December 29, 2019, from https://www.canyonranch.com/tucson/explore-experiences/

Corporate Wellness Magazine (2022). Infusing more "wellness" into workplace events. Retrived March 31, 2022 from https://www.corporatewellnessmagazine.com/article/infusing-more-wellness-into-workplace-events

Envision Festival. (2022). Envision Festival. Retrieved May 30, 2022, from https://www.envisionfestival.com/

Event MB/Maritz Global Events. (2018). 8 ideas to embrace a wellness culture at events. Retrieved December 30, 2019, from https://www.eventmanagerblog.com/wellness-event-ideas

EventEducation.com. (2020). What is an Event? Retrieved February 20, 2020, from http://www.eventeducation.com/what-is-event.php

eventIMPACTS. (2020). The Power of Events. Retrieved February 21, 2020, from https://www.eventimpacts.com/

Eventtia. (2022). Hybrid event trends for 2022 – virtual, hybrid, and in-person. Retrieved May 29, 2022, from https://www.eventtia.com/en/blog/hybrid-event-trends-virtual-hybrid-and-in-person

Global Wellness Institute. (2019). Wellness Definitions. Retrieved December 29, 2019, from https://globalwellnessinstitute.org/what-is-wellness/wellness-economy-definitions/

Hybrid Group Limited. (2020). IRIS: Your Escape. Retrieved February 21, 2020, from https://www.irishkg.com/

MindBodySpirit Festival. (2022a). The MindBodySpirit Festival. Retrieved June 1, 2022, from https://www.mbsfestival.com.au/

MindBodySpirit Festival. (2022b). EveryWoman at the MBS. Retrieved June 1, 2022, from www.mbsfestival.com.au/melbourne/whats-on/ewe-at-mbs-melb/

Mind Body Spirit. (2020). Wellbeing Festival. Retrieved February 21, 2020, from https://www.mindbodyspirit.co.uk/london

MindBodySpirit Festival. (2022c). Healthy Living Hub. Retrieved June 1, 2022, from https://www.mbsfestival.com.au/healthy-living-hub/

Mortier, A. (2019, M). How to plan a wellness event: Actionable guide for good healthy fun. *Billeto*. Retrieved July 8, 2020 from https://billetto.co.uk/blog/how-to-plan-wellness-event/

National Wellness Institute. (2022). National Wellness Conference. Retrieved May 29, 2022, from https://nationalwellness.org/nwc/

Shock, P. J. (2018). Want to boost attendee concentration? The do's and don'ts of attendee comfort. Retrieved December 30, 2019, from https://www.eventmanagerblog.com/attendee-comfort

Smith Center for Healing and the Arts. (2020). Smith Center Washington DC. Retrieved December 29, 2019, from https://smithcenter.org/

Soul Circus. (2020). Soul Circus. Retrieved February 21, 2020, from https://www.soulcircus.yoga/

Telluride Yoga Festival. (2020). Telluride Yoga Festival. Retrieved February 21, 2020, from https://www.tellurideyogafestival.com/

Wanderlust. (2019). Choose Your Adventure. Retrieved December 29, 2019, from https://wanderlust.com/events/

Wanderlust. (2022). Wanderlust. Retrieved May 29, 2022, from wanderlust.com/

Well Insiders. (2019) Well Summit. Retrieved December 29, 2019, from https://wellsummit.org/

Yeung, O. and Johnston, K. (2018). Global Wellness Tourism Economy Monitor October 2018. Global Wellness Institute. Retrieved November 8, 2019, from https://globalwellnessinstitute.org/ industry-research/global-wellness-tourism-economy/

8

9 The Design, Operation, and Management of a Wellness Event

This chapter discusses how to design, operate, and manage a wellness event. It starts with introducing the Sedona Yoga Festival. It defines event management and how to design a wellness event. After defining stakeholders, it explains the importance of the identification of stakeholders for a wellness event. It also covers human resources planning, budgeting, marketing, safety, and managing a wellness event. Finally, it discusses what happens after a wellness event.

Learning outcomes

By the end of this chapter, students should be able to do the following:

1. Introduce the Sedona Yoga Festival.
2. Define and discuss event management and how to plan and design a wellness event.
3. Discuss the basic requirements of designing a wellness event.
4. Identify key stakeholders for a wellness event.
5. Discuss human resource planning for a wellness event.
6. Discuss how to develop a budget for a wellness event.
7. Explain how to market a wellness event.
8. Explain how to manage a wellness event.
9. Discuss the role of safety in designing, operating, and managing a wellness event.
10. Discuss what to do after a wellness event.

Case study: Sedona Yoga Festival

The Sedona Yoga festival has been held annually since 2012 in Sedona, Arizona, with the exception of 2020 and 2021 during the Covid-19 pandemic (2020 ticketholders were given a credit to attend a future event). The goals of the 2022 event were to "nourish our collective soul, address the wounds of a difficult couple of years, and spark joy to encourage the continued sharing of yoga's wisdom and healing."

Attendees at the annual festival receive not only the physical benefits from doing yoga, but also a focus on mental and spiritual growth and recovery from the past years, including the effects of the pandemic. The organizers also offer "a variety of guided land excursions that foster meaningful immersion in Sedona's breathtaking natural beauty." Socially and environmentally conscious vendors are in attendance at a free expo attached to the event, which welcomes friends and family not attending the conference itself. Music, kids experiences, and trainings are offered throughout the conference, and pre- and post-conference immersions into various components of yoga are available as conference add-ons.

One day at the event could look like:

7:00 am – Morning meditation sangha

7:45 am – All levels community practice: rise and shine yoga

8:00 am – Trauma informed yoga training, or kids yoga: yoga happiness

8:30am – On the land experience: Cathedral Rock

Throughout the day – courses, yoga practice, chanting, reiki immersion, etc.

2:30pm – Group panel discussion

6:15pm – Concert sunset satsang

(Sedona Yoga Festival, 2022)

Discussion questions

1. What is unique about this festival?
2. What does the Sedona Yoga Festival offer its attendees?
3. What does the Sedona Yoga Festival offer locals?
4. Are there similar festivals where you live?

9

Planning and designing a wellness event

Event management is a term often used synonymously with event planning, but in reality, it is more than just the planning phase. **Event management** includes planning and building an event, promoting it across multiple channels, managing attendee information and communication, executing the actual event, and measuring its success (Layman, 2019).

A **special event** is a one-time event staged for celebration, typically a unique activity. A **special events company** is, therefore, one that is contracted to put on all or parts of an event, and a **special events production company** may present special effects and theatrical acts for the event (Fenich, 2018). Wellness events are usually small events that do not necessarily require the assistance of a special events company or a production company. However, some large festivals do use them to increase the "wow factor."

An **event planner** is someone who coordinates all aspects of professional meetings and events. This person must understand the goals, needs, and desires of their client must work within the parameters of the location, and needs to have a basic understanding of the community infrastructure, merchandising, promoting, developing sponsorships, and working with media (Fenich, 2018).

How to design a wellness event?

First, it is essential to know the target audience for the event. Some critical questions to ask in order to find out who the target audience is:

- Who is the customer/potential attendee, and what are their needs and wants?
- What other options or choices do they have for wellness events?
- How can they be defined?

Once these questions are answered, the planning, programming, scheduling, and expenses can be directed toward that group. To be more specific, here are some typical steps that are taken to design a wellness event (Fenich, 2018):

1. Set Goals and Objectives: Objectives are the basis of the planning process and drive the planning of the program, from site selection to food and beverage, transportation, room layout and setup, and of course, the programming. Goals and objectives, therefore, should be clear, concise, and measurable, or **S.M.A.R.T.** (specific, measurable, attainable, relevant, and time-based).

Some specific questions to help guide the identification of these goals include:

a) Why would people attend your wellness event (i.e., what is the purpose of the event? Education, health improvement, networking, or conducting business)?

b) Who is most likely to attend your wellness event? Recent studies show that apart from the classic methods of marketing research, social media platforms can be analyzed to understand users' preferences by examining their activity such as posts, likes, and shares. Therefore, it is possible to observe what kind of tendencies users are inclined towards. For example, Akbari et al (2016) examined the social media content of Twitter users and identified which wellness events they followed. Such technological data can be very helpful for wellness event planners to define their participant groups for future events.

c) What segment are you mostly trying to attract?

d) Some popular goals for wellness events include (Mortier, 2019):
   i.   Fitness
   ii. Meditation and well-being exercises
   iii. Women's wellness
   iv. Stress management
   v.   Life coaching
   vi. Medical care and health screening
   vii. Ditching bad habits (e.g., smoking cessation)
   viii. First aid

2. Conduct a Needs Analysis: Once the outcomes and most likely, event attendees have been identified, begin thinking about more specific event requirements, for example:

a) What will attendees expect from your event?

b) Where will the attendees be coming from? What types of lodging and amenities will be required? What about transportation options?

c) Are there any medical or dietary needs that are likely to be common among attendees? Or any other special needs that should be taken into account?

d) What is the estimated budget the attendees will be able to spend?

e) Will attendees likely be coming alone or with others (e.g., friends who will also attend the event, or spouses who may not attend)?

3. Select a site: Choosing the perfect location for a wellness event depends on many different factors, such as:.How many people are expected to attend? Where are the majority of them located?

f) What type of event facility is needed? Should it be indoors, outdoors, or a combination of both?

g) Some popular locations for wellness events include (Mortier, 2019):
   i.   Event centers
   ii. Fitness centers
   iii. Campgrounds
   iv. Resorts or hotels

h) An in-person visit to potential venues (called a **site inspection**) is often essential to choosing the perfect location.

4. Develop a budget: Another major consideration in wellness event planning is the budget. This will be discussed in more detail in section 9.5.

5. Consider the program content: After the objectives are developed, consider the format of the event:.

a) Will one schedule of activities for everyone to participate in be sufficient? Or should tracks be developed, where programs are separated into genres for different interests or skill levels?

     b) Write descriptions of each activity or session.

     c) Tips: do not double-book events, and allow for breaks in between activities or sessions.

     d) Some common activities for a wellness event include (Mortier, 2019):

         i. Health screenings

         ii. Yoga classes

         iii. Healthy meals

         iv. Wellness seminars

         v. Team-building exercises and game sessions

6. Logistical considerations: There are lots of little details to be considered for any size and type of wellness event, such as:.

     a) How will registration information and fees be collected?

     b) How will lodging be arranged? Will attendees make their reservations? Should room blocks at local hotels be set up?

     c) What food will be provided at meals and breaks? Will they be catered?

     d) Will there be any speakers? What information is needed from them, and how do they need to be supported?

This is an overview of some important factors in the planning and design phase of a wellness event. Figure 9.1 features a checklist for designing a wellness event.

Figure 9.1: Design a wellness event checklist (Adapted from Fenich, 2018).

Although each event is unique with its own goals and objectives, there are some common trends currently happening in the wellness event area (Fenich, 2018):

1. *Less is the new more/stylish minimalism*: Wellness travelers are not always looking for loud music, an exhaustive list of activities, and constant motion. Often, they are seeking to slow their lives down and find ways to bring joy and peace to their everyday lives. This means events can be streamlined and

straightforward, as long as they run smoothly and offer attendees what they are looking for.

2. *Your wellness events should have a purpose*: The goals and objectives identified for an event could be related to improving attendees' well-being, but they can also be focused on helping the local community or another particular group in need. As discussed in earlier chapters, wellness travelers often enjoy giving back to the place they are visiting, and this can be incorporated into any event.

3. *Face-to-face is popular, with precautions*: Due to improvements in technology, along with the Covid-19 pandemic and the need for social distancing and virtual work, remote conferencing tools have become very popular for personal and work-related video communications. However, people still enjoy uniting in a common place, and the need for meeting in person safely will bring people together. Personal connections and shared energy and experiences can happen in face-to-face scenarios that simply are not possible through digital communications.

4. *Technology is key in promotion*: Although face-to-face events will remain popular, technology is an environmentally friendly, cost-effective, and efficient way to market and communicate about the event.

5. *Be sustainable*: Wellness consumers care about the environment and the impact their travel is making. Events can be held in eco-friendly locations that are easy to get to by public transit and at venues that are committed to reducing their environmental footprint. The event host can offset the carbon emissions generated by attendee travel, and environmentally friendly decisions can be made during the execution of the event.

6. *Make the entire package an experience*: Wellness travelers are looking for more than just a trip; they want an experience that they feel has improved their life in some way. By considering this at each stage in the travel process from start to finish, a wellness event can fulfill this need.

Developing a budget for a wellness event

Even if making a large profit is not a primary goal of a wellness event, having a budget in place will help reduce the chances of a financial loss. Some key things to remember when budgeting include the importance of tracking every expense, communicating the budget to the event team and controlling who can sign off on payments, and staying within the set limits. Establishing the financial goals of an event early in the planning process is important (Fenich, 2018):

- Determine the financial expectations of the event.
- Goals should incorporate the SMART approach discussed above.
- A budget could be set by the planner, association, corporate mandate, or a combination.
- Consider the three possible financial outcomes: break-even; profit; deficit.

If this is a repeat event, revenue, and expense data from previous ones can be a helpful starting point. For a first-time event, potential expenses and revenue sources include the following (Nielsen, 2019):

Potential expenses

- Indirect cost - overhead or administrative items.
- Fixed cost - expenses incurred regardless of the number of attendees.
- Variable cost - based on the number of attendees.
- Rental costs for venue, space, and equipment.
- Costs for the public (police), private (security firms), and equipment (detectors) in regards to safety and security.
- Catering/food and beverage.
- Photography.
- Signage and decoration
- Production costs for entertainment/talent, audio/visual, lighting, sound, and utilities.
- Labor costs for staff, greeters, registration, ticketing, union contractors, carpenters, electricians, riggers.
- Marketing costs.
- Talent costs.

Potential revenue sources

- Registration fees from attendees.
- Corporate/association funding.
- Private funding.
- Exhibitor fees/sponsorships (see section 9.5.1).
- Donations.
- On-site food and beverage sales.
- Event merchandise.

Sponsorship for wellness events

Sponsorship occurs when another person or organization provides funds or in-kind contributions to receive logo usage and identify with the event (Laker & Roulet, 2021). This can help underwrite the event and defray costs. The association between multiple organizations can also be a strong marketing tool for both the event and the sponsor. Sponsorships are popular because they allow sponsors the ability to target a specific market segment or media group, measure results from the event, and take advantage of the growth of diverse population segments (Fenich, 2018).

Identification of key stakeholders

A **stakeholder** is "a person with an interest or concern in something" (Lexico, 2020a). When it comes to wellness events, for example, stakeholders may be employees or members of the host organization, their customers, or anyone with a vested financial interest. Key stakeholders can also be members of the community. These could be local politicians, business leaders, civic and community groups, media, and other community leaders (Fenich, 2018). Their opinions are important to take into consideration when planning a wellness event, as they will be impacted by the hosting of the event and possibly tasked with communicating about the event and its benefits to the local community.

Employee wellness and human resources planning for a wellness event

The importance of employee wellness is increased due to the restrictions and concerns brought about by Covid-19. This crisis has certainly improved business efficiency with more than 10% productivity in 2020, however, employee mental health and well-being is still suffering. Recent data shows that more than 90% of workers have experienced mental distress in the last 12 months. Most company responses are not very effective since their wellness programs are outdated and simply focus on physical health and wellness. However, some are now paying more attention to innovative wellness programs. For example, organizations are hiring wellness officers, introducing new wellness benefits and events to employees, offering fun wellness meetings, implementing new work-life boundaries, offering interactive wellness resources, emphasizing using vacation days, and showing their workers that the company truly cares about them and wants them to remain healthy (Laker & Roulet, 2021).

No event can run smoothly without the right people being involved. Small and personal events may only need one or two event coordinators, but most will require additional resources and personnel. This could come from a few different sources (Fenich, 2018):

- Regular employees: This group is helpful because they are familiar with and invested in the host organization's mission and event goals. Regular employees who have been part of events before are already trained and experienced.

- Temporary staff: Some additional staff members may need to be hired just for the event, possibly from the local community. However, it is challenging to offer extensive training to temporary staff, so their capacity to help may be limited. They also need clearly defined roles and expectations.

- Volunteers: Although volunteers are often considered to be "free," expenses such as food and beverage or training may still be incurred. In many ways, volunteers need to be treated as an employee; they are also interfacing with attendees, and need to understand and support the event's values and mission. It can also be a challenge to motivate volunteers, and they may need to be supervised more closely than regular employees to ensure quality work.

Marketing a wellness event

The traditional marketing promotional mix models are useful reference tools when promoting a wellness event. **Advertising** is any paid form of non-personal communication about an event, and **direct marketing** is advertising that communicates explicitly directly with target customers with the intent of generating a response. **Sales promotion** includes marketing activities that provide value or incentive with the intention of stimulating sales (Fenich, 2018).

Public relations is the effective management of relationships and communications to influence behaviors and achieve objectives. The purpose of public relations is to systematically plan and distribute information to control or manage image or **publicity**, which is defined as marketing that is not directly paid, nor has an identified sponsor. Publicity is one of the most effective marketing tools to get coverage, as messages appear to come from the communicating agency (e.g., the media), which offers credibility that paid advertising cannot (Fenich, 2018).

Personal selling, or a person-to-person attempt to persuade, may also be a useful wellness event-marketing tool. And of course, **social media** tactics like viral marketing and promoting the event through blogging and networks like Facebook, LinkedIn, Twitter, Instagram, etc. are often requirements for 21st-century marketing. (Fenich, 2018) It may even be helpful to partner or collaborate with a **micro-influencer**, an individual, or "brand" with 1,000 to 10,000 followers and who has a highly engaged following in the area of choice (Bernazzani, 2019), to help promote the event on social media. The micro-influencer can be invited to the event for free in exchange for promotion before and during the event on their social media platform of choice (i.e., Instagram stories if they have an engaged Instagram following or YouTube vlogs if they have engaged subscribers on YouTube).

Operation and management of a wellness event

As discussed above, preparing the logistics for a wellness event typically takes some effort. First, a venue must be secured, and permits (e.g., parade, liquor, sanitation, sales, and fire safety) need to be obtained. Dealing with the public sector can be difficult, and preparing for an event may mean involving government agencies like the health department, security, police, and local committees concerned with the use of space. All vendors and suppliers must be secured in advance, liability insurance needs to be purchased, and other support functions such as ticket sales, accounting, travel planning, and more need to be determined. Many digital tools like online spreadsheets and mobile apps are available for helping plan events (Fenich, 2018)

A lot more goes into the on-site management of a wellness event than is typically seen by attendees. While each event is different, many need to take into account one or more of the following:

1. Registration and lodging.
   a) Will advance registration be required, or will on-site registration be possible? How will payments be accepted?

b) Final registration and housing reports should be completed for tracking purposes

2. Event space preparation.

   a) Each event and function space needs to be set up, checked, and double-checked before attendees arrive. This may include décor, seating arrangements, etc.

   b) All audio/visual equipment must also be set up, checked, and double-checked before the speaker and attendees arrive. Speakers are also encouraged to rehearse in the venue beforehand.

3. Ancillary events.

   a) Activities before and after the main event, or for guests accompanying an event attendee (such as spouses and families) must be planned and coordinated according to expectations

   b) All activities should be appropriate to the age and interests of the attendees

   c) Let the attendees select or plan their activities

4. Communication procedures.

   a) How will organizers communicate with each other and attendees during the event? Written, verbal, visual, and behavioral methods may all apply.

   b) Some guidelines for improving communication within an team include:
      i. Establish the level of priority
      ii. Identify the receiver
      iii. Know the objective
      iv. Review the message in your head
      v. Communicate in the language of the other person
      vi. Clarify the message
      vii. Do not react defensively to a critical response

9

Wellness event safety

Where preparing for these types of events, it is important to think about the safety of the people working and attending the event. When large groups of people are brought together, there are certain risks, especially in a situation like the Covid-19 pandemic. **Event risk** depends on the following factors (Tarlow, 2002):

- Size of crowd.
- Size and nature of the event site.
- Time of day.
- Nature of the event.
- Food and beverage.
- Age of crowd.

- Weather conditions.
- Location of the event venue (urban, rural, etc.).

Since every wellness event will be different, the event planners need to take into consideration all of the above factors when considering the safety of an event. Conducting a **risk assessment** is an excellent way to help prepare for an event (University of the Sunshine Coast, 2020):

- Help consider all foreseeable hazards and detail the controls used to eliminate or reduce the risk of those hazards.
- Detail how an emergency during the event will be handled.

Follow-up activities after a wellness event

Here are some activities that may need to be done as a follow-up(Fenich, 2018):

- Prepare final written report/summary/evaluation.
- Evaluate feedback from attendees.
- Finalize income and expense statement.
- Finalize all contacts and compare to final billing.
- Send media final press release.
- Appropriate thank-you acknowledgments (vendors, talent, sponsors, staff, volunteers).

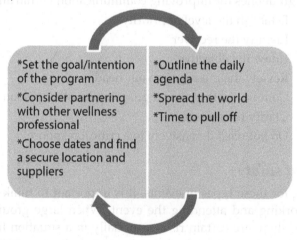

*Set the goal/intention of the program

*Consider partnering with other wellness professional

*Choose dates and find a secure location and suppliers

*Outline the daily agenda

*Spread the world

*Time to pull off

Figure 9.2: Checklist for hosting a wellness event

Bringing it together: Hosting a wellness retreat

Let's take a look at an applied example of the steps above (See Figure 9.3). A wellness retreat is a specific type of event that is becoming very popular; a group of like-minded people gathers together to get away from the stresses, responsibilities, and mad rush of daily life and let the mind quiet down from its daily routine (Jotisalikorn, 2020).

More and more of these are popping up every year in all sizes and hosted by everyone from bloggers to large companies, but they can indeed be a challenge to plan and implement. Bringing a retreat from idea to life requires a few dedicated steps:

1. *Set the goal/mission/intention of the program.* Is it to bring together women who are struggling with trauma in their life, and giving them tools like mindfulness and support systems to help them overcome? Or is it to have an enjoyable trip wandering the Tuscan countryside taking healthy farm-to-table cooking classes and drinking wine while making a conscious pledge to disconnect from mobile devices for 12 hours at a time? Specify what attendees will get out of the event, so the itinerary and marketing messages can be planned precisely.

2. *Consider partnering with other wellness professionals.* Collaborating with a grief counselor, a mindfulness expert, and a nutritionist may be essential for a trauma recovery workshop. A local tour operator may be the best option for a trip around Tuscany. These professionals should be able to demonstrate their ability to help attendees gain the most from the program, and should align nicely with the goal/mission/intention set in step 1.

3. *Choose dates, and find and secure a location and suppliers.* Consider the location your attendees will most likely be coming from and their expected budget, high and low season in the destination, weather, and any events happening at the same time, all of which will impact how the retreat is priced. A healing environment like a spa resort may be an ideal host for a trauma workshop. In contrast, a host of small family-run inns would be more appropriate for a culinary tour around Tuscany. Room blocks need to be negotiated and reserved, speakers and experts need to be engaged, and contracts signed with local tour operators and restaurants or cooking schools.

4. *Outline the daily agenda.* Especially if the event is brand new, attendees will want to know exactly what to expect before they are willing to register and pay a deposit. What activities need to be included? Where will meals come from, and where will ingredients be sourced? How much free time is needed? How many optional activities will be offered? Will transportation be needed throughout the week, or only from and to the airport at the beginning and end of the retreat? A comprehensive timed action plan will include a detailed schedule broken down into increments that clearly state what is optional, what is included in the price, and other details that will be important to potential attendees.

5. *Spread the word.* If a name has not yet been chosen for the event, now is the time to do so. What will catch the attention of attendees while also clearly specifying the purpose? Consider the types of people most likely to be interested in the event. Social media can be an excellent tool to connect like-minded people and promote events to them, and existing email lists can reach potential attendees. Ask friends and colleagues to promote the event on their social media accounts, and post and email consistently but not

9

overwhelmingly with a clear message that communicates the benefits and value of the retreat, and has a prominent call to action and link to register.

6. *Some advice:* Be sure to have some kind of assistance; do not try to do it all! And always have backup plans. Regardless of how tightly things have been planned, caterers can be late, buses can break down, attendees can get ill, and support and a backup plan can help keep things running smoothly. Interact with attendees, share wisdom, ensure that the program brings them value and the ability to return to the world renewed, and, most importantly, listen to their feedback. Ask them to complete post-trip surveys to learn how the event can be improved for next time. Then take that feedback into account and start the planning cycle again.

Summary

This chapter discussed the details of designing, operating, and managing a wellness event. The Sedona Yoga Festival was introduced as an example of a wellness event, then the concept of event management was presented. Planning and designing a wellness event, along with budget considerations, human resources planning, and key stakeholders, were mentioned. Marketing, safety, and operational management were discussed, along with follow-up activities after the event. Finally, an example of hosting a wellness retreat was used to apply the concepts introduced in the chapter.

Definition of key terms

Advertising – Any paid form of non-personal communication about an event (Fenich, 2018).

Direct marketing – Advertising that communicates explicitly with target customers with the intent of generating a response (Fenich, 2018).

Event management – Planning and building an event, promoting it across multiple channels, managing attendee information and communication, implementing the actual event, and measuring its success. (Layman, 2019).

Event planner – Someone who coordinates all aspects of professional meetings and events (CareerExplorer, 2020)

Event risk – Risk associated with involvement in any event (Hendricks, 2020).

Micro-influencer - An individual or brand with 1,000 to 10,000 followers and who has a highly engaged following in the area of choice (Bernazzani, 2019).

Personal selling – A person-to-person attempt to persuade, may also be a useful wellness event-marketing tool (Fenich, 2018).

Public relations – The effective management of relationships and communications to influence behaviors and achieve objectives (Fenich, 2018).

Publicity – Marketing that is not directly paid, nor has an identified sponsor.

Risk assessment – A systematic process of evaluating the potential risks that may be involved in a projected activity or undertaking (Lexico, 2020).

Sales promotion – Includes marketing activities that provide value or incentive intending to stimulate sales (Fenich, 2018).

Site inspection – An in-person visit to potential venues (Fenich, 2018).

S.M.A.R.T. Goals – Goals that are specific, measurable, attainable, relevant, and time-based.

Social media marketing – Tactics like viral marketing and promoting the event through networks like blogging, Facebook, LinkedIn, Twitter, Instagram, etc. (Fenich, 2018).

Special event – A one-time event staged for celebration, typically a unique activity.

Special events company – A company that contracts to put on all or parts of an event (Fenich, 2018).

Special events production company – A company that may present special effects and theatrical acts and hires speakers (Fenich, 2018).

Sponsorship – Occurs when another person or organization provides funds or in-kind contributions to receive logo usage and identify with the event (Fenich, 2018).

Stakeholder – A person with an interest or concern in something (Lexico, 2020).

Discussion questions

1. What are the steps to designing a wellness event?
2. Can you describe the components of a S.M.A.R.T. goal and give an example?
3. What are some current trends in wellness events?
4. How can an event budget be determined?
5. What are some potential expenses and revenue sources of a wellness event?
6. Who are some likely key stakeholders in a wellness event?
7. What types of labor are needed for a typical wellness event?
8. How can a wellness event be marketed?
9. What are some key aspects of operating and managing a wellness event?
10. What are some important variables to consider in regard to event safety?
11. What are some activities that need to be done after a wellness event?

Homework

1. Find a wellness event and evaluate their website to see how they designed, operated, and managed the event. Alternatively, if you have attended a wellness event in the past, discuss the event, what went well, and what could have been improved.

2. Propose a wellness event that you are interested in. Offer discussions and explanations on your concept in terms of design, focus, key stakeholders, human resources, budgeting, marketing, safety, and managing.

References

Akbari, M., Hu, X., Liqiang, N., & Chua, T. S. (2016). From tweets to wellness: Wellness event detection from twitter streams. In *Proceedings of the AAAI Conference on Artificial Intelligence.* 30(1).

Bernazzani, S. (2019, July 15). Micro-Influencer marketing: A comprehensive guide. *Hubspot.* Retrieved March 6, 2020 from https://blog.hubspot.com/marketing/micro-influencer-marketing

CareerExplorer. (2020). What is an event planner? Retrieved February 22, 2020, from https://www.careerexplorer.com/careers/event-planner/

Fenich, G. G. (2018). *Meetings, Expositions, Events & Conventions: An introduction to the industry*, 5th edition. Pearson Higher Ed.

Jotisalikorn, C. (2020). Why you should go on a wellness retreat. Retrieved February 22, 2020, from https://www.spafinder.com/blog/spa-travel/why-you-should-go-on-a-wellness-retreat/

Hendricks, B. (2020). Risk management in event and conference planning. Retrieved March 6, 2020 from https://study.com/academy/lesson/risk-management-in-event-conference-planning.html

Laker, B., & Roulet, T. (2021). How organizations can promote employee wellness, now and post-pandemic. *MIT Sloan Management Review.* ISSN 1532-9194 Available at http://centaur.reading.ac.uk/94575/

Layman, M. (2019). What is event management? Retrieved February 27, 2020, from https://www.cvent.com/en/blog/events/what-is-event-management

Lexico. (2020a). Meaning of stakeholder in English. Retrieved February 27, 2020, from https://www.lexico.com/definition/stakeholder

Lexico. (2020b). Risk assessment definition. Retrieved March 6, 2020 from https://www.lexico.com/definition/risk_assessment

Mortier, A. (2019). How to plan a wellness event: Actionable guide for good healthy fun. Retrieved February 27, 2020, from https://billetto.co.uk/blog/how-to-plan-wellness-event/

Nielsen, F. (2019). How to prepare and manage your event budget like a pro. Retrieved February 27, 2020, from https://billetto.co.uk/blog/how-to-prepare-manage-event-budget/

Sedona Yoga Festival. (2022). Sedona Yoga Festival. Retrieved May 30, 2022, from https://sedonayogafestival.com/

Tarlow, P.E. (2002). *Event Risk Management and Safety*. John Wiley & Sons.

University of the Sunshine Coast. (2020) Risk Assessment / Safety Checklist for Events. Retrieved March 6, 2020 from https://www.usc.edu.au/media/1083076/USC-Event-Risk-Assessment.pdf

9

10 The Management and Upgrading of Wellness Amenities and Facilities

This chapter discusses the management and development of health and wellness destinations, facilities, and amenities in foodservice, hospitality, and tourism businesses. First, it introduces the case study of the Finger Lakes Region of New York State. Next, it defines wellness destinations, facilities, and amenities in foodservice, hospitality, and tourism. Finally, it discusses how those wellness destinations, facilities, and amenities can be developed and managed.

Learning outcomes

By the end of this chapter, students should be able to do the following:

1. Discuss the case study of the Finger Lakes Region of New York State.
2. Define and discuss wellness destinations, facilities, and amenities.
3. Categorize the core resources and competencies that a wellness destination should have.
4. Define and discuss management of wellness destinations.
5. Define and discuss the development of facilities and amenities in wellness destinations.

Case study: Finger Lakes Region, New York

Between New York City, the Adirondack Mountains, and the western New York city of Buffalo, a third of New York State is comprised of the Finger Lakes Region. This part of the state has gone through a transformation from an agricultural paradise to an industrial center anchored by Corning Glassworks, a brief stint as a silent film mecca, and it is now known as a wellness haven. Hiking trails, cycling circuits, yoga studios, herbal apothecaries, and other traditional medicine centers, farm-to-table restaurants, farmer's markets, and more abound in this destination (Steuben County CVB, 2020).

One of the primary cities, Ithaca, is home not only to Cornell University and Ithaca College but also to the North American seat of Namgyal Monastery, the personal monastery of the Dalai Lama. Other parts of the rustic region host vineyards and many water activities centered on the 11 Finger Lakes in the region, as well as cow cuddling and horse therapy. Spas and wellness centers thrive, including the Inns of Aurora, located in Aurora, which has an on-site yoga master and Ayurvedic expert in the role of Director of Serenity, whose only job is to help guests decompress. This resort, in particular, offers guests massages and bodywork, Ayurveda consultations, and serenity sessions for those guests who are visiting and focusing on their wellness (Inns of Aurora, 2020).

Multiple New York State parks make it easy for guests to take advantage of the gorges, waterfalls, and pristine forests of the region (Lippe-McGraw, 2019). There are also many history centers and attractions celebrating such people and events as President Millard Fillmore, Harriet Tubman, the underground railroad, women's suffrage in Seneca Falls, the Erie Canal, and more.

There are several destination management organizations (DMOs) (defined below) in the Finger Lakes Region that oversee the management and development of tourism in the area. This network of organizations monitors the current and potential tourism offerings, coordinates with various destination stakeholders like lodging and restaurants, other local businesses, the State Park network, and more, to help ensure a consistent wellness product and marketing message. They work together in areas such as research and marketing, to avoid overlap and duplication of efforts.

Discussion questions

1. What types of wellness facilities and amenities are available in the Finger Lakes region?

2. What natural resources does this region have to offer visitors?

3. What purposes can destination management organizations (DMOs) serve?

4. What other areas of the United States and the world are similar to the Finger Lakes region?

10

Wellness destinations, facilities and amenities

Chapter 4 of this textbook described some popular wellness destinations around the world, like Sedona, Arizona, Amelia Island, Florida, Bali, Indonesia, and Costa Rica. Although many of those places have been famous for their wellness facilities and amenities for decades and even centuries, to remain competitive in the modern tourism environment, they must continue to innovate by managing and upgrading their offerings. Chapter 7 discussed the development and management of spas and hot springs, but there are many other facilities and amenities a destination can use to compete in the wellness arena. In Chapter 4, a *tourist destination* was defined as a country, state, region, city, or town which is marketed or markets itself as a place for tourists to visit, and a *wellness destination* was defined as a country, state, region, city, town, or event that tourists and residents visit to improve their holistic health.

Coordinating efforts within each destination and between the destination and the rest of the world often are handled by a destination management organization (DMO). While the M in DMO has traditionally stood for *marketing*, in recent years, it has transitioned to *management*, making a DMO the leading organizational entity that may encompass the various authorities, stakeholders, and professionals and facilitates partnerships towards a collective destination vision (WTO 2019a; Destination Think!, 2020). Often, it is recommended that DMOs work alongside their members and stakeholders (hotels, restaurants, activity providers, etc.) to develop an overarching and cohesive strategic plan for marketing and promoting the area (Dvorak et al., 2014). DMOs do not own the destination's tourism product, but are in charge of facilitating its development by encouraging tourism to the region. In addition to the hard skills of designing, planning, and marketing, DMOs perform "soft functions" like instilling trust, calming uncertainties, and creating a sense of community (Sheehan et al., 2016).

DMOs exist in three different capacities and depending on where the wellness destination is located, how large it is, and if it is publically or privately owned. This will affect which type of DMO a destination may reach out to for assistance. First is the national tourism authorities; this type of DMO is responsible for managing and marketing an entire country. If a wellness destination wants to be included in national tourism management and marketing, it will contact this type of DMO. Second are the regional tourism authorities, which are responsible for the management of a specific tourist zone like the French Riviera or French Alps. Lastly, there are local DMOs that are independent regional tourism organizations that are close to all of the local tourism areas. In Central Florida, these would be Experience Kissimmee or Visit Orlando.

The duties of DMOs are as follows (Burnaz et al., 2017):

- **Coordination** – Coordinating many elements (including local, political, civil, business circles, and tourism sector representatives) that constitute the tourism industry to provide a single voice in tourism.
- **Protection** – Leading tourism efforts in local communities and protecting the interests of the tourism industry.

- **Product development** – Helping to develop an attractive mix of touristic possibilities, events, and programs.
- **Providing information** – Helping visitors to provide services such as pre-visit information and additional information on arrival.
- **Stakeholders** – Assisting external organizations, such as meeting planners, tour operators and travel agencies, which bring visitors to the destination.

In addition to the above list, DMOs also participate in strategy development for a destination, economics and finance, marketing, lobbying, research, and event hosting.

It is important to note that as we discuss destination management and development throughout this chapter, each destination has its own destination capability. *Destination capability* is "the ability of destination actors to integrate, reconfigure, and release distributed resources and competencies to generate successful new products" (Sainaghi et al., 2019, p. 518). Destination capability is essential to wellness destinations because it can help to increase the number of services/activities at a destination or aid in increasing the development of wellness products at a destination. Second, it helps increase the perceived value of the destination by ensuring all the stakeholders are involved in the destination management process (Sainaghi et al., 2019).

A destination's health and wellness facilities and amenities are likely to include spas and hot springs (as discussed in Chapter 7); accommodations; restaurants and other dining options; transportation; leisure centers for physical, mental, or spiritual improvement (such as Ashrams, retreat locations, and exercise facilities); parks and hiking areas; event venues; and in some cases hospitals, clinics, and rehabilitation centers with a focus that is not strictly medical (see Chapter 1 for the spectrum of wellness and health tourism). Supplementing these facilities, Voigt and Pforr (2014, pp. 292-296) specify additional core resources and competencies that comprise a wellness destination. Table 10.1 highlights some of these wellness destination core resources and skills.

Table 10.1: Wellness destination core resources and competencies (Adapted from Voigt, 2014)

Natural resources	Geothermal, mineral waters, therapeutic climate, muds, clays, plants, geographical features
Cultural, historical and spiritual resources	Hammam, sauna, cleansing rituals, purification ceremonies, traditional spiritual practices such as yoga
Complementary and alternative medicine offerings	Homeopathy, naturopathy, massage, cupping, transcendental meditation, baleology
Wellness specific superstructure	Beauty spa resorts, lifestyle resorts, spiritual retreat
Wellness related events	Events showcasing various facets of health, community health events
Crossover of wellness with other activities	Wellness service combined with medical activities, local food and beverages

All these offerings can benefit a region promoting itself as a wellness destination. However, they must be carefully maintained and improved upon to ensure their potential is being maximized, but only to a sustainable level that will retain natural resources for future generations. As mentioned previously in this textbook, wellness travelers typically spend more than other travelers, meaning wellness resources are one beneficial way for a destination to attract a lower volume of higher-spend visitors, which also helps decreases the effects of ove-tourism.

Wellness destination management and development

Destination management is "the coordinated management of all the elements that make up a tourism destination (attractions, amenities, access, marketing, and pricing)" (WTO, 2007). It is important to note that destination management is a continuous process. While it incorporates all aspects of a destination, wellness elements are one valuable and robust element of the bigger picture. DMOs and other stakeholders may come up with a destination management plan during the development and management of a destination. A *destination management plan* is "a document that provides a vision and an intent highlighting how a destination will be managed over a period of time, specifying the roles of stakeholders, their specific actions and finding and allocating resources to achieve the intended goals"(Coban & Yildiz, 2019; Visit GREENWICH PR Brief, 2015). This plan helps to ensure that everyone is in agreement during the development and management of a wellness destination.

The core product of a healthy and productive destination includes its culture, reputation, the level of authenticity, and nature, which provides for its natural assets, beautiful scenery, and environment. A location can use this core product as its competitive advantage against similar wellness destinations, but to truly maximize its competitiveness, it must also have a wide selection of quality services that support health and well-being, such as those discussed above (Saari & Tuominen, 2014; Voigt, 2014).

Wellness destination management

Destination management covers the following dimensions (Saari & Tuominen, 2014):

- Coordinating public and private network leadership and actors.
- Understanding the past, current, and future health and well-being tourism concepts and demand.
- Operational activities throughout the destination network.
- Evaluating the quality of the product offered by the destination and monitoring its improvement.
- A DMO is vital for coordinating and communicating between public and private partners, as well as leading the management and development effort.
- A DMO is also a useful central repository for information such as research, for example, on the macro level, looking at all factors that affect the competitiveness and success of a destination. These macro-level factors can be applied to wellness tourism in the following ways:
- *Social/cultural* – On a macro level, societal trends will affect where, how, and when consumers travel. For example, the United Nations World Tourism

Organization reported that some important consumer social/cultural travel trends include "travel to show", i.e., traveling to Instagram-worthy destinations, and "traveling in pursuit of a healthy life", i.e. walking, wellness, and sports tourism (WTO, 2019b). Wellness tourism is an important current trend, and wellness travelers are looking for authentic and sustainable experiences. On a destination level, the more residents that embrace the concept of wellness in their own lives and their tourism product, the more competitive a destination will be in this element. Customer orientation can be measured by evaluating their experiences and satisfaction.

■ *Economy* – The global economy has a considerable impact on travel. From the varying strength of currencies to the health of a country's own internal economy and the overall financial health of a region, many factors influence a wellness traveler's choice of destination. The UNWTO (2017) states that "strong economy drives tourism growth," and in 2018, the favorable economic factors included a 3.6% increase in global GDP, moderate exchange rate changes, and low-interest rates.

■ *Political/legal* – Similar to the global economy, the political environment within a country, as well as its relationship with other countries, affects where and when wellness travelers choose to visit. If a country is viewed as politically unstable or unfriendly to their group, travelers may decide to travel to a different location for safety or convenience reasons. For example, in 2017, the UNWTO cited that Turkey had moved down four spots in the top ten international tourism arrivals for the year because of the failed coup attempt and security issues in 2016.

■ *Ecology/environment* – As mentioned previously, sustainability is an important component for wellness travelers. They want to interact with an authentic and unspoiled natural region, where the local people value and protect their natural resources. In their 2019 report, the UNWTO cited "rising awareness on sustainability" as a consumer travel trend countries should be aware of and catering to.

■ *Technology* – As discussed in Chapter 6, technology integrates with a wellness lifestyle in many ways. When it comes to travel, destinations can choose the level of adoption they want to offer guests. In essence, more may not always be better as wellness travelers are often looking to disconnect and disengage from the stressful modern world. Destinations and DMOs have been measuring tourism in real-time, which allowed for better management (UNWTO, 2017).

To manage a destination, a DMO might use a *destination management system* (DMS), which is a platform that provide networks aimed at optimizing DMOs' internal coordination, destinations' players' collaboration as well as the engagement with the tourism demand. These systems represent a fundamental structure in destination management as they allow the exchange of tourism data. Benefits of DMSs include: "coordinated promotion and distribution of the destination's products, disintermediation and optimization of revenues, coherent and effective development, promotion, visibility, and presence in the global market, and contributions for smart tourism destinations. There are three major challenges that destination management systems face: (1) DMS technology and management models, (2) organization factors, and (3) external environment." (Estevao et al., 2020).

Wellness destination development

Wellness destination development is the process of systematically and continuously planning, developing, managing, evaluating, and leading a destination's brand identity as it relates to wellness tourism. Destination development takes place in four dimensions (Saari & Tuominen, 2014):

- Strategic destination planning in a systematic way that incorporates all relevant parties.
- Developing and managing the destination's brand identity.
- Planning and policymaking at a destination level to support and promote wellness tourism.
- Continually evaluating and leading the development of infrastructure and service offerings.

Differentiating, positioning, and brand strategy are all critical elements of a destination's marketing and development strategy. A DMO is essential here for outlining responsibilities, tracking key performance indicators (KPIs) and metrics, seeking funding, and updating the plan when needed. Endowed resources, such as nature, culture, authenticity, and reputation, are one of the most important factors for a successful wellness destination. During the development process, care must be taken not to overdevelop the location and dilute these resources. Some suggestions for maintaining a destination for future generations include (Saari & Tuominen, 2014):

- Taking action to eliminate pollution and any destruction of nature so that guests can enjoy easily accessible intact natural areas. Regular monitoring is essential so that any damage can be recognized and remedied quickly.
- Incorporating natural resources into the destination's product offering.
- Offering wellness treatments based on indigenous or local health and well-being traditions.
- Ensuring food and beverages that are part of the wellness product are organic and/or locally sourced.
- Highlighting the local culture through events, museums, and sites made accessible to visitors.
- Living up to the expectations created by the destination's marketing campaigns.
- Basing the destination's overall reputation on health and wellness.

Managing and upgrading health and wellness facilities and amenities

Any wellness destination contains a multitude of hospitality-related facilities and amenities. This is often referred to as a *superstructure*, "an umbrella term for facilities and services created especially for tourists, for example, hotels, restaurants, transportation facilities, recreation facilities, and built attraction" (Saari & Tuominen, 2014). For wellness destinations, this includes high-quality accommodations, restaurants, and transportation services, as well as a broad offering of high-quality services to enhance health, well-being, and relaxation (e.g., wellness and medical treatments, sauna and pool facilities, sporting facilities, and opportunities to refresh mentally).

Wellness facilities and amenities management

While the condition and capacity of the physical facilities are important to the overall experience, the services provided are typically considered the most vital component of a wellness destination. They should be viewed as a major pull factor for tourists and can help increase the competitiveness of a destination as well as the guest's overall satisfaction (Turcan et al., 2015). The administration of many public facilities, for example, many of the *onsen* (thermal spas) in Japan, is undertaken by a regional or local government. In other situations, the management of a wellness facility may be outsourced to or operated by a private company. Some examples of services offered at wellness facilities include (Voigt, 2014):

- Spa body treatments (e.g., facials, body wraps).
- Water-based and sweat-bathing therapies (e.g., hot/thermal springs, saunas, Vichy showers, ice grottos).
- Manual-pressure based and manipulative body-based therapies (e.g., acupressure, massages, cupping).
- Natural remedies and herbal medicine (e.g., aromatherapy, local herbal treatments).
- Healthy diet and nutrition (e.g., detoxing, fasting, special diets).
- Exercise and fitness (e.g., personal training, indoor and outdoor activities).
- Mind/body activities (e.g., yoga, Pilates, tai chi).
- Relaxation and meditation techniques (e.g., prayer, transcendental meditation).
- Expressive and creative therapies and arts (e.g., poetry, drumming, dancing).
- Energy and New Age therapies (e.g., healing touch, crystals, Reiki – a Japanese technique for stress reduction and relaxation [International Center for Reiki Training, 2020]).
- Wellness education activities (e.g., workshops and seminars about stress management or work-life balance, counseling).

10

A facility manager at a wellness destination is in charge of providing a safe environment for stakeholders so they can deliver goods and services or experience them. Facility management should be viewed as creating an environment that both employees want to work in, and guests want to experience (Turcan et al., 2015).

Spa management is significantly important in health and wellness tourism. Research has found that industry experts are aware of fundamental issues in this area, revealing management concerns and gaps related to workplaces, employees and customers. Concerns include quality issues pre-visit (information search and booking), during the spa visit (first welcome and experience), post-visit and after-care experiences of spa clients as well as the availability of evidence-based holistic treatments, therapies, fitness, nutrition, and mental wellness practices for healthier lifestyle. From a management perspective, the main issues for spas include the sustainable usage of water, following safety and hygiene protocols, sales, controlling expenditure and monitoring costs, forecasting, training and career development, fair wages, good leadership, and a positive team spirit (Smith & Wallace, 2019). This emphasizes the importance of design, aesthetics, atmosphere, and sustainability in spa management.

Wellness facilities and amenities development in destinations

Similar to the management of wellness amenities and facilities described above, a government or private company can undertake the development of these assets. As an overarching tourism body with a big-picture view of a destination, a DMO is in a position to make recommendations on how to improve the region's health and wellness tourism offerings by (WTO, 2019):

- Ensuring sustainability to maintain its environmental, social and cultural integrity, and its authenticity, resources, and character.
- Strengthening institutional governance and bringing together all stakeholders to make decisions for a collective gain.
- Avoiding overlapping and identifying gaps between entities to avoid duplicating efforts while recognizing areas that need additional attention.
- Spreading the benefits of tourism by increasing and keeping jobs in the local community.
- Building a tourism culture in the destination by giving residents a voice in the tourism development process and encouraging a positive attitude toward visitors.
- Improving tourism yield by optimizing capacity and length of stay, and maximizing distribution.
- Building and delivering a strong and vibrant brand identity that is closely connected to the identified values of the destination.

One key asset of any tourism destination is its people. As discussed previously, wellness travelers often want to interact with and support the local economy and residents. Therefore, how people in a destination welcome and treat wellness travelers are critical, as visitors will be keenly aware of how their presence affects the residents.

A welcoming culture of hospitality is an excellent asset here; destinations that have traditionally welcomed visitors are known for this, and it is seen as an advantage. DMOs and other tourism organizations can foster this kind of culture by educating the residents about the benefits visitors to bring to the local economy. They can also offer suggestions or more formal training on appropriate ways to interact with guests.

Additional considerations

In addition to these physical facilities and amenities, Voigt and Pforr (2014, pp. 292-296) identify core resources and competencies that are intangible. A wellness mindset and wellness-related lifestyle throughout a community (for example, a population with wellness-related values and health-conscious lifestyles) will bring a more authentic feel to a destination's wellness offerings than a community that does not have a wellness mindset and wellness-related lifestyle. Having a qualified labor force to deliver wellness services is also essential for following through on a destination's wellness promises (Voigt, 2014).

Summary

This chapter discussed how health and wellness destinations, facilities, and amenities in foodservice, hospitality, and tourism businesses are managed and developed. First, it introduced the case study of the Finger Lakes Region of New York State. Then, the relationship between destination management organizations (DMOs) and the local wellness community was covered. Lastly, it discussed how those wellness destinations, facilities, and amenities could be developed and managed.

Definition of key terms

10

Destination capability – "The ability of destination actors to integrate, reconfigure, and release distributed resources and competencies to generate successful new products." (Sainaghi et al. 2019).

Destination management – "The coordinated management of all the elements that make up a tourism destination (attractions, amenities, access, marketing, and pricing)." (WTO, 2007).

Destination management plan (DMP) – "A shared statement of intent to manage a destination over a stated period of time, articulating the roles of the different stakeholders and identifying clear actions that they will take and the apportionment of resources." (Coban & Yildiz, 2019).

Destination management organization (DMO) – "The leading organizational entity which may encompass the various authorities, stakeholders, and professionals and facilitates partnerships towards a collective destination vision." (WTO, 2019a).

Destination management system (DMS) – A platform or platforms that provide networks aimed at optimizing DMO's internal coordination, destinations' players' collaboration as well as engagement with the tourism demand (Estevao et al., 2020).

Superstructure – "An umbrella term for facilities and services created especially for tourists, for example, hotels, restaurants, transportation facilities, recreation facilities, and built attractions." (Saari & Tuominen, 2014).

Wellness destination development – The process of systematically and continuously planning, developing, managing, evaluating, and leading a destination's brand identity as it relates to wellness tourism (Saari & Tuominen, 2014).

Discussion questions

1. What is the typical role of a DMO? How has it evolved in recent years?
2. What are some examples of health and wellness facilities and amenities that might be found in a destination?
3. What are some core wellness resources and competencies that a destination can have?
4. Can you describe the components of developing a health and wellness destination, and how they interact?
5. What are the five primary macro-level factors that apply to wellness tourism?
6. Can you describe wellness destination development and its dimensions?
7. What steps can a destination take to maintain itself for future generations?
8. What roles do physical facilities and services play in a wellness destination?
9. What kind of recommendations can DMOs make to improve the region's health and wellness tourism offerings?

Homework

1. Visit a DMO's website (perhaps your home town, or your next vacation destination), and identify the wellness facilities and amenities offered in that area.
2. How could that destination expand its wellness offerings? Which specific facilities or services do they seem to be lacking? How can they take care to preserve their product for future generations?

References

Beirman, D. (2003). *Restoring Tourism Destinations in Crisis: A Strategic Marketing Approach.* Crows Nest, NSW: Allen & Unwin.

Burnaz, E., Kurtuldu, H.S., and Akyuz, A.M. (2017). An organization structure suggestion of national destination management organization for Turkey. *Global Journal of Economics and Business Studies, 6*(12). 46-62.

Coban, G., and Yildiz, O.S. (2019). Developing a destination management model: Case of Cappadocia. *Tourism Management Perspectives, 30.* 117-128.DOI: 10.1016/j.tmp.2019.02.012.

Destination Think! (2020). What does the "M" of DMO mean for your destination? Retrieved March 17, 2020, from https://destinationthink.com/blog/m-of-dmo-destination/

Dvorak, D., Saari, S., & Tuominen, T. (2014). Developing a competitive health and well-being destination. Retrieved February 15, 2020, from https://globalwellnesssummit.com/wp-content/uploads/Industry-Research/Global/2015-developing-a-competitive-health-and-well-being-destination.pdf

Estevao, J., Carneiro, M.J., and Teixeira, L. (2020). Destination management systems' adoption and management model: proposal of a framework. *Journal of Organization Computing and Electronic Commerce, 30*(2). 89-110. DOI: 10.1080/10919392.2020.172765.

Inns of Aurora. (2020). Wellness. Retrieved March 20, 2020 from https://innsofaurora.com/wellness/

International Center for Reiki Training. (2020). What is Reiki? Retrieved March 20, 2020 from https://www.reiki.org/faqs/what-reiki

Lippe-McGraw, J. (2019). Forget Bali: These 7 Destinations Are the Next Wellness Hot Spots. Retrieved February 16, 2020, from https://thepointsguy.com/news/surprising-new-wellness-destinations/

Saari, S., & Tuominen, T. (2014). In Developing a competitive health and well-being destination. Retrieved February 15, 2020, from https://globalwellnesssummit.com/wp-content/uploads/Industry-Research/Global/2015-developing-a-competitive-health-and-well-being-destination.pdf

Sainaghi, R., De Carlo, M., and d'Angella, F. (2019). Development of a Tourism Destination: Exploring the role of destination capabilities. *Journal of Hospitality & Tourism Research, 43*(4). 517 – 543. DOI: 10.1177/1096348018810388.

Sheehan, L. et al. (2016). The Use of Intelligence in Tourism Destination Management: An Emerging Role for DMOs. *International Journal of Tourism Research, Int. J. Tourism Res., 18.* 549-557.

Smith, M., & Wallace, M. (2019). An analysis of key issues in spa management: Viewpoints from international industry professionals. *International Journal of Spa and Wellness, 2*(3), 119-134.

10

Steuben County CVB. (2020). How to have an uncommon health and wellness getaway in Corning and the Southern Finger Lakes. Retrieved February 16, 2020, from www.corningfingerlakes.com/steuben-stories/post/how-have-uncommon-health-and-wellness-getaway-corning-and-southern-finger-lakes/

Turcan, E., Ates, M., and Varol, E.S. (2015). An evaluation related to the effect of strategic facility management on choice of medical tourism destination. *Marketing*. 124-131.

Voigt, C., (2014). Towards a conceptualization of wellness tourism. In: C. Voigt & C. Pforr, eds. 2014. *Wellness Tourism, A destination perspective*. Routledge. Ch. 2.

World Tourism Organization (WTO) (2007), A Practical Guide to Tourism Destination Management, UNWTO, Madrid.

World Tourism Organization (2017). *UNWTO Tourism Highlights: 2017 Edition*, UNWTO, Madrid, doi: https://doi.org/10.18111/978284419029

World Tourism Organization (WTO) (2019a), UNWTO Guidelines for Institutional Strengthening of Destination Management Organizations (DMOs) – Preparing DMOs for new challenges, UNWTO, Madrid. Retrieved February 16, 2020, from https://www.e-unwto.org/doi/pdf/10.18111/9789284420841

World Tourism Organization (2019b). UNWTO Tourism Highlights: 2019 Edition, UNWTO, Madrid, doi: https://doi.org/10.18111/9789284421152

11 Analysis and Management of Health and Wellness Programs and Offerings

This chapter discusses the analysis and management of health and wellness programs and offerings in foodservice, hospitality, and tourism businesses. First, it introduces the case study of the Arctic Bath Hotel and Spa in Sweden. Then, it describes the primary categories of health and wellness programs and offerings. In particular, it looks at specific ways wellness services and experiences need to be reviewed and identifies some key performance indicators (KPIs) to measure. Finally, it suggests ways to gather and analyze data to improve wellness facilities and services to increase customer and stakeholder satisfaction.

Learning outcomes

By the end of this chapter, students should be able to do the following:

1. Describe the wellness programs and offerings that Arctic Bath Hotel and Spa offers its guests.
2. List and explain what wellness programs and offerings hospitality and tourism businesses can contribute to their guests.
3. Explain and discuss key performance indicators to measure the success of these wellness programs and offerings.
4. Describe different ways to gather and analyze data related to customer feedback.

Case study: Arctic Bath Hotel and Spa, Sweden

Found in Swedish Lapland, in the micro-destination of Harads, the Arctic Bath Hotel and Spa welcomes guests year-round with a unique wellness offering. Walking across a cold pool centerpiece, a footbridge brings visitors to cabins and rooms that float on top of the Luleriver in warm weather and freeze in place during the winter. Here guests can experience the Northern Lights during the winter and the midnight sun during the summer. With a focus on local foods, activities, building materials, and spa ingredients, the Arctic Bath Hotel and Spa provides guests with an authentic Scandinavian experience while leaving little impact on the local environment.

Their treatments center on the four cornerstones of wellness: proper nutrition, regular exercise, peace of mind, and care of the face and body. Hotel guests are guaranteed a table in the on-site restaurant, which offers a five-course menu, changing daily depending on what local ingredients are in season. For exercise, guests are encouraged to partake in one of the handpicked local activities such as a nature hike, fishing on River Luleå or through the ice, cycling in the forest, horseback riding, cross-country skiing, or a wilderness ride by snowmobile or traditional dogsled. Caring for the face and body begins with an open-air cold bath alternated with a sauna or hot tub, and continues into luxurious products and professional spa treatments.

The Arctic Bath Hotel and Spa offers a unique accommodation design in a tranquil and beautiful location. Focusing on their natural surroundings and local traditions, the property also partners with local activity companies and food sources to maximize the guest experience. Visiting the hotel is sure to be a bucket list experience for many wellness travelers.

Sources: Arctic Bath (2019); Rosenberg (2020)

Discussion questions

1. What types of wellness facilities and amenities are available in the Arctic Bath Hotel and Spa?
2. What makes the Arctic Bath Hotel and Spa so unique?
3. What natural resources does this hotel offer to its visitors?
4. What can other hotels, spas, and similar businesses learn from the Arctic Bath Hotel and Spa?

Wellness programs and offerings

Throughout this textbook, we have looked at many facets of wellness in hospitality and tourism. The primary categories discussed include destinations, spas, and hot springs, health and wellness facilities and amenities, and events. While planning and implementing health and wellness components is a crucial stage, it is equally as important to monitor them on an ongoing basis to ensure the offering is being managed as well as possible, and clients are still pleased and returning and recommending it to others. First, it may be helpful to review the definitions and scope of the different components of health and wellness tourism.

Wellness destination management and analysis

As noted in Chapter 4, a wellness destination refers to a country, state, region, city, town, or event that tourists and residents visit to improve their holistic health. Again as noted in Chapter 10, wellness destination development refers to the process of systematically and continuously planning, developing, managing, evaluating, and leading a destination's brand identity as it relates to wellness tourism. Destination management is defined as "the coordinated management of all the elements that make up a tourism destination (attractions, amenities, access, marketing, and pricing)" (WTO, 2007). While managing a destination, the following factors should be paid attention to since they are the most important in the eyes of the tourist: "the natural conditions of the destination and the relaxing environment of the hotel, differentiation based on personalized and professional attention, price competitiveness and attractiveness of the offer of wellness treatments and centers" (Medina-Munoz & Medina-Munoz, 2014).

Spa and hot springs management and analysis

Chapter 7 introduced eight different types of spas: resort spa, amenity spa, destination spa, medical spa, club spa, cruise ship spa, day spa, and mineral springs spa. Spas can benefit a destination in many ways, such as attracting more visitors in the off- and shoulder seasons, lengthening the shoulder season and thereby shortening the off-season, giving business guests a reason to extend their stay and return as a leisure guest, enriching spouse/companion programs for business travelers, providing an indoor activity option during poor weather, and more (Mill, 2011). One spa brings their dedication to wellness travelers to the next level; Rocco Forte Spa at the Verdura Resort in Sicily uses four initiatives for a comprehensive approach to wellness:

1. Organics (skincare products made with local ingredients).
2. Rituals (unique spa treatments).
3. Fitness (innovative trainers, equipment, and technology).
4. Nourish (delicious and healthy food).

These four elements are customized to each particular guest upon arrival. All staff and managers are made aware of the resulting program, and every piece of the stay is personalized down to the in-room minibar snacks (Ramani, 2018). Previous studies show that a destination's natural spa resources, cultural resources, attractions, lodging options, food, transportation, and safety and security are key elements for spa and hot spring visitors. In line with that, strategies for destination competitiveness should address the following capacities: capabilities of DMOs, planning and management of a destination, environmental management, experience management, talent management, pricing, marketing and management of a destination (Lee & King, 2008).

11

Wellness value "reflects the benefits of spa experiences in terms of enhancing physical, mental, and spiritual health" (Choi et al., 2015). This wellness value affect spa management and its analysis in terms of the facility, programs, and staff, and it is a compelling predictor of guest satisfaction. While spas typically are owned by individual companies, hot springs are unique as they are often considered public amenities and are regulated by a local government or organization. They are naturally occurring features and have their distinct challenges. Therefore, hot spring visitor satisfaction generally should be measured differently from spa visitor satisfaction. The differences will be outlined in a later section of this chapter.

Wellness facility and amenity management and analysis

Spas and hot springs are one type of health and wellness facility and amenity, but many other businesses and features also fall into this category. Examples include accommodations, restaurants, and transportation services, as well as an extensive offering of high-quality services to enhance health, well-being, and relaxation (e.g., wellness and medical treatments, sauna and pool facilities, sporting facilities, and opportunities to refresh mentally). Like spas and hot springs, these health and wellness facilities and amenities might be privately or publically owned and managed. Both the physical facilities and their accompanying services are essential to consider when analyzing and managing these amenities.

Health and wellness programs incorporating the above specifications are becoming very popular around the world. EVEN Hotels is a brand geared explicitly to business travelers with a wellness orientation, as they offer in-room amenities such as stationary bikes and other exercise equipment and dozens of on-demand fitness videos. Hamilton Hotel in the heart of Washington, D.C., has a fleet of Lopifit electric walking bikes for visitors to use, each with a battery-powered treadmill (Wilson, 2019). Taking spa treatments outside the traditional facility, the Fairmont Empress in British Columbia, Canada, allows guests to learn about and harvest seaweed in the wild before returning to the spa for a seaweed treatment (Travel Channel, 2020).

Wellness event management and analysis

As discussed in Chapter 8, a wellness event is a type of event that focuses on spiritual, social, physical, and/or emotional well-being. It may incorporate physical exercise, mindfulness education, holistic therapies, environmental awareness and engagement programs, and other activities to improve the overall well-being of its attendees. More specifically, primary wellness events can be categorized as events that cater to primary wellness travelers. In contrast, secondary wellness events target secondary wellness travelers with add-ons to their primary travel itinerary or incorporating healthy elements into a larger event. Corporate and industry wellness events encompass activities sponsored by a corporation or industry association and will be discussed further in Chapter 12. The next sections offer suggestions on ways to look at each of these categories through the lens of management and analysis to maximize the satisfaction of both guests and internal stakeholders.

Meeting and exceeding customer expectations

Consumers have so many wellness choices today that it is no longer enough to sell an average quality wellness service and experience. Each one must be thought of as an opportunity to surprise, delight, and exceed customer expectations with a memorable experience. Pine and Gilmore (1998) discuss the concept of experiences as a distinct economic offering in their article "Welcome to the Experience Economy." Experiences go beyond commodities, goods, and services, and into a personalized situation that can be thought of almost like an interactive performance, where customers participate and connect with the "event" at hand. Table 11.1 highlights the key features of the experience economy as dictated by Pine and Gilmore.

Table 11.1: The Experience Economy (Adapted from Pine & Gilmore, 1998).

	Commodities	Goods	Services	Experiences
Economy	Agrarian	Industrial	Service	Experience
Economic function	Extract	Make	Deliver	Stage
Nature of offering	Fungible	Tangible	Intangible	Memorable
Key attribute	Natural	Standardized	Customized	Personal
Method of supply	Stored in bulk	Inventoried after production	Delivered on demand	Revealed over a duration
Seller	Trader	Manufacturer	Provider	Stager
Buyer	Market	User	Client	Guest
Factors of demand	Characteristics	Features	Benefits	Sensation

Pine and Gilmore also discuss the four realms of experience: entertainment, educations, escapist, and esthetic. Wellness experiences fall into the latter two categories since the guests are immersed in the experience versus absorbing it, and some wellness experiences require active participation, while others require passive participation. It is interesting to note that the escapist realm is the realm that is most highly correlated with the overall guest experience (Luo et al., 2018).

Pine and Gilmore suggest five key design principles to keep in mind when developing an experience: theme the experience, harmonize impressions with positive cues, eliminate negative cues, mix in memorabilia, and engage all five senses. Building on these principles, we can recommend the following in designing wellness experiences:

1. *Theme the wellness experience.* Many restaurants do this, for example, medieval-themed restaurants that offer jousting shows while diners experience meals that would have been prepared hundreds of years ago. Hotels in Las Vegas also come to mind, with themes centered on particular cities, performers, or attractions. Wellness facilities and amenities can consider developing their strengths around one specific type of activity.

2. *Harmonize wellness impressions with positive cues.* To support the wellness theme selected, cues such as décor, the script delivered by staff, visual signs, and instructions, can help bring the guest deeper into the wellness experience. This is often seen in spas, with dim lights, calming music, soft and comfortable furnishings, etc.

3. *Eliminate negative cues.* Similar to the above, make sure all cues fit in with the wellness theme and have a positive message. Even items like poorly designed or integrated signage can distract customers and ruin the effect that is being created. In the case of a wellness spa, something as trivial as a flickering light can ruin the experience for a guest.

4. *Mix in memorabilia.* If the wellness experience is engaging and exceptional, guests will want to bring a piece of it home. Tour t-shirts are trendy souvenirs from concerts, Disney visitors purchase all sorts of items, and caps with embroidered logos serve as reminders of a memorable day of golf at a famous resort. When wellness consumers look at or use these items in the future, they are reminded of the wellness experience.

5. *Engage all five senses.* The more senses a wellness experience engages, the more effective and memorable it can be. Pine and Gilmore use the example of a Rainforest Café, a chain of restaurants with a jungle theme. As soon as a guest enters the café, rainforest sounds fill the air, they are surrounded by foliage, tropical smells are piped into the room, audio-animatronic animals come to life across the restaurant, and a gentle mist fills the space. In short, a good wellness experience should engage all five senses.

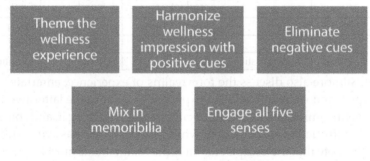

Figure 11.1: Checklist for designing a wellness experience (Adapted from Pine & Gilmore, 1998).

There are four areas of service quality: excellence, value, conformance to specification, and meeting and/or exceeding expectations (Silvestri et al., 2017). Excellence at a wellness destination can be reached if the service at the destination was outstanding or stood out in a guest's mind. Value is perceived if a guest sees the experience, destination, and service as being worth what they paid for it. Conformance to specification considers whether the wellness destination's service complies with the notions a guest already had in their head about the experience. Lastly, the service at the wellness destination should meet or exceed a guest's preconceived expectations. However, it is important to note that one needs to be careful when looking at service quality since the idea of quality and satisfaction is inherently subjective.

As discussed briefly in Chapter 7, wellness services have some features distinctive from tangible goods, which affect the way they need to be analyzed and managed. Services are *intangible*, meaning they cannot be seen, tasted, felt, heard, or smelled before purchase, and it does not result in the customer's ownership of anything. Services are also *variable*; due to the high human component in services, the resulting end product may differ between providers or even vary for the same provider on different days. Lastly, services are *perishable* and cannot be stored for future use. If an appointment is canceled or a time slot, hotel room, or airplane seat is left empty, it cannot be double-booked in the future.

Services are also typically *produced and consumed simultaneously*; the massage therapist gives the massage at the same time the client receives it, meaning the guest is participating in the production process. These defining factors of services make it difficult to measure customer approval and to identify any areas of dissatisfaction specifically. There are some tools available to help address these concerns:

Standard operating procedures

Standard Operating Procedures (SOPs) detail all of the policies and procedures to be followed when carrying out any wellness task of the operation, including client interactions. Beyond guest interactions, SOPs contain policies, procedures, forms, and templates. One document commonly included in SOPs is a treatment protocol manual, or a detailed instruction manual for each of the treatments and services offered in a spa, with information on the products used, and the timing and steps for each treatment. Another common document is a product description manual, which includes a list of ingredients and descriptions for every product sold or used in the facility, along with their uses, benefits, and contraindications. (Wisnom & Capozio, 2020).

Training

Employees need to be trained on the SOPs when they are implemented, when new staff starts, and as a refresher. Developing a curriculum of skills and information that will help staff best do their jobs, important things the team should be aware of, and how they should act will help improve consistency throughout service providers and heighten overall guest satisfaction. A training program should be thorough and delivered in a professional and detailed manner, with follow-up resources available as needed.

When it comes to wellness service delivery, there are multiple points throughout the process where things can go wrong. One approach to beginning to identify possible causes of any client unhappiness is summarized in Table 11.2. Putting SOPs and training in place and using the service quality GAP model offers a helpful starting point. The next step is to consider specific key performance indicators and data gathering and analysis techniques to better fit each organization's particular needs in designing and delivering wellness programs and offerings.

11

Table 11.2: The Service Quality GAP Model

Gap No.	Description	Causes	Example in Wellness
1	Guests' expectations versus managers' perceptions	Managers fail to understand their wellness guests' wants and wishes	Offering Ayurveda and massage when guests request local wellness services
2	Managers' perceptions versus service standards	Managers are aware what wellness guests really want, but they are unable or reluctant to offer such services	Not hiring and keeping talented and expert employees to deliver wellness experiences
3	Service standards versus the service delivery process	Managers know what wellness offerings should be, but employees are reluctant or unable to offer wellness experiences	Employees miss customer orientation sessions. Employees are not engaged and inattentive
4	Service delivery versus communication	The business promises more and specific wellness offerings in its external communication	Limited and inaccurate marketing and promotional efforts and materials on wellness offerings
5	Discrepancy between guests' wellness expectations and their perceptions of the wellness experience delivered	Guests' wellness experiences fall below their wellness expectations	Poor-quality wellness experiences offered
6	Discrepancy between guests' wellness expectations and employees' perceptions	Employees fail to understand what wellness experiences guests expect	Differences in age, culture, health and education between guests and employees
7	Discrepancy between employees' and managers' perceptions	Managers fail to understand employees	Managers expect employees to treat wellness guests as normal guests

Adapted from Smith & Puczkó (2008), and Parasuraman et al. (1985).

Performance indicators for wellness facilities, programs, and offerings

Wellness facilities and amenities can be very expensive to build and operate, and therefore their success must be carefully monitored. Many different models and methods exist for benchmarking, analyzing, and measuring the effectiveness of health and wellness facilities and programs. Some of these Key Performance Indicators (KPIs) and other methods are discussed below.

Key Performance Indicators (KPIs)

We can suggest KPIs that can be used to monitor the performance of wellness facilities, programs, and offerings (Singer, 2009):

- Capture rate (the percentage of guests who use spa services)
- Average treatment rate
- Treatment room utilization
- Therapist productivity
- Revenue per available treatment room
- Revenue per guest
- Revenue per square foot
- Revenue per occupied guest room
- Number of services per guest
- Retail sales as a percentage of treatment revenue
- Market segmentation
- Revenue per available treatment hour (RevPATH).

Adapted slightly to their more individual and unique circumstances, hot springs (or mineral/thermal springs) can also use the same KPIs. All of these indicators can provide useful information to a service manager, but the revenue per available treatment hour (RevPATH) metric may be the most useful. This is calculated either by multiplying the treatment room occupancy by the average expenditure per person or by dividing the revenue received in a set time by the number of treatment-hours during that time (e.g., day, week, month, etc.) (Guo et al., 2016). This ratio can be controlled by the spa if desired; for example, a luxury spa may wish to increase treatment rates and lower occupancy to keep a quiet and selective guest experience, whereas a spa targeting budget-conscious travelers may lower prices and increase occupancy to bring in as many clients as capacity allows (Mill, 2011). Nine specific factors can be used to measure wellness travelers' satisfaction with wellness destinations (Mi et al., 2019). Table 11.3. lists these factors, describes them, and also explains how to analyze and manage them.

Methods of evaluation

One way to holistically evaluate a wellness program or offering is using the Five Ps of Evaluation: participants, personnel, programs and offerings, place, and paperwork (Wisnom & Capozio, 2020; Henderson & Bialeschki, 1995). *Participants* includes everyone involved in the wellness experience and details like their motivations, satisfaction, attitudes, knowledge, skills, and/or abilities, privacy, level of participation, and other characteristics. In a wellness offering, these participants can be everyone in a spa or other wellness facility: staff, guests, and anyone else present in the area. *Personnel*, in particular, includes details about the staff of the facility, like their level of training and development, goal achievement, characteristics, service and sales performance, and guest interactions.

11

To analyze wellness *programs and offerings*, managers can look at the characteristics of wellness services provided, scheduling and timing, promotion techniques, safety and security, and number of and robustness of offerings and programs. Related to programs and offerings is *place*, which includes interior and exterior characteristics, safety and privacy, cleanliness and sanitation, and having ample and adequate facilities. Lastly, *paperwork* is necessary to maintain financial accountability, inventory management, and operational efficiencies. Each organization must consider its situation and identify their key performance indicators. Once they better understand what they should measure to understand customer satisfaction, data can be gathered and analyzed.

Table 11.3: Wellness destination visitor satisfaction

Factor	Description	Analysis and management
Environmental quality	Overall environment assessment of wellness destinations and resorts including location, air condition, and noise	Monitoring and communicating the composition and stability of the water's health benefits to wellness guests
Special resources	Specific wellness natural resources in the region including mineral concentration, chemical composition, and water temperature	
Convenience	How easy it is to purchase or enjoy wellness programs and offerings	Guest satisfaction surveys
Food	Quality and quantity of food and beverages offered	
Service quality	The abstract construct of how wellness services are measured (see the service quality GAP model above)	
Facilities	Physical elements include interior decorations, furniture, food and beverage units, gyms, pools, etc.	
Consumption emotion	The set of emotional responses elicited during product use or consumption of wellness experiences	Interviews, focus groups
Perceived value	Guests' views on wellness products and services' overall quality in relation to what was promised versus what was received/delivered	Guest satisfaction surveys
Target consumers	The different types of wellness travelers who are more likely to use and purchase wellness resort's offering and programs	Guest satisfaction surveys, interviews, focus groups

Adapted from Mill (2011) and Mi et al. (2019)

Data gathering and analysis

In general, clients are willing to share their thoughts and opinions about their experiences; they just need to be asked. One typical way of gathering customer feedback is through *customer satisfaction surveys*, also often called a *guest satisfaction survey* in the hospitality field. More in-depth data gathering methods may also be used, such as focus groups, personal interviews, and online reputation management. Each of these will be discussed in the following sections. For each method, the first steps are to understand what you want to know, and how will the information be used? Who will use the information and make decisions based on the research findings? When should the evaluation be done: before, during, or after the experience? Which clients or stakeholders will provide the most useful and accurate information? (Wisnom & Capozio, 2020).

Wellness customer/guest satisfaction surveys

A **wellness customer satisfaction (and delight) survey** is a survey that often uses rating scales to understand how happy wellness clients are with an organization's wellness products, services, or experiences (Qualtrics, n.d.). Just as a reminder, *customer satisfaction* is the "customers' overall attitude and their emotional reactions about a hospitality business in relation to the differences between what customers expect and what they receive" (Silvestri et al., 2017). These surveys are often self-administered, meaning the guest fills out a card at the time of checkout, or they receive a link via email to take a survey online soon after their experience is complete, and they fill it out on their own (Wisnom & Capozio, 2020). Typically this kind of wellness survey is anonymous and quick and easy to encourage the guest to complete it. These types of surveys are important because satisfaction is a crucial step in the service profit chain. Satisfied, loyal, and productive employees create value for the company, which in turn helps to create satisfied guests, which in turn can create loyal guests (Heskett et al., 1994).

Focus groups and personal interviews

A focus group is typically conducted as a personal conversation, in a one-to-one situation like a personal interview, or a small group discussion (usually 10-12 people maximum). This discussion format can help gather more detailed responses about wellness topics like a previous wellness experience, or even potential modifications or upgrades being considered for a wellness facility (Wisnom & Capozio, 2020).

Natural wellness experiments

A natural wellness experiment can be carried out during a regular course of events, where one change is made to a wellness experience, and the resulting satisfaction is compared to the consistent wellness experience. If the average satisfaction increases or decreases in a significant way, that difference can be attributed to the one experience change. For example, a new type of check-in procedure could be tested, where half the wellness guests randomly get the old procedure, and the other half randomly get the new procedure, and levels of satisfaction can be compared to see which is preferred (Wisnom & Capozio, 2020).

Online reputation management

Because online reviews are so popular, it is essential also to monitor what wellness guests are saying on review sites and social media like TripAdvisor, Yelp, Facebook, Google, and other sites relevant to your business. **Online reputation management** indicates how your organization appears on the internet, both on sites that you control

11

(like your website) and those you do not (like on review sites mentioned above). Consumers rely heavily on online review sites to make decisions, especially when it comes to services, due to their unique features discussed above. It is important to monitor what guests are saying they like and do not like about your offering, to be able to make adjustments as needed.

Using the data and taking actions

One of the most important things to remember is that these insights are only useful as long as they are implemented, monitored, and used to update wellness products and services as needed. Collecting and analyzing data on the quality and performance of wellness programs and offerings should be an ongoing process, and any peaks in positive sentiment or valleys in negative sentiment need to be understood and addressed quickly if possible.

Summary

This chapter discussed the analysis and management of wellness programs in food-service, hospitality, and tourism businesses. First, it introduced the case study of Arctic Bath Hotel and Spa, in Sweden. Then, it described the primary categories of health and wellness programs, looked at specific ways wellness programs and offerings need to be reviewed, and identified some key performance indicators (KPIs) to measure. Finally, it suggested ways to gather and analyze data to improve wellness facilities, programs, and offerings to increase customer and stakeholder satisfaction.

Definition of key terms

Customer satisfaction – "Customers satisfaction refers to customers' overall attitude towards a business, or their emotional reactions to the differences between what they expect and what are served." (Silvestri et al., 2017)

Natural wellness experiment – An experiment carried out during a regular course of events, where one change is made to an experience, and the resulting satisfaction is compared to the consistent experience (Wisnom and Capozio, 2020).

Online reputation management – Indicates how your organization appears on the internet, both on sites that you control (like your website) and those you do not (review sites like Yelp or TripAdvisor).

Product description manual – A list of ingredients and descriptions for every product sold or used in the facility, along with their uses, benefits, and contraindications (Wisnom and Capozio, 2020).

Standard operating procedures – Details of all the policies and procedures to be followed when carrying out any task of the operation, including client interactions (Wisnom and Capozio, 2020).

Treatment protocol manual – Detailed instruction manual for each of the treatments and services offered in a spa, with information on the products used, and the timing and steps for each treatment (Wisnom and Capozio, 2020).

Wellness customer satisfaction survey – Survey that often uses rating scales to understand how happy wellness clients are with an organization's products, services, or experiences (Qualtrics, n.d.).

Wellness value – A reflection of the benefits of spa experience in terms of enhancing physical, mental, and spiritual health (Choi et al., 2015).

Discussion questions

1. What wellness facilities can spas have?
2. What wellness programs and offerings can food businesses and resorts provide for their customers?
3. What steps can be taken to overcome the intangibility, heterogeneity, and perishability of services?
4. How can a wellness facility meet and exceed customer expectations?
5. What types of data gathering and analysis tools are available to wellness facilities, programs, and offerings?

Homework

1. Think about a time when you had a positive wellness experience that was better than you expected it to be. What made it so special?
2. Consider the last bad wellness experience you had, explain what went wrong, and was below your expectations. Using the Service Quality GAP Model, can you identify the gap where the problem (or problems) existed?
3. Find a spa, resort hotel, or a wellness destination and look at their reviews at tripadvisor.com or another social media website. Summarize positive and negative reviews on their wellness facilities, programs, and offerings under different headings and offer specific recommendations on how they can improve their wellness facilities, programs, and offerings.

11

References

Arctic Bath. (2019). Explore Arctic Bath. Retrieved March 26, 2020, from https://arcticbath.se/

Choi, Y. et al. (2015). The role of functional and wellness values in visitors' evaluation of spa experiences. *Asian Pacific Journal of Tourism Research,* 20(3). 263-279. DOI: 10.1080/10941665.2013.877044.

Guo, Y., Denizci Guillet, B., Kucukusta, D., & Law, R. (2016). Segmenting spa customers based on rate fences using conjoint and cluster analyses. *Asia Pacific Journal of Tourism Research*, 21(2), 118-136.

Henderson, K. A. & Bialeschki, D. (1995). *Evaluating Leisure Service: Making Enlightened Decisions*. State College, Pennsylvania: Venture Publishing.

Heskett, J.L., Jones, T.O., Loveman, G.W., Sasser, W.E. & Schlesinger, L.A. (1994). Putting the Service-Profit Chain to Work. *Harvard Business Review, March/April*. 164-174.

Lee, C. F., & King, B. E. (2008). Using the Delphi method to assess the potential of Taiwan's hot springs tourism sector. *International Journal of Tourism Research*, 10(4), 341-352.

Luo, Y., Lanlung, C., Kim, E., Tang, L. & Song, S. (2018) Towards quality of life: the effects of the wellness tourism experience. *Journal of Travel and Tourism Marketing,* 35(4). 410-424. DOI: 10.1080/10548408.2017.1358236.

Medina-Munoz, D.R., and Medina-Munoz, R.D. (2014). The attractiveness of wellness destinations: An importance-performance satisfaction approach. *International Journal of Tourism Research,* 16. 521 – 533. DOI: 10.1002/jtr.1944

Mi, C., Chen, Y., Cheng, C. S., Uwanyirigira, J. L., & Lin, C. T. (2019). Exploring the Determinants of Hot Spring Tourism Customer Satisfaction: Causal Relationships Analysis Using ISM. *Sustainability*, 11(9), 2613.

Mill, R.C. (2011). *Resorts: Management and Operation, 3rd Edition*. Hoboken, New Jersey: John Wiley & Sons.

Parasuraman, A., Zeithaml, V. A., & Berry, L. L. (1985). A conceptual model of service quality and its implications for future research. *Journal of Marketing*, 49(4), 41-50.

Pine, B. J. II & Gilmore, J. H. (1998). Welcome to the Experience Economy. Retrieved March 27, 2020, from hbr.org/1998/07/welcome-to-the-experience-economy

Qualtrics. (n.d.). What are customer satisfaction surveys? Retrieved March 24, 2020, from https://www.qualtrics.com/experience-management/customer/satisfaction-surveys/

Ramani, S. (2018). Well Beyond Spa. Retrieved March 27, 2020, from https://www.organicspamagazine.com/well-beyond-spa/

Rosenberg, M. (2020). Arctic Bath Hotel and Spa, Sweden: Floating Arctic Bath. Retrieved March 26, 2020, from https://www.travelchannel.com/interests/wellness-and-renewal/photos/the-newest-hotel-wellness-offerings

Silvestri, C., Auilani, B., and Ruggieri, A. (2017). Service quality and customer satisfaction in thermal tourism. *TQM Journal, 29*(1). 55-81. DOI: 10.1108/TQM-06-2015-0089.

Singer, J. L. (2009). Spas & Hotels: Compatible, Marketable & Profitable. Retrieved February 12, 2020, from https://www.hospitalitynet.org/opinion/4040816.html

Smith, M., & Puczkó, L. (2008). *Health and Wellness Tourism.* Routledge.

Travel Channel. (2020). Our top 10 hotel wellness offerings. Retrieved March 27, 2020, from https://www.travelchannel.com/interests/wellness-and-renewal/photos/the-newest-hotel-wellness-offerings

Wilson, K. (2019). These 15 wellness programs keep health and fitness goals on track during vacation. Retrieved March 27, 2020, from https://www.goodmorningamerica.com/travel/story/15-wellness-programs-health-fitness-goals-track-vacation-62204379

Wisnom, M. S. & Capozio, L. L. (2020). *Spa Management: An Introduction.* Ann Arbor, Michigan: XanEDU.

World Tourism Organization (WTO) (2007), *A Practical Guide to Tourism Destination Management*, UNWTO, Madrid.

11

12 Management of Health and Wellness Programs for Employees

This chapter discusses the management of health and wellness programs for employees in foodservice, hospitality, and tourism businesses. First, it introduces the case study of the wellness programs and benefits that Rosen Hotels & Resorts offers its employees. Then, it defines health and wellness programs for employees and describes the benefits of these programs to both organizations and employees. Next, it discusses various areas of well-being and gives examples of different employee health and wellness programs. Finally, it describes how to start employee health and wellness programs, how to communicate, measure, and reward program participation, and factors that may affect employee participation in wellness programs.

Learning outcomes

By the end of this chapter, students should be able to do the following:

1. Describe what wellness programs and offerings Rosen Hotels & Resorts provides to its employees.
2. Define health and wellness programs for employees and provide examples of successful programs.
3. Describe the benefits of employee health and wellness programs to both organizations and employees.
4. Name and discuss the various areas of well-being.
5. Give examples of different employee health and wellness programs.
6. Discuss how to start employee health and wellness programs.
7. Describe ways to communicate, measure, and reward health and wellness program participation.
8. Discuss the factors that affect employee participation in wellness programs.

Case study: Rosen Hotels Health and Wellness Program

Harris Rosen, founder of Rosen Hotels and current COO and President, not only believes in a healthy lifestyle but also lives it. Born in 1939, the inspirational icon swims two miles a day and eats a strict and healthy diet. The culture and wellness benefits offered by Rosen Hotels to its employees mirrors this dedication.

The Orlando, FL-based company has an onsite medical center for associates and their families to receive health care like annual exams, basic laboratory work, nutrition program assistance, chiropractic services, and physical therapy. Rosen Medical Center has a complete staff, multilingual services, a state-of-the-art facility, services for students of a local college, occupational medicine, access to specialists, in-house ultrasound and x-ray capabilities, case management, a full gym and fitness center, pharmacy, physical and occupational therapy, and more.

The company even has its self-insured healthcare model, RosenCare®, which saved the company over $340 million between the years 1991 and 2018 (latest data available). The program combats rising healthcare costs by offering comprehensive benefits to its employees while incorporating ongoing wellness programs to maintain improved overall health to reduce costs throughout the system. Employees also benefit from low co-pays, affordable specialists, free (or inexpensive) medications, low premiums, same-day services, paid medical visits, transportation, 24-hour information, and more.

Wellness incentive programs allow employees to earn points to redeem for gym equipment and other gifts. Each month has a health theme, like heart health or walking, and employees are given information and inspiration to participate. Community walks and runs to benefit charities and free weekly fitness classes encourage associates to exercise together outside of work for both intrinsic and extrinsic reasons.

Nutrition services at the Rosen Medical Center include a registered dietician on staff to assist with healthy eating choices and weight loss at no cost to the patient. Weight Watchers programs are easily accessible, as well. Healthy food options are stocked throughout their corporate headquarters and their hotel properties, including in vending machines. All menus at company events are approved by the Rosen Medical Center to be both nutritious and tasty and accommodate various dietary restrictions. The Orlando campus even has a healing garden with a small pond and spacious area where fruits and vegetables are grown, including blueberries, blackberries, raspberries, grapes, mangos, avocados, banana, kumquats, key limes, and citrus.

The benefits of this program are visible from the first year, where healthcare costs per employee were immediately reduced from $2,300 to $875, and the "cost per covered life" as of 2018 was $5,500, roughly half of the nation's $11,000-$12,000 average. Rosen's workers' compensation costs are much less than the average hotel company, and employee turnover is in the teens, compared to an industry average of 70-80%. RosenCare® has won multiple industry and governmental organizations and is often recognized as an excellent example of an employee health and wellness program.

12

Health and wellness programs for employees

Companies of all sizes, in all industries, can offer their employees successful health and wellness programs. In the U.S., approximately half of employers offer wellness initiatives. Larger employers are able to introduce more complex wellness programs to their employees; these programs often include health screening activities and interventions to promote healthy lifestyles. Most employers (72%) view health and wellness programs as a combination of screening activities and interventions. The programs are offered to employees either directly by employers themselves or by third-party vendors. (Mattke et al., 2013).

Employee wellness programs fall under more significant company initiatives like health promotion, which include actions and initiatives to facilitate and encourage healthy eating, exercising and similar actions among employees and managers (Mathis et al., 2019). The goals of these programs can range from quitting smoking, to losing weight, to learning coping strategies to deal with stress. While many health insurance companies offer similar incentives, these are often long-term and more formal; this chapter will focus on how individual organizations can help improve their employees' health (Bean-Mellinger, 2019). Employee health and wellness programs are essential because the workplace is crucial for employees and managers to achieve their health goals and improve their overall health and well-being (Hall et al., 2016). Employees themselves need to be well before they can offer wellness activities to their guests.

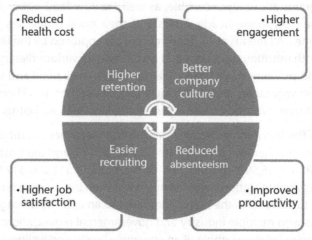

Figure 12.1: Key benefits of employee wellness programs. Adapted from Zojceska (2019)

Defining employee health and wellness

An **employee health and wellness program** is one that helps employees stay healthy, or helps them to improve their health. Such programs can be managed by the internal Human Resources department or similar or can be outsourced to third-party organizations that specialize in this area. Health and wellness programs can be as short as a workshop on meditation, to as long as an ongoing weight-loss or fitness competition. Large companies with a corporate office building may offer an onsite gym for employees to use, and smaller organizations might provide a fully paid or subsidized membership to a local fitness center (Bean-Mellinger, 2019).

Successful companies with good wellness programs

Workplace health is not only a slogan, but also a concept that defines the company culture and helps in guiding employees' path to success. A well-organized wellness program can increase productivity, reduce burnout, and increase overall employee engagement. The following section details companies known for their good wellness programs.

Asana

Silicon Valley-based Asana sells project management software that allows organizations to organize their tasks and employees in many flexible and powerful ways (Asana, 2020). Although Asana is not a wellness product retailer, they offer many health and wellness programs to their employees. Some are on the traditional end of the spectrum, such as a retirement plan and executive coaching, but other perks stretch the normal boundaries. For example, like some other Northern California tech firms, Asana has a company cafeteria with free food for employees; theirs serves healthy breakfasts, lunches, and dinners made from scratch with local and seasonal ingredients. Additional food outlets throughout their campus provide staff with snack options like local kombucha on tap and homemade chips. Daily yoga, free gym memberships, in-house massage and reiki, and an excellent health insurance plan support the concepts of healthy eating and healthy living (Zurer, 2017).

Beyond this nutritious food and exercise, Asana has "nap rooms" where employees can rest, recharge, and de-stress. If more rest is needed, the company gives personnel unlimited paid time off and paid sick leave, four months of paid parental leave, and a six-week paid sabbatical after every three years of employment. When a new employee starts, they are given a $10,000 budget to set up their workspace with whatever furniture and tools work best for them. Workshops on health topics are held consistently, and the company prides itself on its culture of mindfulness and compassion (Zurer, 2017). Due to all these reasons and more, Asana was named one of Inc.'s 2019 Best Workplaces (Inc., 2019), and their headquarters location is rated 4.7 out of 5 stars on Glassdoor.com (2022).

12

Google

Another Silicon-Valley tech firm, Google, is famous for its flexible working programs and employee empowerment. They also have an all-encompassing wellness program within their campus that offers onsite healthcare facilities like fitness centers and community bicycles, and services like physicians, chiropractors, physical therapists, and masseuses. Beyond these physical health benefits, their campus cafes use smaller plates to help with portion control and offer nutritious color-coded meals and snacks to help employees easily make better food choices. For personal improvement, Google supplies its employees with courses on topics like cooking classes, coding degree programs, and guitar lessons, among others. To round out their offerings, Google also has financial wellness resources for its employees, like financial planning services and financial advisors (Martis, 2020).

Zappos

Making wellness more fun is the goal of Zappos' wellness coordinator, Kelly Maher. While this firm offers more traditional health benefits like gym memberships and fitness classes, they also encourage employees to do fun activities during their lunch break. Their main campus has activities like laser tag, basketball, golf, and trampolines to get employees active in ways beyond the typical boring treadmill. In this spirit of fun activities, Zappos also has a program called Recess Tuesdays, where the office plaza is filled with playground toys like tetherball, giving employees easy access to activities that get them moving without feeling like a chore. (Rise, 2019a).

For mental wellness, Zappos offers a program they call *ikigai*, which supports employees in their quest for learning through online courses, shadow sessions, and life coaching opportunities. They also offer paid paternity leave and extended prenatal care and pet adoption fee reimbursement and events. Their Destination Wellness program began in 2017 and encourages employees to undertake challenges like money-saving, mental fitness, and physical fitness exercises; completing these earns points to earn special experiences (Christofferson, 2019).

Benefits of employee health and wellness programs

Because so many companies are offering health and wellness programs to their employees, it is important to be competitive in this area. Competitive programs can help attract and retain good employees who are looking for this benefit and can also improve the company's bottom line. Here are a few ways an investment in employee health and wellness programs pays back:

1. Productivity losses related to personal and family health problems have been estimated (pre-Covid-19) to cost U.S. employers $1,685 per employee per year, or $225.8 billion annually (ODPHP, 2017). Wellness programs can reduce absenteeism, as healthier workers will not need to call in sick as often, therefore reducing the loss in productivity. Healthier workers also lessen the chance of an infected person coming to work and spreading the illness among their co-workers (Bean-Mellinger, 2019).

2. Exercise and mental well-being also contribute to a more positive outlook in general, and increased endorphins (the "feel-good" chemical in the brain), meaning workers are more energetic, positive, and productive (Bean-Mellinger, 2019). Physically active employees are healthier in general, and workplace wellness programs have been proven to assist in ways like improving physical activity, nutritional intake, and reducing body weight, cholesterol levels, and blood pressure (ODPHP, 2017).

3. Health and wellness programs can also help a company save money on health insurance costs and in other areas. One study found that for every dollar invested in wellness activities and programs, employers saved $3.27 in health-care costs (Bean-Mellinger, 2019), and another agreed that the return on investment ranged from $2-$4 per dollar spent on the program. Workplace health programs can reduce the overall sick leave, health insurance, and workers' compensation and disability insurance costs by approximately 25%. Some states also offer tax incentives to encourage small businesses to offer wellness programs (ODPHP, 2017). These combined benefits allow employers to save money, and to pass those savings on to their employees, giving them another incentive to participate in the health and wellness programs offered.

Areas of well-being: physical, emotional, social, and financial

While traditional health and wellness programs have focused on physical health with perks like gym memberships and weight loss, the other areas of well-being cannot be ignored. A person's health combines physical, emotional, social, and financial aspects, and a good employee wellness program incorporates all of these. A well-rounded support function will help improve employee health and reduce employer costs, benefiting both sides.

Physical well-being

As discussed in the examples above and the Rosen Hotels & Resorts case study, there are many things an organization can do to support the physical well-being of its employees. **Physical well-being** is more than the absence of disease; it also includes lifestyle behavior choices to ensure good health and avoid preventable diseases and conditions (AANA, 2020). This is an essential component of health, as a person's physical well-being contributes significantly to their ability to do their job and live a healthy life. Onsite fitness centers, medical facilities, and dining areas with healthy food options are popular ways for large companies to offer health benefits to their employees, but smaller companies can provide similar benefits; this will be discussed in the next section.

12

Emotional well-being

Emotional well-being is the ability to practice stress-management techniques, be resilient, and generate emotions that lead to good feelings (Davis, 2019). This textbook offers many examples of emotional well-being to its readers. Individual travelers with a primary or secondary wellness focus will look for opportunities to improve their mental well-being while they travel, doing activities like visiting beautiful areas of nature, taking meditation or yoga classes, or attending specialized healing or self-improvement retreats. Mindfulness is currently a popular buzzword in emotional well-being; maintaining an in-the-moment focus can help reduce stress by not worrying about the past or the future. More concrete examples of emotional health and wellness programs will be covered in the next section.

Social well-being

Social well-being is the ability to communicate, develop meaningful relationships with others, and maintain a support network that helps overcome loneliness (Davis, 2019). It can include some components also covered under physical and emotional well-being. For example, tobacco and alcohol usage in the form of smoking and drinking are often social activities but also include factors like healthy relationships and making good life choices. A corporate culture of trustworthiness can make employees feel more secure in their work-life; people at high-trust companies report 76% more engagement, 74% less stress, 29% greater life satisfaction, and 13% fewer sick days than those at low-trust companies. Improved connections and working relationships with co-workers also strengthens the working atmosphere and helps efficiency and productivity. When employees feel this support structure at work, they are more able to focus on improving the same areas in their personal lives. (CHC Wellbeing, 2020).

Financial well-being

Like social well-being, financial well-being can be an underlying area of stress for many people. **Financial well-being** is about being in control of day-to-day finances and having the financial freedom to make choices that allow a person to enjoy life (CABA, 2020). When employees are stressed about their finances, it directly impacts their physical, emotional, and social health. Improving financial confidence and, therefore, a person's financial position can be done through educational programs on topics like budgeting, bank accounts, student loans, credit cards, and retirement. When an employee is financially stable and confident, they are more able to focus on other areas of well-being. They, therefore, will be better able to contribute to both their responsibilities and their job (CHC Wellbeing, 2020).

Examples of employee health and wellness programs

There are many different components and ideas that a company can incorporate and mix and match to create their ideal health and wellness program. Here are a few popular examples of things a company can offer its employees (Aldana, 2020; DiNardi, 2020; Rise, 2019b; SHRM, 2012, 2020; SnackNation, 2020; WorkplaceTesting Inc., 2019):

1. *Onsite fitness center.* As mentioned earlier, this is a traditional yet effective way to encourage employees to stay active. Offering them a convenient location to exercise, with opening hours that match their schedule, removes some of the barriers to physical activity. Advanced amenities like fitness classes, swimming pools, rock climbing walls, and access to personal trainers may encourage a higher usage rate. Many companies have a locker room and shower facilities, and some offer paid exercise time, so employees are working out "on the clock." Smaller companies without space or resources to start an onsite fitness center could offer free or reduced-cost passes to a nearby gym, join a local sports league, or participate in 5k fun runs.

2. *Onsite medical and paramedical services.* Rosen Hotels & Resorts and the other examples mentioned throughout this chapter show the growing popularity of onsite medical and paramedical (e.g., massage therapy) services. These facilities offer convenient and cost-effective ways for employees to get the health and wellness services they need.

3. *Smoking cessation programs.* Another traditional, but still necessary, way to improve employee health is to encourage them to quit smoking. Team members who smoke cost their employers more on average in healthcare costs. A multi-faceted approach of coaching and behavioral modifications, incentives and rewards, and pharmaceutical support, when needed, has shown to be effective in reducing smoking rates.

4. *Transit options.* Especially for city-based companies or those with limited parking, offering alternative transportation options for staff can be mutually beneficial. Employees may be encouraged to walk or bike to work, rideshare, or be reimbursed for public transportation costs. On large campuses like Google and Facebook, offering a bike-sharing program has been proven to encourage that mode of transportation over driving from one part of campus to another.

5. *Healthy dining options.* Large companies may incorporate healthy local food options in their onsite dining facilities. Still, even small companies can contribute here by providing healthy options in their vending machines or break rooms.

6. *Employee assistance programs.* For emotional, mental, and social well-being, an employee assistance program can provide support for issues like stress, depression, anxiety, and substance abuse. These plans can take the form of confidential phone counseling, longer-term programs, or more advanced support if needed.

12

7. *Time to relax and recharge.* It is becoming more and more popular for companies (like Asana, mentioned earlier) to offer napping or other recuperation time for employees. Sleeping facilities could be rooms set up for power naps or longer rests during stressful times like a product launch. Or recharging could take a different form, like a peaceful area to take an afternoon walk outside, or a game room to talk strategy over a game of ping pong.

8. *Wellness challenges.* These challenges could focus on goals ranging from a step challenge to drinking more water to meditating every day to losing weight. Employees can opt-in as individuals or teams, and this offers a way for them to reach personal goals, interact with their colleagues, and improve their wellness habits. Challenges can even take the form of a charitable activity like a can drive, gratitude exercises, or random acts of kindness, encouraging social and mental well-being.

9. *Gather and communicate information about healthy options.* Sometimes people are looking for easy ways to improve their health and wellness, but do not know where to start. One low-cost and straightforward way for a company to support their employees in this way is to research and distribute information about local health resources. Periodically publishing a workplace wellness newsletter is a great way to keep this content fresh. For example:

   ■ Compile a list of healthy dining options within a two-mile list of the office as suggestions for lunch destinations.

   ■ Post maps for outdoor walking trails, including distance and energy level required.

   ■ List tips to help reduce back and eye strain while working at a computer.

   ■ Assemble a list of local farmer's markets, farm stands, or community-supported agriculture (CSA) organizations nearby where employees can obtain healthy local food.

   ■ Go a step beyond by organizing CSA share buy-ins or even delivery to the office to make it even easier.

10. *Offer flexible schedules and workspaces.* Encourage employees to maintain a healthy work-life balance by allowing them to work flexible hours and from varied locations like their home, or even co-working spaces at the office. Also, encourage them to use their vacation time and even offer opportunities to volunteer for a cause of their choice while getting paid. Standing desks can be a great way to keep employees moving even while in their office working, and plants liven up an office and help improve air quality.

11. *Give employees autonomy.* Take a cue from luxury hotel chain Ritz-Carlton, which allows their team members to spend up to $2,000 per guest to resolve customer issues. Rather than having to go through layers of management for approval, which takes time and leads to reduced guest happiness, the employee is empowered to resolve a problem themselves immediately. This leads to not only increased guest satisfaction but also improves employee satisfaction with

their job and overall better performance. As one Ritz Carlton employee said, "the hotel leadership tells me what they expect of me, but they let me create what I need to for the guest. I am not told what to do; I can figure that out for myself," (Michelli, 2008). That level of autonomy leads to less stress in the workplace, and higher levels of employee satisfaction.

12. *Offer onsite health events.* Even without a medical center, companies can still organize a small health fair or other events with health screenings. A health fair is a "workplace event that features educational activities related to a variety of health issues" (WorkplaceTesting Inc., 2019). It can be extended to a **health and wellness fair** by considering non-physical issues as well. Features could include risk assessments for things like high blood pressure, education on topics like nutrition, or smoking cessation. Optional vaccinations could also be offered as a convenient way to receive a flu shot or other recommended inoculation. Holistic health components can also be included, like chair massages and other vendors that offer alternative medicines like acupuncture, acupressure, or reiki. Local gyms, spas, emergency medical services, and restaurants may also be interested in participating. Workshops could be offered on topics like feng shui, reflexology, meditation and mindfulness, and more (Episcopal Church Medical Trust, 2011). Keep the content educational and interactive, and try incorporating raffles, demonstrations, and other fun activities. Promoting the event is essential to increasing attendance; try voicemail message reminders, table tents in shared spaces, emails, announcements at company meetings, intranet posters, flyers throughout the premises, etc. (Moda Health, 2020).

13. *Encourage small changes.* Wellness programs do not have to be large and costly events; they can be as small as encouraging employees to take the stairs, maybe starting a competition or offering a self-tracking mechanism. Facilitate a healthy potluck lunch and recipe exchange, create a healthy office cookbook, bring in a chef to teach an easy cooking class, or coordinate a "healthy snack of the month" club. Encourage staff (including upper management) to hold walking meetings outside and offer coordinated stretch break times throughout the day. Even a step challenge among office workers can help bring small changes to employees' lives.

Adapted from: Rise, 2019b; Aldana, 2020; DiNardi, 2020; SHRM, 2012, 2020; SnackNation, 2020; WorkplaceTesting Inc., 2019.

All of these are potential programs that companies of all sizes could consider. They can be modified to fit each organization's needs and resources. Techniques and suggestions for starting, communicating, measuring, and rewarding programs such as these are discussed in the following sections.

12

How to start employee health and wellness programs

Employee health and wellness initiatives can vary in scope from a single hour-long workshop taught by an in-house expert to a multi-year overarching plan. Although the programs vary greatly, the necessary steps for planning and implementing generally remain the same. Setting a well-being strategy takes multiple steps (CHC Wellbeing, 2020; Bean-Mellinger, 2019; SHRM, 2020).

1. *Conduct Assessments.* As with any program, a baseline measurement must be taken to understand the current situation. This sets a benchmark to measure future results against. It also allows a company to identify its current biggest weaknesses and strategic areas to focus on first. Here are a few examples of the types of assessments that may be appropriate:

    a. Survey employees to evaluate their wellness interests and needs

    b. Conduct a health risk assessment

    c. Conduct an organizational assessment to determine which types of programs would be appropriate to offer

    d. Review group health plan utilization rates, both medical and pharmaceutical

    e. Evaluate health culture and conduct environmental audits of the workplace in general

2. *Obtain Management Support.* This is an essential step for any successful wellness program. Management needs to not only approve the costs but a lso to lead by example and participate in the program themselves. Consider the following questions in this step:

    a. What are the organization's short- and long-term strategic priorities?

    b. What benefits can be expected from the wellness initiative, and what is the potential value to the organization?

    c. What are the leadership styles, pressures, strengths, and weaknesses of the organization's senior-level executives?

3. *Strategize.* Based on the assessment from step one, set a long-term plan to reach the program's goals. The length of this plan can range in time, but benchmarking points should be placed along the way to measure progress. A few things to consider in this step include:

    a. Does a committee need to be established to oversee the program's progress?

    b. What are the goals and objectives of the program? Broad goals could be to reduce healthcare costs or reduce absenteeism. Specific objectives need to be measurable and time-limited to make it easy to determine if they have been achieved. For example, reduce the number of employees who smoke by five percent in this fiscal year.

    c. What is the budget for this program? How much can the company afford to spend right now, and what is the anticipated return on that investment?

Does the program need to be outsourced to a third party to do it right, or could a few motivated and organized employees that are passionate about that wellness topic take control?

4. *Design Program Components.* It is essential to include a variety of components that target risk behaviors and the needs and interests of the employees. Do employees need health risk assessments or screenings? Would they benefit from nutrition education or smoking cessation programs? It is important to note that programs are subject to some legal and compliance issues like prohibiting discrimination, HIPAA privacy law concerns, and fairness to all types of employees. Lastly, in this step, wellness program incentives and rewards need to be determined; this will be discussed more in the next section.

5. *Engage and Communicate.* Communicate the program's benefits and goals to the potential participants, and motivate them to join in. Surround employees with tools for improving their overall well-being and the focused strategic areas. This will be discussed more in the next section.

6. *Measure and Evaluate.* As with any program, it is essential to evaluate the effectiveness of the wellness program on an ongoing basis. This can be through wellness program evaluation tools like HERO Scorecard or WELCOA's 7 Benchmarks or informally at the organization level (Cheon et al., 2020). This will be discussed more in the next section.

Companies seeking to implement employee health and wellness programs may encounter some challenges. For physical fitness activities, some employees may not feel comfortable wearing exercise clothing or performing exercise moves around others, especially when they are just starting. Others may not join in if they have small children at home or other commitments that prevent them from spending more time on work activities. Or sometimes they just are not interested in the programs being offered.

To overcome these challenges, ask employees what would benefit them the most and fit best into their lifestyle. Solutions may include providing a variety of program options for all fitness levels and through various channels (e.g., give employees links to online classes that they can do at home when they have time), making sure social support is available when needed, offering appropriate and valued motivating incentives, and making it part of the overall company culture (BurnAlong, n.d.).

Communicating, measuring and rewarding achievements

When it comes to communicating a wellness plan, it needs to be done with a clear and concise message (Figure 12.2). It should include the reason for the plan, the responsibilities of the organization and the employee, and the rewards and incentives available. Communicating a specific program should also be part of a broader social culture where health and wellness are valued. This might include an attention-generating program rollout, logos and slogans, visible promotion by upper management, sustaining and repeating the message and program over several years, and communicating through multiple channels. (SHRM, 2020).

12

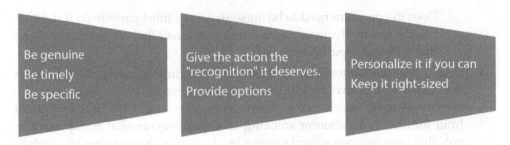

Figure 12.2: Guidelines for recognition. Adapted from Harvard (2020)

At pre-determined points along the way, measure the progress of the wellness program. This may include a weigh-in for a weight loss competition, a survey of financial health taken after a workshop has been offered, etc. Adjust the program if needed to reach the goals set. Also, be sure to ask for employee feedback – what do they think of the program? What improvements would they suggest? Sample metrics include participation rates, program completion rates, reduction in health care costs, and percentage of employees who stopped smoking or lost weight. Employers may also want to measure the return on investment (ROI).

Rather than the traditional approach of using incentives like a single lump-sum amount for a single action (e.g., completing a health screening), ongoing rewards programs are the more popular way to maintain employee engagement. Strategic ongoing programs reward participants over time, encouraging loyalty, and creating long-term healthy habits rather than one-time actions. Consistently doing actions over time builds and establishes the habit, making it a way of life. Some questions to consider while developing a reward system for achievements include (CHC Wellbeing, 2020):

- What are the rewards being used?
- How frequently are rewards granted?
- How much value does each reward carry?
- What mix of activities and/or outcomes are being rewarded, and why?
- How are rewards verified to confirm specific behaviors and actions have occurred?

All of the programs discussed in this chapter can help employees reach their true potential, both at work and in their personal lives, which are closely related when it comes to health and wellness. This can result in thriving, contributing, learning, and connecting individuals, lower healthcare costs and increased productivity, and a culture built on trust where people do their best work. Reaching one's true potential is about establishing a fresh perspective, shaping a trustworthy culture, nurturing healthy habits, and overall living their best life.

Factors affecting employee participation

As mentioned previously, employee wellness programs can reduce employee absenteeism as well as decrease health insurance expenses, increase employee productivity, employee satisfaction, and reduce turnover. But several things may affect employee participation in such programs. These include (Fink et al., 2020):

- "Employee perception of the value of employee wellness programs."
- "Employer's role in employee wellness and employee's responsibility for their own wellness."
- "Commitment of the CEO, senior leaders, and company leaders to employee wellness."
- "Employer offered resources for maintaining wellness."
- "Support for achieving wellness goals."
- "Incentives for participating in programs."

Other demographic factors like race or ethnicity and income level can make employees not want to participate in employee wellness programs because of "healthcare cost-shifting." Hall et al. found in a 2016 study that employees would be motivated to participate in wellness programs if they were compensated for their time participating in the program, i.e., paid to work out or paid to attend seminars. Knowing these factors and characteristics of employees can help employers create programs that better fit the needs of their employees, so it is important to keep these things in mind when crafting an employee wellness program (Hall et al., 2016).

Summary

This chapter discussed the management of health and wellness programs for employees in foodservice, hospitality, and tourism businesses. First, it introduced the case study of the wellness programs and benefits that Rosen Hotels & Resorts offers its employees. Then it defined health and wellness programs for employees and described the benefits of these programs to both organizations and employees. It discussed various areas of well-being and gave examples of different employee health and wellness programs, and finally described how to start employee health and wellness programs, how to communicate, measure, and reward program participation, and what may influence an employee's decision of whether or not to participate in an employee wellness program.

Definition of key terms

Emotional well-being – The ability to practice stress-management techniques, be resilient, and generate the emotions that lead to good feelings (Davis, 2019).

Employee health and wellness program – A program that helps employees stay healthy, or helps them to improve their health (Bean-Mellinger, 2019).

Financial well-being – Being in control of day-to-day finances and having the financial freedom to make choices that allow a person to enjoy life (CABA, 2020).

12

Health promotion – Supportive approach to facilitating and encouraging healthy actions and lifestyles among employees (Mathis et al., 2019).

Health and wellness fair – A workplace event that offers educational and training activities and materials about physical and non-physical health and wellness issues.

Physical well-being – More than the absence of disease; it also includes lifestyle behavior choices to ensure good health and avoid preventable diseases and conditions (AANA, 2020).

Social well-being – The ability to communicate, develop meaningful relationships with others, and maintain a support network that helps overcome loneliness (Davis, 2019).

Discussion questions

1. How are health and wellness programs for employees defined?
2. Describe the benefits of employee health and wellness programs to both organizations and employees.
3. What are some examples of successful health and wellness programs?
4. What are the benefits of employee health and wellness programs to both organizations and employees?
5. What are the four areas of well-being?
6. Discuss how to start employee health and wellness programs.
7. Describe ways to communicate, measure, and reward health and wellness program participation.
8. Why would employees decide not to participate in employee wellness programs?

Homework

1. Find an example of a company with a good employee wellness program online, preferably from the hospitality and tourism industry that was not mentioned in this chapter. What do they offer to their employees in terms of health and wellness? What do you particularly like about their health and wellness program? How can they further improve their program?
2. Find an example of an employee wellness program online (that was not mentioned in this chapter) and describe how you would communicate the program to employees. How do you think this organization measures the results and incentivizes participants?
3. Consider the four areas of well-being in your own life. Rank them in order from strongest to weakest and discuss why and how you could improve.

References

AANA. (2020). Physical well-being. Retrieved April 4, 2020, from https://www.aana.com/practice/health-and-wellness-peer-assistance/about-health-wellness/physical-well-being

Aldana, S. (2020). 17 employee wellness program ideas and tips to transform your workplace. Retrieved April 4, 2020, from https://www.wellsteps.com/blog/2020/01/02/employee-wellness-program-ideas/

Asana. (2020). Why Asana? Retrieved March 30, 2020, from asana.com/company

Bean-Mellinger, B. (2019). What is an employee wellness program? Retrieved March 31, 2020, from https://smallbusiness.chron.com/employee-wellness-program-1349.html

BurnAlong. (n.d.). Learn from the best: 5 ways to create a corporate wellness program that engages all employees. https://www.burnalong.com/

CABA. (2020). What is financial well-being? Retrieved April 4, 2020, from https://www.caba.org.uk/help-and-guides/information/what-financial-well-being

CHC Wellbeing. (2020). The roadmap to true potential. Retrieved April 1, 2020, from https://www.chcw.com/media/1320/chc_whitepaper_2018.pdf

Cheon, O., Naufal, G., & Kash, B. (2020). When workplace wellness programs work: Lessons learned from a large employer in Texas. *Journal of Health Education,* 51(1). 31-39. DOI: 10.1080/19325037.2019.1687366.

Christofferson, T. (2019). Wellness benefits that keep Zapponians happy And healthy. Retrieved March 31, 2020, from https://www.zappos.com/about/stories/employee-wellness-benefits

Davis, T. (2019). What is well-being? definition, types, and well-being skills. Retrieved April 4, 2020, from www.psychologytoday.com/us/blog/click-here-happiness/201901/what-is-well-being-definition-types-and-well-being-skills

DiNardi, G. (2020). 11 employee wellness programs that work. Retrieved April 4, 2020, from www.cultureamp.com/blog/11-employee-wellness-programs-that-work

Episcopal Church Medical Trust. (2011). Health & wellness fair planning guide. Retrieved April 4, 2020, from https://www.episcopalhealthministries.org/files/resources_attachments/health-fair.pdf

Fink, J., Zabawa, B. & Chopp, S. (2020). Employee perceptions of wellness programs and incentives. *American Journal of Health Promotion,* 34(3). 257-260. DOI: 10.1177/0890117119887687.

Glassdoor.com. (2020). Working at Asana. Retrieved March 30, 2020, from https://www.glassdoor.com/Overview/Working-at-Asana-EI_IE567443.11,16.htm

Hall, J.L., Kelly, K., Burmeister, L. & Merchant, J. (2016). Workforce characteristics and attitudes regarding participation in worksite wellness programs. *American Journal of Health Promotion,* 3(5), DOI: 10.44278/ajhp.140613-QUAN-283.

12

Harvard (2020) Recognizing and rewarding your staff, Human Resource Department. https://hr.fas.harvard.edu/recognition

Inc. (2019). The 346 best places to work in 2019. Retrieved March 30, 2020, from https://www.inc.com/best-workplaces-2019.html

Martis, L. (2020). 7 companies with epic wellness programs. Retrieved March 31, 2020, from https://www.monster.com/career-advice/article/companies-good-wellness-programs

Mathis, R.L. et al. (2019). *Human Resource Management*. Cengage.

Mattke, S., Liu, H., Caloyeras, J., Huang, C. Y., Van Busum, K. R., Khodyakov, D., & Shier, V. (2013). Workplace wellness programs study. *Rand Health Quarterly*, 3(2).

Michelli, J.A. (2008). *The New Gold Standard: 5 leadership principles for creating a legendary customer experience courtesy of the Ritz Carlton Hotel*. McGraw Hill.

Moda Health. (2020). Wellness and health fair planning guide. Retrieved April 4, 2020, from https://www.modahealth.com/pdfs/wellness/health_fair_planning_guide.pdf

National Institute of Health (2021) 6 strategies for improving your emotional health. https://www.nih.gov/health-information/emotional-wellness-toolkit

ODPHP. (2017). Five reasons employee wellness is worth the investment. Retrieved March 31, 2020, from https://health.gov/news-archive/blog/2017/05/five-reasons-employee-wellness-is-worth-the-investment/index.html

Rise. (2019a). List of companies with wellness programs: 10 amazing workplaces. Retrieved March 31, 2020, from https://risepeople.com/blog/10-companies-with-amazing-workplace-wellness-programs/

Rise. (2019b). 10 great examples of workplace wellness programs. Retrieved April 4, 2020, from https://risepeople.com/blog/workplace-wellness-programs/

Rosen Hotels & Resorts. (2020). About us: Health & wellness. Retrieved April 2, 2020, from https://www.rosenhotels.com/about-us/health-wellness/

Rosen Hotels & Resorts. (2018). Rosen Hotels & Resorts Associate Healthcare Program fact sheet. Retrieved April 2, 2020, from https://www.rosencare.com/wp-content/uploads/ROSEN_MedicalCenterFactSheet_6-12-18.pdf

SHRM. (2012). Promoting employee well-being: wellness strategies to improve health, performance and the bottom line. Retrieved April 4, 2020, from https://www.shrm.org/foundation/ourwork/initiatives/the-aging-workforce/Documents/Promoting%20Employee%20Well-Being.pdf

SHRM. (2020). How to establish and design a wellness program. Retrieved April 4, 2020, from https://www.shrm.org/resourcesandtools/tools-and-samples/how-to-guides/pages/howtoestablishanddesignawellnessprogram.aspx

SnackNation. (2020). 121 employee wellness program ideas for your office. Retrieved April 4, 2020, from https://snacknation.com/blog/employee-wellness-program-ideas/

WorkplaceTesting Inc. (2019). Health fair. Retrieved April 4, 2020, from https://www.workplacetesting.com/definition/986/health-fair

Zojceska, A. (2019). 8 Key benefits of employee wellness programs. www.talentlyft.com/en/blog/article/273/8-key-benefits-of-employee-wellness-programs

Zurer, R. (2017). How Asana designs its successful, authentic company culture. Retrieved March 30, 2020, from https://consciouscompanymedia.com/workplace-culture/developing-talent/asana-designs-successful-authentic-company-culture/

12

13 Wellness Management during Crises and Pandemics

The Covid-19 pandemic that began in early 2020 changed the world. With over 532 million reported cases and 6.3 million reported deaths (the actual numbers are likely much higher) as of June 2022 (WHO, 2022a), people around the globe felt isolated by forced quarantining and social distancing, yet united by fear of the disease and the unknown. This chapter opens with a case study of G Adventures' Wellness Tours, then defines relevant terms around a crisis and pandemic, outlines the phases of a crisis, and discusses wellness management during times of crisis.

Learning outcomes

By the end of this chapter, students should be able to do the following:

1. Discuss G Adventures' Wellness Tours and how they encourage all kinds of wellness.
2. Define a crisis and a pandemic, and the phases of a crisis.
3. Understand complications and concerns in travel's recovery from a pandemic.
4. Describe the physical, emotional, occupational, intellectual, and spiritual components of wellness.
5. Discuss the future of the wellness economy

Case study: G Adventures' Wellness Tours

In 2018, adventure tour operator G Adventures introduced Wellness Tours. Although they were paused during the Covid-19 pandemic along with most other travel around the world, as of June 2022 Wellness Tours are planned in Iceland, Bali, and Costa Rica (G Adventures, 2022a). One important effect of the Covid-19 crisis is the emphasis on a broad definition of wellness—it's not only about being physically healthy, but also includes emotional, spiritual, social, occupational, and intellectual health (this chapter will go into more details about each of those categories), and G Adventures' Wellness Tours include components of each.

G Adventures' 2022 Wellness Tours range in price from $1,349 USD for 9 days in Bali to $2,719 for 7 days in Iceland (not including flights). All are small group tours, meaning an average of 12 people and a maximum of 16 people, and they require all travelers to be fully vaccinated against Covid-19. The physical intensity ratings range from 2 (light) to 3 (average), meaning the itineraries have some light hiking, biking, rafting, or kayaking, but nothing too strenuous. The Wellness Tours are in an upgraded service level category, meaning they include higher-level accommodations, private transportation, and elevated meals.

Each tour incorporates elements from various aspects of wellness, not only physical activity. In Costa Rica, guests can practice yoga overlooking the Arenal Volcano, visit hot springs and take mud baths, enjoy healthy local food experiences, visit the Mi Cafecito Community Coffee Plantation and a G for Good project supporting 200 local farmers, try paddleboard yoga and surfing, enjoy extended meditation periods, and more (G Adventures, 2022b). These activities are specially designed to encourage not only physical movement, but also emotional and spiritual growth and practice. Connecting to local communities through experiences like the Community Coffee Plantation visit and project, and facilitating interactions among guests in a small tour encourage social wellness. The actual act of taking a vacation aids in occupational wellness by encouraging work-life balance, and intellectual wellness is gained through learning about other cultures and taking in new experiences.

Discussion questions

1. Who are G Adventures' target market segment(s) for their Wellness Tours?
2. What other activities could G Adventures include in their Wellness Tours?
3. What impacts (positive and negative) do these Wellness Tours have on the local communities hosting visitors from these groups? Could G Adventures do anything to mitigate the negative impacts?

13

Definitions of crisis and pandemic

As of 2022, the world is still recovering from the effects of the Covid-19 (or Coronavirus) pandemic, and it is possible that more crises affecting wellness in tourism and hospitality will occur in the future. This section will discuss the definitions of a crisis and pandemic, and the following sections will look at the phases of a crisis, and management of all facets of wellness during these times.

Description of a crisis

A **crisis** as it relates to wellness in tourism and hospitality can be defined as "a condition of instability or danger, as in social, economic, political, or international affairs, leading to a decisive change" (Dictionary.com, 2022a). Covid-19 certainly falls in this category, as it has the potential to dangerously affect every person in the world. This caused global instability and an almost complete standstill in travel for months during 2020 and 2021, to try to avoid the spread of the virus with so many unknown attributes and effects. As of mid-2022 the decisive change has primarily been to require and document vaccinations as much as possible (although the challenges of this will be discussed later in the chapter), and to encourage more socially distanced travel.

Description of a pandemic

A **pandemic** is a type of crisis, generally related to health, defined as "a disease prevalent throughout an entire country, continent, or the whole world" (Dictionary.com, 2022b). Covid-19 meets this definition precisely, with cases being reported in every country around the world (BBC, 2022).

Phases of a crisis

While there are multiple frameworks and ways to divide a crisis into stages, some are very simplistic (e.g., pre-crisis, during crisis, post-crisis), and others do not align well with the topic of wellness in tourism and hospitality. Therefore, for the purposes of this book, Mitroff's five-stage model for crisis management (see Figure 13.1) will be discussed in more detail, the phases being: (1) signal detection, pursue to detect threatening signs and search for preventative actions; (2) probing and prevention, work on initiating to eliminate/limit threatening factors; (3) acute/crises/damage containment, after crisis occurs, actions are taken to limit its spread and its negative impacts; (4) recovery, efforts to return to normal operations; and (5) learning, reviewing all crisis management efforts including its causes and learn from the process. (Mitroff, 1994).

Figure 13.1: Mitroff's five-stage model for crisis management. Adapted from Mitroff, I. I. (1994)

Phases of the Covid-19 pandemic

Mitroff's framework can be applied to the Covid-19 pandemic and its effects on wellness in tourism and hospitality (Centers for Disease Control & Prevention, 2022):

1. December 2019: Signal Detection:
   a) December 12, 2019: A group of people in Wuhan, China began to experience shortness of breath and fever.
   b) December 31, 2019: The World Health Organization (WHO) was informed of a number of cases of pneumonia with an unknown cause.
2. January 2020: Probing and Prevention:
   a) January 2, 2020: The WHO activated its incident management system across the three levels of WHO (country office, regional office, and headquarters).
   b) January 5, 2020: CDC's National Center for Immunization and Respiratory Diseases (NCIRD) activates a Center Level Response for novel pneumonia of unknown cause.
   c) January 7, 2020: CDC establishes a 2019-nCoV Incident Management Structure to guide the response. It follows previously established MERS-CoV preparedness plans for developing tests and managing cases.
   d) January 13 & 15, 2020: The first cases are reported in Thailand and Japan, respectively.
   e) January 17, 2020: CDC begins screening passengers on direct and connecting flights from Wuhan, China at San Francisco, New York City, and Los Angeles, and plans to expand screening to other major airports. CDC deploys a team to Washington state to assist with contact tracing efforts in response to the first reported case of 2019-nCOV in the U.S. (confirmed through laboratory testing on January 20).
   f) January 21, 2020: CDC transitions from a Center-led Incident Management Structure to an Agency-wide Structure and activates its Emergency Response System.
   g) January 22, 2020: The WHO confirms human-to-human spread of the novel coronavirus. The WHO International Health Regulation Emergency Committee meets and decides to not declare the novel coronavirus a Public Health Emergency of International Concern, instead to monitor the situation and reconvene in 10 days to re-discuss.
   h) January 27, 2020: The United States Food and Drug Administration (FDA) announces that it will take "critical actions to advance development of novel coronavirus medical countermeasures" with interagency partners, including CDC.
   i) January 29, 2020: The White House Coronavirus Task Force is established with U.S. Health and Human Services Secretary, Alex Azar, as the head of the Task Force.

13

j) January 31, 2020: Alex Azar declares the SARS-CoV-2 virus a public health emergency and the White House 2019 Novel Coronavirus Task Force announces the implementation of new travel policies to be effective February 2, 2020. The WHO International Health Regulation Emergency Committee reconvenes and declares the coronavirus outbreak a Public Health Emergency of International Concern.

3. February 2020-December 2021: Damage Containment (Centers for Disease Control & Prevention, 2022; WHO, 2022b)

a) February 2020: The U.S. FDA approves the Emergency Use Authorization (EUA) PACK for the CDC developed SARS-CoV-2 diagnostic test. The WHO announces the official name for the disease that is causing the outbreak: Covid-19 (an abbreviated version of 'coronavirus disease 2019').

b) February 26, 2020: CDC's Dr. Nancy Messonnier, Incident Manager for the Covid-19 Response, holds a telebriefing. During the telebriefing she braces the U.S. for the eventual community spread of the novel coronavirus and states that the "disruption to everyday life may be severe."

c) March 11, 2020: The WHO declares Covid-19 a pandemic.

d) March 13, 2020: U.S. President Donald J. Trump declares a nationwide emergency.

e) March 14, 2020: CDC issues a "No Sail Order" to all cruise ships. The order calls for all cruise ships in waters that the U.S. has jurisdiction over to cease activity.

f) March 15, 2020: U.S. states begin to shut down to prevent the spread of Covid-19.

g) March 17, 2020: First human trial of a vaccine to protect against pandemic Covid-19 begins in the U.S. at Kaiser Permanente research facility in Seattle, Washington.

h) April 3, 2020: At a White House press briefing, CDC announces new mask wearing guidelines and recommends that all people wear a mask when outside of the home.

i) April 13, 2020: Most U.S. states report widespread cases of Covid-19.

j) May 2, 2020: World Health Organization renews its emergency declaration from three months prior calling the pandemic a global health crisis.

k) May 9, 2020: U.S. unemployment rate at 14.7%, the worst rate since the Great Depression. With 20.5 million people out of work, hospitality, leisure, and healthcare industries taking the greatest hits.

l) June 25, 2020: CDC expands list of people at risk for severe Covid-19 illness by removing the specific age threshold from the older adult classification, noting that risk increases with age. CDC also includes people with chronic kidney disease, COPD, obesity, immuncompromised from solid organ transplant, serious heart conditions, sickle cell disease, and type 2 diabetes are also at increased risk of severe Covid-19 illness.

m) December 11, 2020: Food and Drug Administration issues an Emergency Use Authorization (EUA) for the first Covid-19 vaccine – the Pfizer-BioNTech Covid-19 vaccine.

n) December 18, 2020: The U.S. Food and Drug Administration issues an Emergency Use Authorization for the second Covid-19 vaccine – the Moderna Covid-19 vaccine.

o) December 30, 2020: AstraZenica and University of Oxford's vaccine approved for emergency use in the UK and will begin distribution in the New Year.

p) January 27, 2021: Worldwide Covid-19 cases surpass 100 million.

q) February 27, 2021: FDA approves emergency use authorization for Johnson and Johnson one shot Covid-19 vaccine.

r) March 13, 2021: U.S. surpasses 100 million vaccinations administered.

s) April 2, 2021: CDC announces fully vaccinated individuals can travel safely domestically in the U.S. without a Covid test first.

t) August 18, 2021: CDC announces a new center, the Center for Forecasting and Outbreak Analytics, to improve the U.S. government's ability to forecast and model emerging health threats, such as pandemics.

u) October 7, 2021: WHO launched the 'Strategy to Achieve Global Covid-19 Vaccination by mid-2022', which outlines a plan for achieving WHO's targets to vaccinate 40% of the population of every country by the end of 2021 and 70% by mid-2022.

v) November and December, 2021: WHO continues to issue emergency use listings for Covid-19 vaccines to increase availability around the world.

4. January 2022-Current: Recovery

a) As of June 2022, the world is still in the recovery phase from the Covid-19 pandemic. Although domestic and international tourist arrivals are improving over 2020 and 2021 numbers, they are still drastically down from 2019's pre-pandemic arrivals (UNWTO, 2022a). Europe and North America are recovering the strongest, likely due to high vaccination rates and health precautions (UNWTO, 2022b). More about this will be discussed later in this section.

5. Forthcoming: Learning

a) As of June 2022, it is yet to be seen how the world will learn from the unprecedented Covid-19 pandemic. While the WHO remained the leading guide and information center, each country, state, and local area set their own specific rules. Although vaccines were developed quite quickly, there were many flaws in the distribution process. Testing and reporting processes were not well-defined, and treatment recommendations also varied greatly. Overall the long-term effects of Covid-19 on the health of people, the economy, and tourism remain to be seen.

13

Complications and concerns in travel's recovery

Although the tourism industry (including wellness tourism) is in the recovery process as of June 2022, many complications remain. One of the primary concerns is vaccine inequity. While vaccines are readily available in most high-income countries, low-income countries are having a more difficult time obtaining access: as of June 10, 2022, 66.3% of the world population has received at least one dose of a Covid-19 vaccine, but only 17.8% of people in low-income countries have received at least one dose (Our World in Data, 2022). This means traveling to low-income countries can expose their unvaccinated populations to Covid-19, putting them at a very high risk, especially due to the lower quality of medical testing and treatment available. For example, as of June 10, 2022, 99% of the population of the United Arab Emirates (UAE) had received at least one dose of a Covid-19 vaccine, but only 1.6% of the population of Haiti had received at least one dose (only 1.15% were fully vaccinated).

As mentioned in previous chapters, overtourism is also a risk. Although the standstill in travel during the Covid-19 pandemic gave destinations a chance to reassess their tourism policies, many places are desperate to have tourism dollars return, leading them to be less strict than before. Tourists are also looking for more rural and remote areas that allow for better social distancing, which will bring people away from cities and into regions that may not have the infrastructure, capacity, or desire to receive multitudes of tourists. These are the areas that have traditionally been havens for travelers looking for wellness solutions, and now they may be overrun by mass tourists. The next section of this chapter discusses how individuals can manage and support their own wellness and others' wellness during and after a pandemic.

Wellness management during and after a pandemic

The Covid-19 pandemic led to many changes in perspective, priorities, and practice. The need for lockdowns, quarantines, and social distancing meant many workplaces and personal activities shifted from face-to-face to virtual. Technology became even more important to daily life, with tools like video communication moving from occasional to commonplace. Related to wellness, in-person exercise classes moved online with consumers purchasing in-home fitness equipment, at-home beauty care became more popular instead of going to spas, and demand for mental wellness tools increased sharply (Global Wellness Institute, 2021). Thinking of wellness as separate components of physical, emotional, occupational, intellectual, and spiritual can be helpful to ensure hospitality and tourism programs are including all aspects.

Managing physical wellness during a crisis and pandemic

Physical wellness consists of "recognizing the need for physical activity, healthy foods, and sleep, as well as preventing illness and injury or managing chronic health conditions" (Northwestern University, 2022a). Although physical wellness encompasses the more salient components of exercising and diet, it also involves managing medical issues and chronic health conditions, food insecurity, tension or conflict with household members possibly leading to domestic violence, and more. Pandemics and crises, particularly those involving isolation and lockdowns, can exacerbate existing conditions and even lead to new problems that did not exist before (Harvard, 2022).

To maintain physical wellness, individuals can follow these suggestions (Harvard, 2022; Missouri Western State University, 2022):

- Understand how and why your body works
- Feel comfortable with your physical appearance
- Make informed choices about your body and sexuality
- Feel competent at physical activities
- Develop well-balanced and healthy eating habits
- Become a responsible drinker or a non-drinker
- Become aware of how a lack of sleep, stress, and non-activity affect your body
- Become aware of how food, beverages, drugs, chemicals, additives, and caffeine affect your body
- Engage in regular movement to improve flexibility, strength, aerobic, and cardiovascular health
- Develop and cultivate leisure activities
- Seek medical care when needed for illness, injury and preventative care.

All of these techniques can benefit your physical health, which is an essential foundation for creating and maintaining health in other areas of life.

Managing emotional wellness during a crisis and pandemic

As defined by the National Institutes of Health (NIH, 2021), **emotional wellness** is "the ability to successfully handle life's stresses and adapt to change and difficult times." This is especially challenging during a crisis or pandemic—during Covid-19, routines have been interrupted, people have been isolated from friends and family, and worries abound. Not taking care of emotional wellness can lead to feelings of panic, overwhelm, sadness, anger, frustration, hopelessness, and many other negative emotions. Underlying emotional concerns can cause difficulty with sleep, appetite, concentration, physical illness, strained relationships, and thoughts of self-harm (Sanford Center for Aging, n.d.).

Recent studies conducted in different occupational groups revealed varying rates of depression and stress. For example, burnout and acute stress rates are higher among healthcare providers who care for Covid-19 patients than those who do not, and that Covid-19 frontline healthcare providers are at higher risk for common psychological disorders, including depression (Jaconia et al., 2022). Unemployed individuals, women and younger workers were more negatively affected by the crisis during the pandemic (Chen, 2020). Therefore, especially in the travel industry, tourism and hospitality services should provide information on barrier mechanisms to reconcile anxiety and rumination during any crisis, providing a new perspective to view travel-related

13

health, wellness and well-being threats (Yang & Wong, 2020). Studies have also found that the primary factors determining an individual's loyalty and revisit intention in tourism activities are the restorative environment and wellness experiences, which contribute to positive emotions and life satisfaction (Backman et al., 2022).

The NIH (2021) recommends six strategies to improve emotional health:

1. Develop ways to brighten your outlook
2. Identify healthy ways to cope with stress
3. Get quality sleep
4. Learn to cope with grief and loss
5. Strengthen social connections
6. Practice mindfulness to live more in the present

A daily routine and check-in on your emotions can help implement and monitor the strategies listed above. It is also important to make time for rest, engage in healthy activities, stay connected to friends and family, and reframe thoughts to look at the positive side of things (Sanford Center for Aging, n.d.). Setting limits on media consumption (e.g., social media and news) and looking for accurate health information from reputable sources can help reduce stress around things outside of your control (National Suicide Prevention Lifeline, 2022). Many more resources for emotional wellness can be found online.

Managing occupational wellness during a crisis and pandemic

Occupational wellness is "the ability to achieve a balance between work and leisure in a way that promotes health, a sense of personal satisfaction and is (for most people) financially rewarding" (University of Nebraska Omaha, n.d.). This balance involves the following (Washington State University, n.d.a):

- Engaging in motivating and interesting work
- Understanding how to balance your work with leisure time
- Working in a way that fits into your personal learning style
- Communicating and collaborating with others
- Working independently and with others
- Feeling inspired and challenged at work
- Feeling good at the end of the day about the work you've accomplished

To accomplish occupational wellness, the experts suggests these tips:

- Don't settle, keep motivated, and work towards what you want
- Increase your knowledge and skills to accomplish your goals
- Find the benefits and positives in your current job
- Enjoy what you do, do what you enjoy
- Create connections with your co-workers

- Write out goals, create a plan to execute them, then start work on your plan
- Look for something new and/or talk to a career counselor if you feel stuck or unhappy

These tips are especially relevant during and after a pandemic, especially with the fluctuations in the job market and unemployment that resulted from Covid-19. One 2021 survey found that over half (52%) of U.S. workers were considering a job change, and as many as 44% actually had plans to do so. Many of these people are incentivized by remote work and work-from-home options, which are valued by 68% of currently employed workers (Fast Company, 2021).

The main source of professional well-being is the work environment, particularly relationships with colleagues. In many professions, small problems in daily work activities can cause a person's career choice to lose value and meaning and lead them to be dissatisfied with their current job. Occupational health tries to identify these stressors so workplaces can work to negate or bypass them in daily life. A range of tools and assessments are helpful in employee self-discovery and embarking on a path towards an enlightening and fulfilling career (American Association of Equine Practitioners, 2022).

However, it is clear that minimizing health and wellness issues in workplaces is not easy. For example, there are a lot of challenges in the tourism and hospitality industry. Theme parks (e.g., Disney, Sea World, Universal, and LEGOLAND) and the many different attractions in them, restaurants, nightclubs, wineries, hotels and resorts, golf courses and millions of visitors keep employees very busy, often leading to physical and mental exhaustion. Although all theme parks and restaurants implemented changes to keep their guests and employees healthy during the Covid-19 pandemic, daily concerns arose for employees in these workplaces. Theme parks are thought of as some of the happiest places on earth, however, the reported files show that these parks are actually miserable workplaces for many of their employees. Multitudes of abuse cases have been reported in theme parks; the guests push boundaries and the cast members serve as emotional targets for visitors. They have to tolerate tourists' screams, punches and even gropes. The guests yell, insult, grab the employees and push them. Therefore, employees in the tourism and hospitality industry have to develop a callousness to endure these bad behaviors. Other problems are poverty-level wages and unstable working schedules. Due to poor scheduling, nearly two in three workers cannot find a second job to improve their income.

When the Covid-19 pandemic was layered onto these pre-existing and ongoing problems, employees' burdens and additional workplace stressors increased with rocket speed. The most common workplace stressor is encountering the Covid-19 virus at work; the fear often triggers employee absence. Moreover, alcohol and drug use, depression and anxiety are often increased due to work and personal stress. Almost all companies and foodservice operators offer employee assistance programs but they are not often well-suited for the serious mental health and stress problems of today's employees. Undoubtedly, this creates employee disengagement and lower team confidence. The US Bureau of Labor Statistics reported less productivity during the Covid-19 pandemic, and the CDC reported workplace fatigue, stress, depression, anxiety and chronic insomnia linked to changes in work schedules and routines and worries about economic stability. In addition to mental health issues, some nutrition problems, poor eating habits, stress eating and food insecurity triggered the fear of health problems such as infection disease, heart problems and obesity. According to the CDC, 19% of young people from 2 to 19 years and 40% of adults have clinical obesity in the United States, which can cause heart disease, type 2 diabetes, and some cancers. Obesity costs the US health care system about $147 billion dollars a year.

Problems related to the Covid-19 pandemic increased the skilled labor shortage and staff turnover in the tourism and hospitality industry, and employees are often forced to deal with long and sometimes irregular working hours (Sariisik et al., 2022). Few employees are able to work virtually in the hospitality industry, and there is no magic solution for resolving the mental and physical health issues here. However, some simple measures can improve the lives of workers and may boost work productivity. Although these measures do not guarantee success, it is always beneficial to try improving employees' situations. Business operators should build a more resilient organization with some proactive steps, such as making mental health training mandatory; including mental health coverage as part of the healthcare plan; establishing an employee assistance program; offering a meditation room, mindfulness training, and/or yoga classes at work, and encouraging employees to use their vacation time. Employees can then participate in these programs and share their difficulties with health experts and peers in their workplaces.

Although employees' mental health issues are currently a big problem for companies, many people do not want to share or discuss their mental health or emotional concerns due to fear of losing their job. This is another reason why tourism and hospitality employers and theme park professionals are currently and actively seeking permanent solutions. Tomorrow's employees may face these issues, especially mental health issues, more frequently, as the world continues to recover from Covid-19 and adapt to the new normal. Companies need to develop new projects and find solutions for the future workforce. (Hojjati, 2020; Karatepe et al., 2021; Xiong et al., 2022).

Managing the office environment

Criteria for healthy and comfortable buildings have been developed using methods, tools and concepts focused on the prevention of health and comfort problems in general. Research into these methods, tools and concepts shows that there is a lot of room for improvement. According to experts, there is a need for a different, or at least adapted, approach to assessing the health and comfort of indoor workers: an integrative multidisciplinary approach that takes into account positive an d negative stimuli and deals with peoples' "real" needs is essential in improving work environments (Bluyssen, 2010). For example, Forooraghi et al. (2022) investigated employees' perceptions of their office environment, finding that people do not find their office environment to be understandable and meaningful, and that negative effects caused by bad design choices are not easily reversed. For this reason, office design should be approached with balanced attention to clarity, manageability and meaningfulness.

Recent discoveries regarding the effects of light on human health raise new demands and the need for improved lighting solutions. In addition to visual comfort criteria (e.g., adequate work lighting, limited glare), additional non-visual criteria should be formulated. The non-visual effects of light include the biological clock and direct stimulation of the human brain. Triggering of these effects occurs via receptors recently discovered in the human eye. Vertical lighting in this process is an important factor for the eye. In terms of light dynamics, intensity and spectral composition play an important role throughout the day (Ariës & Zonneveldt, 2004). In addition to poor lighting, poor indoor air quality in buildings can reduce productivity, adding to the dissatisfaction of employees. It is generally more energy efficient to eliminate sources of pollution rather than increase outdoor air supply rates (Wyon, 2004). Similarly, particulate matter (PM), known as a byproduct of commercial cooking, has been reported as one invisible factor aggravating health risks in restaurants. Commercial cooking is known as the main source of excessively harmful particulate matter pollution indoors for customers and employees in foodservice settings (Chang et al., 2021). Many types of physical hazards can threaten the health and safety of workers. For example, electrical hazards, ergonomic risks (e.g. repetitive movements, improper posture or excessive force), radiation exposure, machine-related injuries, and the risks of a work-related motor vehicle accident. It is important to recognize, assess, minimize, eliminate or control these hazards to enhance the physical wellness in workplaces (Stoewen, 2016).

Managing intellectual wellness during a crisis and pandemic

Intellectual wellness is "engaging the individual in creative and stimulating mental activities to expand their knowledge and skills to help them grow their potential" (Washington State University, n.d.a). This type of wellness encourages learning, exploring new ideas, being curious about new things, and developing a better understanding of the world. To improve your intellectual wellness, the experts encourages asking yourself these questions:

- Are you open to new ideas?
- Do you seek personal growth by learning new skills?
- Do you search for learning opportunities and stimulating mental activities?
- Do you look for ways to use creativity?

During a pandemic, especially when socially isolated or in lockdown, intellectual wellness can thrive. Covid-19 led many people to read lots of books, start a garden, take classes virtually, do creative projects, maintain and improve their homes, and learn more about topics they were interested in.

13

Managing spiritual wellness during a crisis and pandemic

Northwestern University (2022b) defines **spiritual wellness** as "expanding a sense of purpose and meaning in life, including one's morals and ethics. It may or may not involve religious activities." To develop your spiritual wellness, they suggest to:

- Explore your personal values
- Question and clarify your values
- Become aware of how values develop and change from life experiences
- Become aware of the differences in others' values
- Search for meaning in your own life
- Develop integrity by acting in ways that are consistent with your values
- Explore the issues related to mortality and your own life and death

The above descriptions can apply to both managing one's own wellness, and helping tourism guests and employees manage theirs. All of these components can also be considered when developing wellness products for hospitality and tourism, as travelers often seek multiple benefits from a wellness trip. The demand for wellness solutions will only continue to grow as people value their own health and wellness more and look for wellness-friendly solutions from hospitality and tourism organizations.

The future of the wellness economy

As the world recovers from the Covid-19 pandemic, the wellness economy is expected to boom, especially tourism. The Global Wellness Institute and IMF estimate that from 2020-2025, the expected average annual growth rate for wellness tourism will be 20.9% (see Table 13.1), helping the wellness economy overall grow to a value of nearly $7.0 trillion USD in 2025 (Global Wellness Institute, 2021).

Table 13.1: Projected average annual growth rate by sector, 2020-2025. Adapted from Global Wellness Institute, 2021).

Sectors	Annual Growth Rate
Wellness tourism	20.9%
Thermal/mineral springs	18.1%
Spas	17.2%
Wellness real estate	16.1%
Physical activity	10.2%
Mental wellness	9.8%
Personal care & beauty	8.1%
Traditional complementary medicine	7.1%
Healthy eating nutrition and weight loss	5.1%
Public health prevention and personalized medicine	5.0%
Workplace wellness	3.8%

Although Covid-19 shocked the wellness industry temporarily, the underlying forces for a heightened need for wellness remain: "the growing global middle class, population aging, the ongoing rise of chronic disease, and expanding consumer interest in and awareness of healthy lifestyles" (Global Wellness Institute, 2021). The pandemic has also brought a "growing awareness of the role of the built environment in health, a growing focus on mental health and well-being, a rethinking of the balance of work and life, an expanding focus on social justice and environmental sustainability, and much more." However, health services and wellness services are different. Wellness services are not new for many hotels but there is still some confusion between wellness hotels and health retreats. While a health retreat "offer[s] a purposefully designed program of therapies and activities, guided by leading health and fitness experts," "a wellness hotel is a luxury hotel that offers wellness facilities, such as a spa or fitness center." More and more hotels are describing themselves as wellness hotels these days, as this concept has become trendy among travelers, especially after the pandemic (Health and Fitness Travel, 2022). According to the results of a consumer survey conducted by the World Tourism Association covering 48 countries and territories, more than 24% of consumers are "highly likely to book a wellness vacation in the next two years" and 78% have already booked reservations with wellness related hotels and services. Health-conscious travelers spend up to 130% more on wellness facilities than other guests. On top of that, the growth rate of the wellness industry grew 6.5% per year from 2015 to 2017, more than double the growth rate for general tourism. In 2017, international health tourists spent an average of $1,528 per trip, or 53% more than the average. US domestic wellness travelers spent $609 per trip, which is exactly 178% more than the typical domestic tourist (Wendt, 2022).

Summary

This chapter discussed the concept of a crisis, specifically the Covid-19 global pandemic and how it affected (and continues to affect) wellness tourism. G Adventures' Wellness Tours were given as an example of a wellness tourism program. The chapter then offered suggestions for managing wellness during and after a pandemic, from physical, emotional, occupational, social, intellectual and spiritual aspects.

Definitions of key terms

Crisis – "A condition of instability or danger, as in social, economic, political, or international affairs, leading to a decisive change." (Dictionary.com, 2022a)

Emotional wellness – "The ability to successfully handle life's stresses and adapt to change and difficult times." (National Institutes of Health, 2021)

Intellectual wellness – "Engaging the individual in creative and stimulating mental activities to expand their knowledge and skills to help them grow their potential." (Washington State University, n.d.a)

Occupational wellness – "The ability to achieve a balance between work and leisure in a way that promotes health, a sense of personal satisfaction and is (for most people) financially rewarding." (Washington State University, n.d.a)

Pandemic – "A disease prevalent throughout an entire country, continent, or the whole world." (Dictionary.com, 2022b)

13

Physical wellness – "Recognizing the need for physical activity, healthy foods, and sleep, as well as preventing illness and injury or managing chronic health conditions." (Northwestern University, 2022)

Spiritual wellness – "Expanding a sense of purpose and meaning in life, including one's morals and ethics. It may or may not involve religious activities." (Northwestern University, 2022)

Discussion questions

1. What other crises are happening in the world right now beyond the ongoing effects of Covid-19?
2. How can tourism's return hurt and help destinations around the world as they welcome travelers again?
3. How can you take precautions for mental wellness in the tourism and hospitality sector?
4. How can you organize an exemplary and healthy office environment?

Homework

1. Discuss at least two ways (each) you can maintain your physical, emotional, occupational, intellectual, and spiritual wellness during the recovery from the Covid-19 pandemic.
2. Design a trip incorporating at least one (each) physical, em otional, occupational, intellectual, and spiritual wellness component.
3. Discuss the differences between health and wellness hotels and leisure hotels. Which one is more beneficial for guests' health and wellness?

References

American Association of Equine Practitioners (2022). Occupational wellness. Retrieved June 13, 2022, from https://aaep.org/wellness/occupational-wellness

Ariës, M. B. C., & Zonneveldt, L. (2004). Architectural aspects of healthy lighting. In *21th Conference on Passive and Low Energy Architecture, Netherlands* (pp. 1-5).

Backman, S. J., Huang, Y. C., Chen, C. C., Lee, H. Y., & Cheng, J. S. (2022). Engaging with restorative environments in wellness tourism. *Current Issues in Tourism*, 1-18.

BBC. (2022). Covid map: Coronavirus cases, deaths, vaccinations by country. Retrieved June 10, 2022, from https://www.bbc.com/news/world-51235105

Bluyssen, P. M. (2010). Towards new methods and ways to create healthy and comfortable buildings. *Building and environment*, 45(4), 808-818.

Centers for Disease Control and Prevention. (2022). CDC Museum Covid-19 Timeline. Retrieved June 10, 2022, from https://www.cdc.gov/museum/timeline/covid19.html

Chang, H. S., Capuozzo, B., Okumus, B., & Cho, M. (2021). Why cleaning the invisible in restaurants is important during Covid-19: A case study of indoor air quality of an open-kitchen restaurant. *International Journal of Hospitality Management*, 94, 102854.

Chen, C. C. (2020). Psychological tolls of Covid-19 on industry employees. *Annals of Tourism Research*. doi: 10.1016/j.annals.2020.103080

Dictionary.com. (2022a). Crisis definition & meaning. Retrieved June 10, 2022, from https://www.dictionary.com/browse/crisis

Dictionary.com. (2022b). Pandemic definition & meaning. Retrieved June 10, 2022, from https://www.dictionary.com/browse/pandemic

Fast Company. (2021). Is now a good time to change careers? More workers are feeling good about it. Retrieved June 10, 2022, from https://www.fastcompany.com/90607167/is-now-a-good-time-to-change-careers-more-workers-are-feeling-good-about-it

Forooraghi, M., Cobaleda-Cordero, A., & Babapour Chafi, M. (2022). A healthy office and healthy employees: A longitudinal case study with a salutogenic perspective in the context of the physical office environment. *Building Research & Information*, 50(1-2), 134-151.

G Adventures. (2022a). Wellness Tours. Retrieved June 5, 2022, from https://https://www.gadventures.com/travel-styles/wellness/

G Adventures. (2022b). Wellness Costa Rica. Retrieved June 5, 2022, from https://www.gadventures.com/trips/wellness-costa-rica/6573/

Global Wellness Institute. (2021). The Global Wellness Economy: Looking Beyond Covid. Retrieved June 10, 2022, from https://globalwellnessinstitute.org/industry-research/the-global-wellness-economy-looking-beyond-covid/

Harvard. (2022). Mental and emotional well-being during the Covid-19 pandemic. Retrieved June 10, 2022, from https://hr.harvard.edu/mental-and-emotional-well-being-during-covid-19-pandemic

Health and Fitness Travel (2022). What is the difference between a health retreat versus a wellness hotel. Retrieved June 13, 2022, from https://www.healthandfitnesstravel.com/retreats-guide/health-retreat-vs-wellness-hotel

Hojjati, P (2020). Mental health in the workplace during Covid-19: How can employers help? https://healthblog.uofmhealth.org/wellness-prevention/mental-health-workplace-during-covid-19-how-can-employers-help

Karatepe, O. M., Saydam, M. B., & Okumus, F. (2021). Covid-19, mental health problems, and their detrimental effects on hotel employees' propensity to be late for work, absenteeism, and life satisfaction. *Current Issues in Tourism*, 24(7), 934-951.

13

Missouri Western State University (2022). Retrieved June 10, 2022 https://www.missouriwestern.edu/student-life/griffon360/

Mitroff, I. I. (1994). Crisis management and environmentalism: A natural fit. *California Management Review*, 36(2), 101-113.

National Institutes of Health. (2021). Emotional wellness toolkit. Retrieved June 10, 2022, from www.nih.gov/health-information/emotional-wellness-toolkit

National Suicide Prevention Lifeline. (2022). Emotional well-being during Covid-19. Retrieved June 10, 2022, from https://suicidepreventionlifeline.org/current-events/supporting-your-emotional-well-being-during-covid-19/

Northwestern University. (2022a). Physical wellness. Retrieved June 10, 2022, from https://www.northwestern.edu/wellness/8-dimensions/physical-wellness.html

Northwestern University. (2022b). Spiritual wellness. Retrieved June 10, 2022, from https://www.northwestern.edu/wellness/8-dimensions/spiritual-wellness.html

Our World in Data. (2022). Coronavirus (Covid-19) vaccinations. Retrieved June 10, 2022, from https://ourworldindata.org/covid-vaccinations

Sanford Center for Aging. (n.d.). Taking care of your emotional well-being during a pandemic. Retrieved June 10, 2022, from https://med.unr.edu/aging/news-information-resources/emotional-well-being-during-a-pandemic

Sariisik, M., Sengul, S., Okumus, B., Ceylan, V., Kurnaz, A., & Kapucuoglu, M. I. (2022). In-house responses and anxiety levels of commercial kitchen employees towards new Covid 19 food safety regulations. *Journal of Foodservice Business Research*, 1-28.

Stoewen, D. L. (2016). Wellness at work: Building healthy workplaces. *The Canadian Veterinary Journal*, 57(11), 1188.

University of Nebraska Omaha. (n.d.). Occupational wellness: Learning & contributing. Retrieved June 10, 2022, from https://www.unomaha.edu/student-life/presidents-wellness-committee/occupational-wellness-tips.php

UNWTO. (2022a). UNWTO tourism recovery tracker. Retrieved June 10, 2022, from https://www.unwto.org/tourism-data/unwto-tourism-recovery-tracker

UNWTO. (2022b). Tourism enjoys strong start to 2022 while facing new uncertainties. Retrieved June 10, 2022, from https://www.unwto.org/news/tourism-enjoys-strong-start-to-2022-while-facing-new-uncertainties

Washington State University. (n.d.). Intellectual wellness. Retrieved June 10, 2022, from https://spokane.wsu.edu/wellness/intellectual-wellness/

Washington State University. (n.d.a). Occupational Wellness. Retrieved June 10, 2022, from https://spokane.wsu.edu/wellness/occupational-wellness/

Wendt, M (2022). Delivering wellness in the hospitality industry. Retrieved June 13, 2022, from www.amadeus-hospitality.com/insight/covid-19-wellness/

World Health Organization. (2022a). WHO Coronavirus (Covid-19) Dashboard. Retrieved June 5, 2022, from https://covid19.who.int/

World Health Organization. (2022b). Timeline: WHO's Covid-19 response. Retrieved June 10, 2022, from https://www.who.int/emergencies/diseases/novel-coronavirus-2019/interactive-timeline

Wyon, D. P. (2004). The effects of indoor air quality on performance and productivity. *Indoor Air*, 14, 92-101.

Xiong, W., Chen, S., Okumus, B., & Fan, F. (2022). Gender stereotyping and its impact on perceived emotional leadership in the hospitality industry: A mixed-methods study. *Tourism Management*, 90, 104476.

Yang, F. X., & Wong, I. A. (2020). The social crisis aftermath: tourist well-being during the Covid-19 outbreak. *Journal of Sustainable Tourism*, 29(6), 859-878.

13

14 Conclusions: The Future of Wellness Management

This chapter draws conclusions from the previous chapters and offers suggestions for current and future wellness management in foodservice, hospitality, and tourism businesses. It starts by introducing the wellness programs that EVEN Hotels offer. Next, it revisits wellness management concepts in hospitality and tourism, looks at generations of travelers and their travel preferences, and discusses future trends.

Learning outcomes

By the end of this chapter, students should be able to do the following:

1. Describe what wellness programs and offerings EVEN Hotels provides to its guests.
2. Draw conclusions from previous chapters.
3. Discuss current and future generations' expectations of health and wellness.
4. Offer discussions and recommendations on the future of wellness concepts.

Case study: EVEN Hotels

EVEN Hotels' tagline is "Where wellness is built in." This is embodied throughout a traveler's stay, as EVEN offers ways to stay healthier and happier away from home. Their employees are wellness-savvy, and their fitness offerings, healthy food choices, and relaxing spaces combine to help guests stay active and productive. This well-rounded approach to wellness encourages their guests to incorporate physical, mental, and social health while traveling.

EVEN Hotels boast about their best-in-class Athletic Studio, in-room training zone, online instructional videos, and group classes. Simple and natural food options like smoothies, gluten-free snacks, and even organic signature cocktails are available at the Cork & Kale™ Market and Bar found at each property. Like many hotel brands, rooms at EVEN Hotels feature premium sleep systems, but theirs go beyond an adjustable bed and into the territory of natural eucalyptus fiber bedding. Other room amenities include comfortable, eco-friendly products to help ensure a good night's sleep and a balanced stay. Free WiFi and lots of calming workspaces around each property help their guests accomplish their goals during their stay. (EVEN Hotels, 2020).

IHG, the parent company of EVEN Hotels, offers plenty more tips for wellness travel on their blog, Wellwellwell. The blog features articles on "keeping well, eating well, resting easy, and accomplishing more" (IHG, 2020). For example, one article on getting a solid night's sleep in a hotel room encourages travelers to eat foods rich in melatonin and tryptophan, complete a quick pre-bedtime yoga routine, sleep on sheets with a blend of natural eucalyptus and cotton fibers, and enjoy relaxing scents like lavender and sage (Russock, 2017). While many large hotel brands are now offering wellness-focused products, EVEN Hotels was one of the pioneers.

Discussion questions

1. What do EVEN Hotels offer to improve guests' physical, mental and social wellness?
2. Who would like to stay at EVEN Hotels, and why?
3. What improvements could EVEN Hotels make to their wellness offerings?
4. What other topics could IHG/EVEN Hotels discuss on their wellness blog?

Revisiting wellness management concepts

Common themes have been mentioned throughout this textbook as current trends in health and wellness travel. The main ones will be summarized in this section briefly, and the next sections will look at upcoming future trends. Generational differences in health and wellness expectations will also be considered.

Primary and secondary wellness travel

The concepts of primary and secondary wellness travel have been discussed throughout this text. Retreats will become more popular, as people look for time away from their stressful workplaces and daily lives and seek ways of better managing and balancing their days in all areas of wellness (Smith & Puczkó, 2008). Wellness travel offerings that mix primary and secondary travel are also becoming more common, allowing each person in a party to customize their own experience (Rokou, 2019). For example, a business traveler may only be able to partake in exercise classes and healthy dining options, but their accompanying partner might seek a fully immersed wellness experience.

Identifying a destination's unique wellness offerings

Every destination has its history, traditions, and unique amenities to offer health and wellness travelers. This may serve underdeveloped destinations particularly well, as these travelers are often seeking places that remove them from their developed

14

concrete world and bring them back to nature with exercise, play, rest, nutrition, and mindfulness in peaceful settings that run at a slower pace (Rokou, 2019).

Customization and personalization

While this is a general trend in hospitality and tourism, wellness travelers, in particular, are looking for customized and personalized trips that address their individual goals. Some travelers are looking for complete silence, mindfulness, and nature to reverse the effects of constant digital noise and connectivity; 'silent zones' are becoming popular at spas, restaurants, fitness centers, and airports. Others are looking for ways to embrace their creativity through classes that encourage painting, writing, and other creative outlets (Hill, 2017). Even nutrition will become personalized, using science, low-cost medical testing, and new technologies (Insider's Guide to Spas, 2019).

Wellness food

As mentioned in Chapter 6, the health and wellness food market was valued at $733 billion in 2020 and is estimated to be worth $1 trillion in 2026 (Statista, 2021). Special diets are becoming the norm, for example, limited-ingredient diets like vegetarianism, veganism, plant-based, pescetarianism, and the Paleo diet (Innovation Group, 201a). Younger generations expect products to be available that are GMO-free, organic, natural, and sustainable, and they want locally sourced farm-to-table dining experiences (UnityPoint Health, 2018). The healthy beverages market is moving past smoothies and cold-pressed juices and into non-alcoholic spirits and teas. Foods filled with serotonin and other "happiness hormones," high-fiber and high-antioxidant foods, and fermented foods with naturally occurring probiotics are increasing in popularity as well (Innovation Group, 2017b). Immersive and sensory food experiences like food festivals and add-ons like virtual reality (VR) and augmented reality (AR) are becoming more popular, and technology is also being used to decrease production time, create new products, and confirm trustworthiness (Mintel, 2019).

Wellness spas and hot springs

Trends in the spa and hot springs industry are moving more toward individualized treatments and addressing specific visitor needs. For example, mineral springs have curative properties when ingested or bathed in, and different types of mineral contents address different skin, joint, and other bodily concerns (Erfurt-Cooper, 2010). Some springs have radon, which in low doses of exposure may improve the body's metabolism, immunity, antioxidant functions, and natural healing capabilities (Misasa Onsen Ryokan Cooperative, 2020). Wellness travelers are also looking for eco-tourism friendly accommodation and attractions, and spa and hot spring facilities need to be designed and built accordingly (Mill, 2011).

Wellness events

Chapters 7 and 8 discussed primary, secondary, and corporate wellness events in detail. Primary wellness events like retreats give wellness travelers a way to immerse themselves in wellness for a few days or even a few hours, and many resorts like

Canyon Ranch are offering customized packages (Canyon Ranch, n.d.). Large festivals and trade shows bring together like-minded people to exchange ideas and gather inspiration. Secondary wellness elements can be incorporated into any kind of gathering, with features like locally sourced food, creative seating arrangements in meetings, and optional add-on activities like pre-breakfast yoga sessions or running groups (Event MB/Maritz Global Events, 2018). Corporate and industry wellness events can address physical and mental wellness through screenings, webinars and seminars, other informational presentations, team-building exercises, and more.

Workplace wellness

The concept of workplace wellness will also continue to grow as younger generations expect more offerings from their place of employment (discussed further in the next section). As discussed in Chapter 12, employees want workplace wellness benefits and programs that support their physical, emotional, social, and financial well-being. They will also expect to be able to customize their health and wellness benefits by choosing from a la carte-style menus that fit them best, such as fitness club memberships, flexible schedules and paid time off, or similar offerings (Smith & Puczkó, 2008).

Current and future generations' expectations from health and wellness

The Silent Generation, Baby Boomers, and Generation X

The Silent Generation (born before 1945), Baby Boomers (born approximately 1946-1964), and Generation X (born approximately 1965-1979) will continue to play an important role in wellness travel. They are still active travelers and currently make up around one-third of the global population (United Nations, n.d.). They are more traditional travelers, often looking for standardized itineraries and guided tours, but have their own unique needs and preferences. These three groups are more likely than younger generations to define health and wellness as being physically fit, alert, and bright-minded, not being ill, having the energy for an active lifestyle, feeling good about themselves, leading a balanced lifestyle, and being happy and cheerful (Hartman Group, 2017).

Gen X women, in particular, are looking for a respite from their hectic lives on a relaxing retreat involving activities like meditation, mindfulness, spa treatments, yoga, healthy eating, and outdoor activities (AFP Relax News, 2019). They are most likely to travel solo or with a group of friends, and to stay in the United States (especially in the Southwest), but are also venturing abroad to places like Bali and Thailand (Riddle, 2020). Future wellness concepts as the topic relate to older generations will be discussed in a later section of this chapter. While these three segments are vital, looking to the future, Generations Y, Z, and Alpha comprise the remaining two-thirds of the global population and are more deeply interested in health and wellness travel.

14

There are variations between research sources as to the specific date ranges of each generation. For the sake of consistency, the cohorts and age range defined by research firm McCrindle Research Pty Ltd (Fell, 2020) will be used, as they are credited with naming Generation Alpha and not all research sources (e.g., Pew Research) yet recognize a cohort following Generation Z. Numbers such as population sizes and percentages are approximations due to these variations. Statistics describe consumers in the U.S. unless otherwise specified. Also, as Generation Z and Alpha are still emerging, conflicting research is found on their psychographics and buying habits; the purpose of the information here is to demonstrate the general trends of each segment.

Generation Y

Generation Y was born between 1980-1994, and there are approximately 1.75 billion members globally, and 73 million in the U.S. Gen Y are also commonly called Millennials, and sometimes are also referred to as Gen Me, Gen We, and Echo Boomers (Fell, 2020). Millennials value experiences and authenticity, and many vacations alone, with their friends, or with their parents (Hertzfeld, 2019). When it comes to customization, many Gen Yers are interested in services that recommend experiences based on their personality first and their budget second (SiteMinder, 2020).

Members of the Generation Y cohort are looking for experiences with the buzzwords 'Authentic,' 'Connected,' and 'Dynamic' (Kerr, 2017). They want to share photos and videos of their trips on their social networks. Millennials admit that they want to be more like the "idealized versions" of themselves that they portray on social media, and look for social validation through peer responses to their posts.

When it comes to health and wellness, Generation Y is famous for its love of yoga, meditation, and expensive boutique fitness classes (Ducharme, 2019). They smoke less and exercise more than previous generations, and almost half consider healthy eating a lifestyle choice instead of a goal-driven diet. Millennials are often more likely than older generations to use technology and apps to manage their health and to spend more on health and fitness. Gen Yers prioritize work-life balance and view it as a major career concern, expecting perks like flexible work schedules, wellness tools and supports that contribute to their physical, mental, and emotional well-being; and casual dress codes that promote comfort and movement throughout the day (Nermoe, 2018). However, some studies show that Millennials over the age of 27 may be *less* healthy than the previous generation (Gen X) was at the same age. Endocrine, cardiovascular issues, and a rise in obesity seem to be partially the cause. They also struggle with and are more open about their mental health issues like depression, anxiety, and loneliness, and often are unable to pay for health care (Ducharme, 2019). These health concerns may encourage them to seek wellness opportunities and solutions when they travel.

From a wellness travel perspective, Millennials want more than fluffy robes at a spa; they want to be transported to a yoga pavilion in Bali. They want to attend a retreat with a famous fitness influencer, guided meditation practice with a spiritual leader, forest bathing in a remote location, challenging hikes and hot springs, and other unique experiences. Personalization is also disrupting the wellness travel industry, a trend that will continue to grow with future generations, and that will be discussed further in the next sections (Dimon, 2020).

Generation Z

Generation Z was born between 1995-2010; there are approximately 1.85 billion of them worldwide, and 74 million in the U.S. (United Nations, n.d.). Other names for this generation include iGeneration, Post-Millennials, Homeland Generation, Generation Connected, and Dot.Com Kids (Fell, 2020). Members of Generation Z are young, fiscally conservative, and digitally connected. They are relatively brand agnostic and often use the sharing economy while traveling. Even though Gen Zers are price-conscious, they will reduce their costs in one area of a trip to splurge for value-enhancing extras in another part (Biesiada, 2018). They travel approximately three times per year and embrace the YOLO (you only live once) mentality (Travel Agent Central, 2018).

Generation Z is likely to take a holistic view of health, paying attention to physical fitness, healthy eating, and mental well-being. They use apps and wearable technology to track workouts and manage their health and often prefer high-protein, low-carb diets with minimal sugar and plant-based preferences. Technology also comes into play with Gen Z's healthcare preferences; over half of the respondents in one study preferred telemedicine to traditional in-person options, and they are more willing to consider alternative medical treatments like acupuncture and yoga (Vennare, 2020).

They are also more socially conscious than previous generations, and many volunteer regularly and are concerned about humanity's influence on the planet. This consciousness can lead them to be very sensitive to stressors like sexual harassment, immigration, and gun violence, making them the most likely of all generations to report poor mental health. Nearly 48% of Gen Zers are from communities of color, making them the most racially and ethnically diverse generation. Workplace wellness programs need to offer financial support programs to help this group overcome their worries about finances, volunteer opportunities to connect to their social consciousness, eco-friendly office initiatives, and an overall culture of wellness to combat stress (Kohll, 2019).

Even more than Generation Y, Gen Z's constant social media presence makes them a "generation of influencers." They want to be engaged in the travel process and recognized as having unique needs from their parents. This group also understands the value of **bleisure** travel or adding a personal stay on a business trip (Maritur, 2020); as they enter the workforce soon, they are expected to take advantage of options to extend a business trip and enjoy the destination further on their own. Generation Z takes the experience component of travel one step further than Millennials. Instead of simply wanting to try a cocktail made with local ingredients, Gen Zers want to take a mixology class to learn how to make the cocktail so they can replicate it at home. They are concerned about the environment and look for eco-friendly trips, sustainable hotel practices, and ways to do good in the local community they are visiting (Whitmore,

14

2019). Overall, this generation likes health and wellness experiences that are personalized specifically for them. In the same way Amazon and Netflix use algorithms to suggest things to buy and watch, and Airbnb is beginning to recommend places to visit and stay, this trend will continue to become more popular (Dimon, 2020).

Generation Alpha

Generation Alpha is currently the youngest generation, born starting in 2011 and estimated to reach 2 billion by the likely 2025 year of transition to the next generation (United Nations, n.d.). The first cohort to be born entirely in the 21st century, other nicknames for the group include Digital Natives and Generation Glass (Fell, 2020). Although this group is still young and reliant on their parents, they want to be involved in the travel process, and their parents take their input seriously (Menze, 2019). They are often only children and, therefore, may be more likely to be selfish and expect instant gratification (Carter, 2016). Because this generation is still so young, it is difficult to identify their feelings toward health and wellness. Yet, they are expected to embrace experiences and personalization at an even higher level than previous generations.

Future of wellness concepts

Health and wellness travel is predicted to continue to become even more popular in the future. As Generations Y and Alpha grow older and begin to travel more on their own, new trends will likely emerge. This section discusses some trends on the horizon in the next few years.

Taking on overtourism

Overtourism is becoming a commonly heard word in the travel industry, as tourists overwhelm popular destinations. Skift coined the term in 2016, as "a new construct to look at potential hazards to popular destinations worldwide, as the dynamic forces that power tourism often inflicts unavoidable negative consequences if not managed well" (Ali, 2018). Overtourism has been discussed for years in conjunction with sustainability, and it has become even more prominent in response to the Covid-19 global pandemic crisis. Experts expect the future of travel to be changed forever due to the pandemic, with destinations being allowed to recover from past overtourism during the lull in global tourism. When travel returns, smaller groups and eco-friendly individualized experiences are likely to be the new norm, and wellness travel is perfectly positioned for this new way of tourism (Froelich, 2020).

Digital detoxing

The definition of 'detoxify,' often shortened to 'detox,' refers to ridding the body of poison or the effects of a dangerous substance. Traditionally most commonly used in the medical vernacular to describe healing from substances such as poison, drugs, or alcohol, 'detox' has become more popularly used in the mainstream lexicon as a way to reduce the presence and effects of less dangerous elements as well, for example battling an addiction to technology. The full scope of detrimental effects of overuse of the internet or smartphones is not yet clear. Still, so far, negative consequences have been identified pertaining to psychological, physical, and social factors. Psychological effects include "poor memory, concentration and decision-making, anxiety, procrastination, and sleep disturbance," and physical dangers are possible such as harm resulting from accidents, poor posture, and repetitive strain injury (van Velthoven et al., 2018). The fear of being out of contact with a mobile phone or computer has been given the psychological term 'nomophobia' (Bhattacharya et al., 2018).

Social effects are another well-acknowledged result of too much smartphone use. Pew Research identified that users are being distracted by their devices while trying to spend personal time with others, with 82% acknowledging that using a phone in social settings frequently or occasionally hurts the conversation, yet 89% admitted to using their phone during the most recent social gathering they attended (Rainie & Zickuhr, 2015). Even having a smartphone present has been found to decrease the perceived value of a conversation. In sum, "digital communication is felt to be eroding our ability to concentrate, to empathize, and to have meaningful conversations: ultimately threatening the qualities that make us human" (Sutton, 2017).

To help guests overcome this addiction to technological devices, some travel companies are offering experiences centered on digital detoxing. Hotels are restricting cell phone usage in spaces like spas, libraries, and galleries. The Wyndham Grand brand's Reconnected Family Experience targets families with young children; a special non-digital kit includes interactive props like a flashlight, an Instax Polaroid camera, a shadow-puppet book, materials to build blanket forts, and a timed lockbox to pack away phones during dedicated family time. Optional programs abound at hotels, encouraging guests to surrender their phones for some time or when using specific amenities like a hotel pool, or during meals. One activity company, Austin Adventures, offers multi-day digital detox programs. To set guests' minds at ease, they provide emergency contact information where guests can be reached at any time by family and friends back home, and a professional photographer takes pictures throughout the trip and posts on the activity company's official social media accounts, where family and friends can follow along with the travelers (Killion, 2019).

Figure 14.1: Digital detox signs. Adapted from Healthy Hildegad (n.d.)

Role of technology on future wellness concepts

While digital detoxing is one trend in wellness travel, technology is a double-edged sword as it also offers new primary and support services for wellness management for both travelers and hospitality and tourism businesses. For example, technology

14

allows consumers to track their physical health and fitness levels using wearable devices and apps. Emotional, mental, and social health can also benefit from technological features like mindfulness and meditation apps, and apps that connect people to avoid loneliness and other social challenges.

A focus on sleep

Hotels, wellness resorts, and airlines have long promoted their custom beds, fancy linens, lavender soaps, and complimentary eye masks as one way to fight sleep deprivation. Consumers are also starting to get on board in their daily lives, with new technology helping them adjust their sleep cycles to the natural circadian rhythm of sunlight. Apps are becoming available that help people reach their goals of adjusting to a new shift at work, a new time zone while traveling, and more. As wellness travelers continue to seek ways to improve their overall health, sleep is likely one area that will be embraced (Global Wellness Summit, 2020).

Inspiration from other cultures

Wellness travelers have long taken cues from other cultures. Japan, in particular, is well known for its wellness culture, with the highest number of centenarians per capita of any country. The concepts of Japan's *onsen* hot springs and *ikigai* (the lifelong pursuit of finding one's real purpose) have been discussed in this textbook. It is expected that wellness travelers will take a more holistic approach to Japanese culture by also incorporating other elements like tea ceremonies, *Wabi-sabi* (embracing imperfection and transience), and traditional ways of eating with contemplation (Global Wellness Summit, 2020).

Incorporating health, wellness, and daily life

As discussed in Chapter 1, health and wellness are similar concepts, with *health* focused more on the physical, or medical aspect. Blending these two with facilities like hospitals and spas or 'wellpitals,' allows guests to receive both medical and wellness care or recuperation in one attractive, appealing, and relaxing location. Health and wellness are also likely to be incorporated more into consumers' daily lifestyle communities that offer spas, outdoor recreation, Feng Shui-designed apartment complexes, nutritional dining facilities and wellness centers, and more (Smith, M., & Puczkó, 2008).

Wellness and sustainability

Sustainable travel "means finding a way that tourism can be maintained long-term without harming natural and cultural environments" (Charlie on Travel, 2019). As discussed throughout this book, current and future generations value both wellness and sustainability. Wellness travelers are looking for concepts, products, and services that do not have negative impacts on the sustainability of communities, businesses, animals and the natural environment, but instead support healthy and ongoing growth. Future wellness and sustainability concepts go hand-in-hand, and health and wellness travel is likely to contribute to the sustainability movement.

Aging well

As Baby Boomers continue to age, they are looking for ways to do it well. They have the time and money to be active, engaged in enjoying life, and continually achieving goals like running marathons and traveling (Global Wellness Summit, 2020). Travel companies are embracing this wellness trend by going beyond physical health opportunities and offering ways to fulfill the mind and spirit through learning prospects, shared immersive experiences, and celebrating life.

Impact of crises, disasters, and pandemics on wellness concepts

The worldwide pandemic of Covid-19 starting in 2020 has brought the hospitality and tourism industry to a crashing halt. During this unprecedented time, governmental orders to stay at home and general fear of the dangerous virus caused travelers to cancel their trips and become more hesitant to travel in large groups or to popular destinations. The same effect happened, albeit to a much lesser extent, during the earlier avian influenza in 1997, SARS outbreak of 2003, swine flu of 2009, Ebola outbreak of 2014, and other global-reaching epidemics. As people worry about their short-term safety, wellness initiatives often become deprioritized.

In the short-term, people are likely to cancel or postpone upcoming trips to wellness destinations or facilities, to lessen their risk of exposure. Instead, they may move their plans to a closer facility, such as a local spa or retreat center, or may simply stay home. In times like these, wellness businesses must communicate with their clientele, offer incentives to postpone their trip rather than cancel it altogether, and move their offerings online whenever possible. Maintaining a cash reserve is also essential in case of situations like these. In the mid-term and long-term, people will continue to travel. They may focus more on ongoing wellness initiatives like boosting their immune systems and improving their overall health to protect themselves in the case of future pandemics. They are also likely to continue practicing social distancing by traveling to wellness places with fewer people.

While pandemics are often devastating to hospitality and tourism businesses, they also offer a chance to recover from the effects of overtourism and refocus their efforts on what is best for their destination and business. Previously, health and wellness tourism was often associated only with elite and educated people with a higher socio-economic level but Covid-19 changed that perspective.

As the pandemic wanes, people are thinking of traveling for their wellness so health and safety measures have gained even more importance. Due to these growing health perceptions, destinations should offer tour packages with traditional wellness activities such as detox, acupuncture, naturopathy, and panchakarma. Promoting and marketing those traditional methods will increase wellness customer demand and sales of wellness destinations (Tiwari & Hashmi, 2022).

14

Student wellness

Stress and burnout are a serious threat to the emotional health of many students. According to the research of Vazquez Morgan (2021), post-burnout symptoms among medical students and residents are quite high in normal conditions, and more than half of them show symptoms of stress, anxiety and depression. The Covid-19 pandemic has exacerbated this situation and demonstrated that there is a critical need to assess challenges to self-care, well-being and wellness in medical students and trainees.

Similar studies have also shown that due to the pandemic, students have had a hard time adapting to this unprecedented change. They are dissatisfied with the new online education and the sudden transition to online education increased fear, anxiety and uncertainty, especially in the K-12 environment (Kundu & Bej, 2021). While Covid-19 has affected everyone, its impact on people with disabilities, especially students was particularly hard.

Having challenges like ADD/ADHD, eating disorders, learning problems, anxiety, PTSD and various physical limitations weaken the body and mind and sometimes increase anxiety. Students both with and without disabilities face many problems in these difficult times, such as job loss, isolation, financial concerns, and other mental and social issues. Moreover, students with disabilities also experience their own unique high stressors (Gibilisco, 2020).

This is a global issue and whether it is developed or developing countries, being caught unprepared for crises has a great effect on students' health and well-being. Therefore, some simple wellness tips are provided here focused on student relationships and well-being in Table 14.1. These are simple strategies that can be used in communicating with students. These simple steps can reduce their anxiety and help build stronger student relationships.

Student-focused wellness tips

- Avoid eye contact—it is often too threatening
- Consider taking a walk while you talk
- Have regular positive exchanges to build an environment of mutual respect
- Use the existing curriculum to implement conversations that are personally relevant to students
- Use open-ended questions
- Don't judge
- Build a community of care within your classroom
- Make connections between older and younger students
- Share student concerns to build support for the child
- Be flexible, creative and willing to relinquish control
- Remember it is not necessary to always be your student's best friend

- Know your limits
- Be honest in a gentle way
- Take all issues seriously
- Connect students with resources
- Respect every student's individuality
- Determine the student's support groups
- Meet with parents early to suggest available services
- Positive champions need to be encouraged and supported
- Plan events that engage students in discussions of personal wellness
- Know the limits of confidentiality when safety concerns arise.

Table 14.1: Student wellness tips. Adapted from PHE Canada (n.d.)

Summary

This chapter concluded the previous chapters and also offers suggestions for current and future wellness management in foodservice, hospitality, and tourism businesses. It started by introducing what wellness programs EVEN Hotels offers. Next, it reflected wellness management concepts in hospitality and tourism, discussed the effects of upcoming generations on hospitality, and considered future trends.

Definitions of key terms

Bleisure travel – Where travelers mix their business trips with leisure time.

Generation Y / Millennials – Born between 1980-1994, there are approximately 1.75 billion members globally and 73 million in the U.S.

Generation Z – Born between 1995-2010; there are approximately 1.85 billion of them worldwide, and 74 million in the U.S.

Generation Alpha – Currently, the youngest generation, born starting in 2011 and estimated to reach 2 billion worldwide by the likely 2025 year of transition to the next generation.

Overtourism – The concept of too many visitors overwhelming and ruining a particular destination.

Sustainable travel – "Finding a way that tourism can be maintained long-term without harming natural and cultural environments" (Charlie on Travel, 2019).

14

Discussion questions

1. Discuss the wellness management concepts summarized in this chapter.
2. What are the characteristics of Gen Y, Gen Z, and Gen Alpha?
3. What impact do the Silent Generation, the Baby Boomers, and Generation X have on wellness travel?
4. What impact do Generations Y, Z, and Alpha have on wellness travel?
5. What are some examples of future trends in health and wellness?
6. How can crises and disasters affect wellness, hospitality, and tourism?

Homework

1. Design a health and wellness program for a spa or resort that would attract the older generations of travelers (Generation X and above).
2. Design a health and wellness program for a spa or resort that would attract travelers from Generation Y and Z.
3. Describe the impact Generation Alpha currently has on health and wellness travel and what you think they might expect in the future.
4. Choose one future trend mentioned above and find three examples of destinations or organizations currently implementing it.

References

AFP Relax News. (2019). Generation X women to drive wellness travel trend in 2020. Retrieved April 10, 2020, from https://news.yahoo.com/generation-x-women-drive-wellness-travel-trend-2020-170116762.html

Ali, R. (2018). Overtourism: Why we came up with the term and what's happened since. Retrieved April 10, 2020, from https://skift.com/2018/08/14/the-genesis-of-overtourism-why-we-came-up-with-the-term-and-whats-happened-since/

Bhattacharya, S., Bashar, M. A., Srivastava, A., & Singh, A. (2019). NOMOPHOBIA: NO MObile PHone PhoBIA. *Journal of Family Medicine and Primary Care*, 8(4), 1297–1300.

Biesiada, J. (2018). They're not millennials: Targeting Generation Z. Retrieved April 9, 2020, from https://www.travelweekly.com/Travel-News/Travel-Agent-Issues/Targeting-Generation-Z

Canyon Ranch. (n.d.). Explore Experiences. Retrieved December 29, 2019, from https://www.canyonranch.com/tucson/explore-experiences/

Carter, C.M. (2016). The complete guide to Generation Alpha, the children of millennials. Retrieved from https://www.forbes.com/sites/

christinecarter/2016/12/21/the-complete-guide-to-generation-alpha-the-children-of-millennials/#397dd2ae3623

Charlie on Travel. (2019). What is sustainable travel? (and how to be a sustainable traveler). Retrieved April 10, 2020, from https://charlieontravel.com/what-is-sustainable-travel/

Dimon, A. (2020). How Millennials are disrupting the wellness travel market. Retrieved April 9, 2020, from https://www.travelmarketreport.com/articles/How-Millennials-Are-Disrupting-the-Wellness-Travel-Market

Ducharme, J. (2019). Millennials love wellness. but they're not as healthy as people think, report says. Retrieved April 9, 2020, from https://time.com/5577325/millennials-less-healthy/

Erfurt-Cooper, P. (2010). The importance of natural geothermal resources in tourism. In *Indonesia: Proceedings World Geothermal Congress Bali*. pp. 25-29.

EVEN Hotels. (2020). Meet EVEN® Hotels. Retrieved April 8, 2020, from https://www.ihg.com/evenhotels/hotels/us/en/reservation

Event MB/Maritz Global Events. (2018). 8 ideas to embrace a wellness culture at events. Retrieved December 30, 2019, from https://www.eventmanagerblog.com/wellness-event-ideas

Fell, A. (2020). Generation next: Meet Gen Z and the Alphas. Retrieved April 10, 2020, from https://mccrindle.com.au/insights/blog/generation-next-meet-gen-z-alphas/

Froelich, P. (2020). Why the travel industry will be stronger and better after coronavirus. Retrieved April 10, 2020, from https://nypost.com/2020/03/29/why-the-travel-industry-will-be-stronger-and-better-after-coronavirus/

Gibilisco, A (2020). The Impact of Covid-19 on Students with Disabilities. Retrieved April 5, 2022 from https://diversity.unc.edu/2020/06/the-impact-of-covid-19-on-students-with-disabilities/

Global Wellness Summit. (2020). Global Wellness Summit Releases In-Depth Report, "The Future of Wellness 2020." Retrieved April 10, 2020, from https://www.globalwellnesssummit.com/press/press-releases/gws-releases-in-depth-report-the-future-of-wellness-2020/

Hartman Group. (2017). Older consumers: redefining health and wellness as they age. Retrieved April 10, 2020, from https://www.forbes.com/sites/thehartmangroup/2017/10/31/older-consumers-redefining-health-and-wellness-as-they-age/#79558ff515fd

Healthy Hildegad (n.d.) https://www.healthyhildegard.com/digital-detox/

Hertzfeld, E. (2019). Millennials choosing hotels based on social media, technology. Retrieved April 10, 2020, from https://www.hotelmanagement.net/tech/millennials-are-choosing-hotels-based-social-media-tech

Hill, L. (2017). 8 future wellness trends according to the Global Wellness Institute. Retrieved April 10, 2020, from https://www.welltodoglobal.

14

com/8-future-wellness-trends-according-to-the-global-wellness-institute/

IHG. (2020). Wellwellwell. Retrieved April 12, 2020, from https://www.wellwellwell.com/

Innovation Group. (2017a). The Future 100: 2018. Retrieved December 7, 2019, from https://www.jwtintelligence.com/trend-reports/the-future-100-2018/

Innovation Group. (2017b). New trend report: Food and Drink 2017. Retrieved December 7, 2019, from https://www.jwtintelligence.com/2017/05/new-trend-report-food-drink-2017/

Insider's Guide to Spas. (2019). The future of wellness: 8 most important trends of 2019. Retrieved April 10, 2020, from https://www.insidersguidetospas.com/the-future-of-wellness-8-most-important-trends-of-2019/

Kerr, F. (2017). Millennial travel trends to watch. Retrieved April 10, 2020, from https://www.cntraveller.com/gallery/millennials-travel-trends

Killion, C. (2019). Digital detox: hotels and travel companies give guests space to unplug. Retrieved December 29, 2019, from https://lodgingmagazine.com/digital-detox-hotels-and-travel-companies-give-guests-space-to-unplug/

Kohll, A. (2019). Is your employee wellness program ready for Generation Z? Retrieved April 9, 2020, from www.forbes.com/sites/alankohll/2019/06/12/is-your-employee-wellness-program-ready-for-generation-z/#4338e50b5c7c

Kundu, A., & Bej, T. (2021). Covid-19 response: students' readiness for shifting classes online. *Corporate Governance: The International Journal of Business in Society.* 21(6), 1250-1270. https://doi.org/10.1108/CG-09-2020-0377

Maritur DMC. (2020). What is bleisure travel? Retrieved April 9, 2020, from https://www.maritur.com/blog/en/what-is-bleisure-travel/

Menze, J. (2019). What to know about Gen Alpha, the new generation influencing travel decisions. Retrieved from https://www.phocuswire.com/expedia-group-media-solutions-generation-alpha

Mill, R.C. (2011). *Resorts: Management and Operation, 3rd Edition.* Hoboken, New Jersey: John Wiley & Sons.

Mintel. (2019). Mintel announces global food and drink trends for 2030. Retrieved February 5, 2020, from https://www.mintel.com/press-centre/food-and-drink/mintel-announces-global-food-and-drink-trends-for-2030

Misasa Onsen Ryokan Cooperative. (2020). One of the world's richest radium springs. Retrieved February 12, 2020, from https://spa-misasa.jp/eng/radium/

Nermoe, K. (2018). Millennials: The 'wellness generation'. Retrieved April 9, 2020, from https://news.sanfordhealth.org/sanford-health-plan/millennials-wellness-generation/

RPHE Canada (n.d) https://phecanada.ca/sites/default/files/content/docs/teach-resiliency/StudentFocusedWellnessTips.pdf

Przybylski, A. K., & Weinstein, N. (2013). Can you connect with me now? how the presence of mobile communication technology influences face-to-face conversation quality. *Journal of Social and Personal Relationships*, 30(3), 237–246.

Rainie, L. & Zickuhr, K. (2015). Americans' views on mobile etiquette. Retrieved December 29, 2019, from https://www.pewinternet.org/2015/08/26/americans-views-on-mobile-etiquette/

Riddle, H. (2020). How Generation X fuels wellness travel. Retrieved April 10, 2020, from whereverfamily.com/how-generation-x-fuels-wellness-travel/

Rokou, T. (2019). The future of wellness travel: 12 trends to watch in 2020. Retrieved April 10, 2020, from https://www.traveldailynews.com/post/the-future-of-wellness-travel-12-trends-to-watch-in-2020

Russock, C. (2017). 8 solid hours anywhere. Retrieved April 8, 2020, from https://www.wellwellwell.com/8-solid-hours-anywhere/

Shock, P. J. (2018). Want to boost attendee concentration? the do's and don'ts of attendee comfort. Retrieved December 30, 2019, from https://www.eventmanagerblog.com/attendee-comfort

SiteMinder. (2020). Millennials & Travel: 20 interesting stats we learned about millennial hotel guests. Retrieved April 10, 2020, from https://www.siteminder.com/r/trends-advice/hotel-travel-industry-trends/millennials-travel-20-interesting-stats-millennial-hotel-guests/

Smith, M., & Puczkó, L. (2008). *Health and Wellness Tourism*. Routledge.

Statista. (2021). Health and wellness food market value worldwide in 2020 and 2026. Retrieved May 29, 2022, from https://www.statista.com/statistics/502267/global-health-and-wellness-food-market-value/

Sutton, T. (2017). Disconnect to reconnect: The food/technology metaphor in digital detoxing. *First Monday*, 22(6).

Tiwari, R. & Hashmi, H. (2022). Integrating concepts of destination image, travel motivations, expectation, and future behavior to create a model of wellness travel intentions. *International Journal of Spa and Wellness*, 1-22.

Travel Agent Central. (2018). Stats: Gen Z travelers take 2.8 leisure trips per year. Retrieved April 9, 2020, from https://www.travelagentcentral.com/resources/stats-gen-z-travelers-take-2-8-leisure-trips-per-year

United Nations (n.d.). *World Population Prospects 2019*. DESA / Population Division. Retrieved April 10, 2020, from https://population.un.org/wpp/DataQuery/

UnityPoint Health. (2018). How the farm to table trend can create a healthier lifestyle. Retrieved February 5, 2020, from https://www.unitypoint.org/desmoines/article.aspx?id=cf426bcc-5b52-4109-9a16-e53bf37ddf8a

van Velthoven, M. H., Powell, J. & Powell, G. (2018). Problematic smartphone use: Digital approaches to an emerging public health problem. *Digital Health*, 4, 1–9.

14

Vazquez Morgan M (2021) Promoting student wellness and self-care during Covid-19. *Frontiers of Psychiatry* 12:797355. doi: 10.3389/fpsyt.2021.797355

Vennare, J. (2020). Gen Z: The Ultimate Wellness Consumer. Retrieved April 9, 2020, from https://insider.fitt.co/gen-z-wellness/

Whitmore, G. (2019). How Generation Z is changing travel for older generations. Retrieved April 9, 2020, from www.forbes.com/sites/geoffwhitmore/2019/09/13/how-generation-z-is-changing-travel-for-older-generations/#ef4780278f78

Index